FOREIGN AID SAFARI

Journeys in International Development

FOREIGN AID SAFARI

Journeys in International Development

George Guess

ATHENA PRESS
LONDON

FOREIGN AID SAFARI
Journeys in International Development
Copyright © George Guess 2005

ISBN 1 84401 406 1

First Published 2005 by
ATHENA PRESS
Queen's House, 2 Holly Road
Twickenham, TW1 4EG
United Kingdom

Printed for Athena Press

To Regula, Andy, Marty, Benny and Calvin
who were always there when I came home from overseas missions

Contents

I. Introduction

Ken, you were always the switched-on, stable academic, weren't you? You hinted long ago, with dismissive grins and piercing inquiries, that my life plans were that of a global itinerant. I would end up shipwrecked someplace like all the other world-weary aid types. Nevertheless, I began bouncing around the world doing aid work that never jibed with your favourite economic theories. You never ceased to imply that I was wasting my time and that the organisations I worked for were wasting valuable resources. Where should they have gone, Ken? Into higher faculty salaries? And it didn't matter to you that I used to teach graduate students too – but in political science, an inferior field, you noted, that lacked the theoretical rigour of economics! The field was so flabby that they even created a new word – "governance" – to replace "government" and no one noticed! You had a point. But you shouldn't forget "institutions", Ken! That's how we brought in individual irrationality, tribal politics, and the quaint, often self-destructive cultures with which I dealt. You ignored the centrality of political institutions for economic development, didn't you? You took yourself so seriously, labelling all this "inefficiency". Antiseptic terms like that hid more than they revealed – except about you and your pitiful obsession with grand theories and elegant mathematical models. It all appeared quite scientific to the outsider! But we've been through all this before.

Remember when you actually tried your hand at foreign aid field work? You ran a big aid project for a year and were unceremoniously sacked. Too theoretical and perfectionist,

I believe was the reason they gave you. I won't blame you for that. If you reach fifty and haven't been sacked at least five times, you really aren't worth a shit, are you? Was it the civil society types who brought you down? Didn't you tell me once they were all zealous amateurs, trying out their theories overseas? Didn't you say all they wanted was to fly the plane even though they weren't pilots? You thought they wanted to pull the levers of power and instantly change whole countries. Or was it the constant harassment of spineless, toadying officials demanding more measurable results when they didn't know what was to be measured or why? Was it the home office of the development firm that demanded more "profitability" on its aid project? You got burned by all these opposing forces, I recall, and went back to the safety of your university classroom. I don't blame you. I've been trying to deal with these types for the past thirteen years – long after you left the business.

As a kind of "foreign aid captain's log", or a set of living memoirs, this book will describe to you how I got into this work, what the work entailed, and where I am now on my foreign aid safari. It is not another scholarly and reference work on the determinants and impact of aid. There are plenty of those available. For instance, I wrote one myself.[1] No, this is a personal safari. A safari, of course, is a journey and often means someone is far away and out of touch. Often this was true and nobody knew my exact whereabouts. A difficult feature of foreign aid work is that you are out of touch – executing your terms of reference alone except for local officials. This is also the most invigorating part as you are free of the bureaucratic crap from headquarters, donor offices, or your own project office.

---

[1] George M Guess (1987) *The Politics of United States Foreign Aid* (New York, St Martins)

As will be evident, I began as an idealist who believed one could improve the world by sharing his knowledge and skills. I believed naively that organisations such as USAID and World Bank spent funds wisely and innovatively to help the poor and to develop economies. Such views were the product of looking beyond the cynical readings and professors of my graduate programmes. I believed I could make a difference where they might have failed. I would do it differently. The officials and local peoples would like and understand me. We would work together and solve what had not been solved by others. The paternalism and benign arrogance of this view escaped me at the time.

My work over the past several decades fits the pattern of regular journeys – some bad and some good; some successful, many failures; some for well-designed projects, others disastrous and problem-creating rather than solving; some with good colleagues, others with real hustlers and incompetents. It is based on what I've experienced and read while on aid projects overseas. I could be wrong.

This safari log also includes my views of aid workers (or "foreign aides") in institutional settings in which we all have worked. I accumulated a lot of views on the aid business. Many have changed and do not follow a consistent pattern. Much depends on the project itself, which becomes like a microcosm of the aid business. My work overseas was contracted through donors directly (e.g. World Bank) or for a private firm (Development Alternatives, Inc. – DAI). There are several types of aid workers and despite their "community" they become tribal in the field and often do not cooperate with each other. Donors rarely cooperate, so why should their workers?

Who are the foreign aides? Some foreign aides work for the aid bureaucracies overseas and mostly administer projects. These are the USAID and World Bank bureaucrats assigned from headquarters to administer their programmes in the field. They push paper and rarely go beyond the capital city restaurants and embassy circuits. Their link with the projects is through administration – ensuring that work plans are completed; that personnel perform and interact positively with locals; and monitoring and measuring project results. Then there are the embassy types who have all the answers and few questions. In the case of the US Embassy, it is clear that they view aid field workers (those on AID projects) as subhuman. The field workers are the ones who get their hands dirty – "nobody we know", one might hear at an embassy cocktail party. The NGO workers run all kinds of projects from AIDS eradication, to food aid (Oxfam), social services (World Vision), medical assistance (Doctors Without Borders) and environmental/forestry conservation (Nature Conservancy). They tend to be true believers in their causes (as they should be), and often look down on aid project workers (from World Bank, British DFID, or USAID) unless they are getting money from those organisations themselves. NGOs view others as "aid capitalists" in it for the expense accounts and corporate profitability. Of course, firms like Chemonics and Development Alternatives, Inc. (DAI) (for whom I worked most of the time), make profits. Non-governmental organizations (NGOs) have managed to avoid balances in their accounts at the end of each accounting period, as expenses just match revenues from donations and grants – there are no profits. But higher expenses can often avoid reported profits, allowing NGOs to achieve billing rates similar to for-profit firms. NGOs have more flexibility and can in principle get more done in the field than firms.

There are many criticisms of foreign aid, and some are really off the wall. Critics often have axes to grind and may be obsessed with single issues – like US destruction of the world environment – which distorts their view of most other issues. Probably the most venomous criticism is

Graham Hancock's *Lords of Poverty: The Power, Prestige and Corruption of the International Aid Business* (1989). This is a long but well-researched tract that attacks the World Bank and its projects. It is so extreme that one wonders if he was put on the shit list of incompetent consultants before it was written. Other observers are more circumspect. Paul Theroux, for example, sees aid workers (especially NGO types) as "agents of virtue" out to save the world and live it up in the process,[2] ranging in quality from selfless idealists to the laziest boon-dogglers. He likens them to Dickens' Mrs Jellyby types with her "Africa Project" from Bleak House.[3] This was a dreamy make-work scheme that put together cottage industries and improved very little except her sense of worthy philanthropy. Most foreign aid workers, like Mrs Jellyby, don't stay long enough in countries to realise their efforts have failed. If they did, they would note that they have turned problems into permanent conditions. Like many writers, Theroux reserves most of his venom for the client governments – the corrupt kleptocracies that actually cultivate poverty in order to obtain aid funds that keep them in power.[4] This produces dependency on aid for even the most basic work and staggering debts that cut into funding available for local services and programmes. Countries are nicknamed, for example, the "Donor's Republic of Nicaragua". What to do about this? Without intending to, perhaps, Theroux notes that failure by local client governments and their aid handlers to control public expenditures perpetuates the corruption that robs funds from much-needed social services.

---

[2] Paul Theroux (2003), *Dark Star Safari: Overland from Cairo to Capetown* (London: Penguin), p.190
[3] Ibid., p.456
[4] Ibid., p.333

For example, he is told by Malawians that they are not really into accounting and business practices such as keeping inventory. They found out after kicking out the Indians and taking their shops that they "are not cut out for this shop-keeping and book-keeping".[5] It's just not in their "heritage" in contrast with Indians, who "know no other life". Since cultural heritage prevents Malawis and other Africans from making profits, nevertheless donors should keep on giving them sinecure funds to preserve their heritage. Described by Theroux as "bullshit",[6] this keeps the worst aspects of the donor-client government charade going. The more donors are manipulated into funding "indigenous cultures" and their native practices by venal clients, the more real growth and development is prevented.

Single-issue fanatics in the West, which include some NGOs, have often been accused of not having an off switch. Nothing that donors can do will ever satisfy them so they keep the pressure on. Screamers! Moral purists who see the world in black/white terms. You used to rant about the smog, humourless, earnest types who scoffed at you if you disagreed with them. But, this tenacity is one of their virtues. It can also destroy delicate quid-pro-quo deals worked out between donors and officials in poor countries that could benefit from aid. So in Uganda, you reminded me five years ago, environmental zealots blocked a World Bank Nile River electricity project that would have benefited millions of poor people. The single-issue purists held it up for the usual environmental reason – potentially disastrous flooding of the catchment area. It turned out that the only people in country really opposed were those people *outside* the catchment area who didn't receive payments from the World Bank! Such people have been labelled

---

[5] Ibid., p.339
[6] Loc. cit.

"agents of virtue" for their zeal. OK, they are screwed up. A lot of us are…

You've accused me of being a naïve virtue agent. Naturally I could be a closet virtue agent. I am zealous about getting started on changes to improve quality of life and to stimulate development – e.g. public budgeting and financial management. With all my years of experience, I have a lot of doubts about my own work. I have few absolute answers and a lot of questions on how aid in this area might be improved. Through it may not be obvious from the following anecdotes, I've been fixing up governments, improving "governance", strengthening public financial management systems and helping country officials allocate resources better. My stays over the past thirteen years varied from a few days to eight months in particular countries. I have also worked abroad on Organization of American States (OAS) and Fulbright fellowships. These provided enough time to perform the required work, meet officials socially, and get a feel for the operation of the international donor community. The major constraints to accomplishing work objectives were either the donor bureaucrats and their regulations (e.g. excessive zeal for field reporting; inability to modify budgets) or central government officials (inaccessible and often obstructionist, especially in the area of fiscal decentralisation). It was much more enjoyable and fruitful to work with local finance and public works officials as well as the mayors. They often were ahead of me in their desire for reform and made major changes that would have been unthinkable in the past (e.g. installation of multi-year budgeting and planning systems accompanied by transparent documents available to citizens' groups). By encouraging officials to take professional risks, our aid work was valuable. You disagreed with me on this and thought that balanced budgets, open markets, and privatisation was all that was needed.

It's hard to know about a place going in, and one has to read a lot of background reports, which provide the necessary feel and texture as well as knowledge base. Acquisition of book knowledge gave me the confidence to move ahead boldly and make assertions that, often later, I realised were either flat wrong or implausible. But at the time, if they weren't correct, they should have been – the officials liked them, and that's often all that matters when you are far away from home and in uncertain mental territory.

Bucharest, Romania, 2004

II. Views from the Trenches
Living it Up in Albania

Dear Harry—

I'd never seen the grid tubes on a portable electric heater look like glowing embers before. The hotbars, turned up to a high reddish-orange, had flickered down to almost nothing. They were almost black with a few yellowish patches. The large, damp hotel room encased in cracked plaster was full of chills that cut through me like a knife. This morning I woke up in bed watching my breath, rolled up in my stiff, frozen blanket like a taco shell. What a shit hole! It was as if a team of prison workers were getting tired of cranking the hand generator. You could tell they were almost ready to stop as the electric embers dropped down to flickers. It must be some kind of DC voltage system left over from the Soviet Union, I thought, part of Lenin's great plan to spread the communist system via electrification. Street lights were barely visible; little flickering embers in the night that shined no more than fireflies. So it was that we carried our little portable heaters with us everywhere in the Albanian winter. Often it wasn't that cold – rather it was the humidity and windblown rain near the freezing point that made it seem worse. The hotel rooms normally leaked and wind whistled though the cracks, day or night.

Ismail Kadare described these kinds of places in his amazing tale *The General of the Dead Army*.[7] To him they were

---

[7] Ismail Kadare (1986), *The General of the Dead Army* (London: Quartet Encounters), p.31

brothels, not hotels, and the barman didn't just look peculiar – he had a serene round face like a cut-out moon between two dishes piled high with oranges and apples! With these kinds of characters floating on and off stage, I had entered a crude but magical world: the world of the foreign aide!

An important psychological survival tool for me over the years has been literature. I should tell you that reading the works of such trenchant observers of other cultures as William Boyd, Somerset Maugham, Leo Tolstoy, Ken Follett, VS Naipaul and Paul Theroux has been good therapy. They catalogue the struggles of "civilised" people in rough places, and this provided me with spiritual and intellectual sustenance. Every foreign aide should carry at least one of these for armament. In Kadare's novel, two generals led crews around rural Albania after WWII, digging up the remains of their respective Italian and German soldiers killed during the war. In winter they slept in tents or in old state hotels that couldn't have been any better than this one – fifty years later! We weren't digging up corpses, just trying to survive like the generals and their crews.

Working with mayors and city finance department personnel was OK. Frequently the day would kick off with a shot of their homemade raqia. It's how they survived the hopelessness of the Hoxja regime and the uncertainty of the "transition" period. Misery loves company and the sight of our Albanian staff and counterparts enduring even worse shit, despite their culture and solid education, pushed us ahead. Tolstoy once said in Anna Karenina: "There are no conditions to which a man cannot get accustomed especially if he sees that everyone around him lives in the same way". Still, their obvious destitution produced guilt in us for living as well as we did there – at least we had running water, albeit cold – they didn't! Some of the international "experts" in such areas as local government tax admin-istration talked too much. Who else could they find to listen to their war stories? They often had no homes or even friends in the US anymore, drifting from overseas job to overseas job. They needed the outlet of company, of willing listeners. This kind of negative camaraderie probably happens in foxholes during war. When you aren't shooting, you strike up a conversation – the guy would suddenly stare at you with a distant look and proclaim: "You've never lived unless you saw the winter in Boise, Idaho, 1967. That was a winter." *Beam me up Scotty...*

Normally my partner and I worked days with city officials, interviewing, dining, conversing – all about their fiscal problems and how they could use our latest systems, methods and tools to get around the reality that they were broke and so was the central treasury. It all reminded me of Dilbert's budget consultant punch-line: "I'll have to run some chaos and complexity simulations, but it looks as if you need more money." So as a budget consultant, I talked expansively and positively to these poor bastards about sale and leaseback options and other techniques they could use, if they could prove they owned the property, if the law said OK, and if they were willing to take the risk of bringing in legions of corrupt government "supervisors", "controllers" and "inspectors" to look at the books. Most mayors weren't because they couldn't buy them off with anything – there was no money and no goods left.

At night, alone in the hotel room with a flickering heater, time slowed down, letting in waves of depressing thoughts. It could get you down if you let it.

The anguish and despair would set in. I would ask myself, How is it that these cultured and educated people in Albania, for the most part, have absolutely nothing? They had a vicious past of treachery from spies and neighbours, long imprisonments for nothing and enforced labour. Their future almost depended on their ability to escape to Italy, Greece or beyond. There was nothing now but corruption, civil war and a residual failed state. And they had come through remarkably unscathed for a people living under a brutal, totalitarian regime. It won't take Albanians long to heal the psychological scars of this experience and begin to trust one another again.

I had worked in the third world and rationalised the terrible poverty as something that happens to others – to people culturally different and uneducated. Naturally it's terrible that after all the aid to Africa, poverty and governance problems still persist. But places like Albania were different. It contained all your old girlfriends and neighbours, only Albanian clones. That's not just *any* luscious young waitress smiling at me each day and who talks in broken English, it's Janice Moore, my high school flame from twelfth grade. Great that she's here after all those years. She dumped me then because I didn't know what I was doing – couldn't perform, but I can try again, here, now, forty years later, and she hasn't aged a bit – still seventeen. The waitress has the same shapely, golden legs, suggesting strong sexual athletic prowess, just hidden by her loose white outfit. She also throws the same clever, secret glance, the classy neck with head held high.

"Another coffee?" But is that all you want? We could go back to the hotel? The mind wanders during these down periods. Back to the hotel? The thought of taking anyone to that shit hole wrenches me back to the present with a jolt!

So, through technical assistance, training and attention to waitresses, you can help them. The American taxpayer is subsidising an aid time-warp for many of us. This was a major piece of motivation for me – I really wanted to help Albanians, most of whom are poor. Nothing much we can do about Africa any time soon, but other regional experts would disagree with this assessment. Maybe their old girlfriends or boyfriends are in Africa…

Still, it's clear after a few weeks in the mud and rain of

Albania that there is very little we can actually do. Lots of inputs and activity – but not much to show for it other than plans and paperwork. Can't give them millions of dollars to rebuild streets or raise incomes. Not in our TOR. We are showing them how to fish, not giving them the actual fish – that's the rationale. Here, we are giving them virtual fish which are supposed to act as incentives. It may work. But dark thoughts reduce my energy levels. Sometimes I just can't do it anymore. This is really bullshit – maybe the major impact is to give them the drive to emigrate to something better, across the bay to Italy, for example, in one of the evening boat runs. We are not here to tell them that sort of thing – just the opposite. But it happens almost daily. They ask for advice – I tell them what I am supposed to say, then what I'd do – "Clear out fast. You are young and you have only one life."

But the injustice of this place – people enslaved in prisons for looking toward Italy or talking with foreigners. The cultural history of deep and sustained physical and mental repression – Sigurimi secret police and informants everywhere from Hoxja's regime. His was the original hermit kingdom – not Kim's North Korea! Perhaps from long experience of keeping their heads low and not speaking out, my Albanian colleagues are humble and they look to us for all the answers. In exchange, they watch over us and protect us from the many local dangers – con artists, muggers and so on. Day after day, we talk with officials who have nothing left now. What little savings they squirreled away disappeared during the transition around 1991 – and then again in the pyramid scheme collapse of 1996.

"What should we do?" asked the finance director of one town in 1996. You couldn't tell him to demand all his cash at once – that would set off local panic.

"Try and get as much as you can back over the next few weeks."

21

These conversations really hit hard. What else could I be doing? The whole business is a sham. We aren't really helping here. I started drinking more wine at dinner. Over time, my system would fill up with alcohol like a jug, producing mood swings, facetiousness, deafness and prickliness. I'd start picking at the other international experts – for putting on airs, trying out their theories here, ramming a lot of technical crap down their throats on programme budgeting and accrual accounting. For roughly the same reasons, they would pick back. I was turning into a slob. Last night I saw three locals fall in a slithery pile in the corner of a nearby bar. All were drunk, swaying in almost choreographed rhythm. Their unintended dance brought them together in a pile in one motion. I was cutting myself off, speaking the gibberish of my colleagues and behaving like the drunken locals. It was not cultural sensitivity; it was depravity.

It started to take control and became a burden during everyday interactions. Over the months, I started losing it. I couldn't control the emotions. Fits of crying came over me at night – I couldn't control their destiny or even my own. I became suspicious of the other expatriate consultants. Why were they here? Stupid fuck – what is he telling them that for? I need to kick his ass later. What the hell could they bring these people? To these depths I would descend – the ultimate form of thinking inside a small box of my own making. Of course, the other ex-pat specialists brought as much as I did, but the grinding effects of working with culturally advanced people in tattered clothes, who hadn't taken a hot shower in months, wore me down. I could feel the loss of control in sudden outbursts against my colleagues for minor infractions. I knew that others had been evacuated from Albania from stress and self-destructive tendencies. One guy, isolated in a mountain village on an EU project, drank himself into oblivion. They found him on the floor of his office, still alive, and shipped him back to Finland. Like he, I had became possessive of the locals. These particular people were my wards, my responsibility, and fuck the project and its work plan. I found myself stealing software and office supplies from other donor projects and giving them to our city people. Time to come up for air – to depressurise.

The heater finally flickered down from tiny ember to blackish nothing. I have my little torch – as all of us do, to avoid falling into large round holes along the street created by the thriving market for stolen manhole covers. Now, where's my taco blanket?

Shkoder, Albania, January, 1995

III. Getting Into Overseas Aid Work
Motives

Hey Jim—

You used to do this shit for a living. Why would educated, middle-class people still go into overseas development work, often in sub-Peace Corps conditions? Why not do real work? You know; nine to five, processing invoices, managing underlings through appropriate postures and gestures, preparing briefs in badly lighted offices, wearing power suits... With these kinds of challenging options, why does one do development – become a foreign aide? Isn't that clever? "Aide" as in foreign aid. Is it to befriend the natives, to return gloriously later to the village in hopes of being praised in song and story by them? Is this the kind of dreamy nonsense that got us into the business? Or is it the opposite – raw cynicism? How can you really change anything when the world is rigged by global oil firms and their appointed leaders, there is no justice, and globalism is nothing but a capitalist conspiracy? So, go overseas and give the natives the real message – the "real guide" that the world actually sucks. Or are we in it to "do" democracy? Democracy can cure anything – insert reform-minded princes and politicians, set up a model parliament, identify the many good people in rotten systems who want to root out corruption and so on. So we try the incremental approach – an election here, an NGO there, a stronger media someplace else. It all works if we can buy off the local and national elite to share the booty. If not, brute authoritarianism and major corruption continue as a way of life. Many young people believe strongly in the democratic mission, and this may be one of our defining characteristics as a nation, along with our famously proud vulgarity.

I got into this from a mixture of credulous sentimentality and crass materialism. I believed that poor people needed help and that as an educated person who taught at a university and had worked in and with government, I could help out. I also needed the money as universities didn't pay people like me very much. I was not an academic all-star and commanded a rather measly nine-month salary that barely covered the mortgage and living expenses. Aid work pays pretty well for short-term consultants living from job to job. You live out of a suitcase, pay your own medical and social insurance and keep the rest. It's an individualistic existence in pursuit of the common good – world development. For long-term overseas work (twelve-month contracts minimum), the US government tax code still allows a credit for the first eighty thousand dollars earned overseas if you stay out of the US for at least eleven months per year. That means a hundred thousand dollar salary is only twenty thousand dollars of taxable income! Not bad for putting up with the wonders and perils of overseas cultures! Other country foreign aid programmes offer similar fiscal incentives. I was also enthusiastic about the people I was meeting overseas – many of whom were tenured university professor drop-outs. They had switched careers – so did I. The people I met and exchanged stories with for two years on leave from my university were the most interesting people I have ever met. Sure, it was artificial. It was like a chance meeting at a campfire in the wilderness. You stay up all night drinking, singing and telling stories you've never told anyone. In the morning, you part ways and never meet again. In fact, it hasn't been that – I keep meeting the same people overseas in the oddest places. It is a wild business.

Still, the situation over the past four years has ratcheted up negative sides of the business. We are now into deliberate nation and democracy-building by war and regime change – Serbia, Kosovo, Bosnia, Iraq – next up maybe North Korea and Iran. This missionary zeal has always been just below the surface in US foreign policy – coming and going: Vietnam (yes), Iraq I (no). It's the hubris of Pyle in *Quiet American* and the clumsiness of Lonnie in *Of Mice and Men* – wanting to spread American values and purpose a là Walt Whitman circa 1871 in *Democratic Vistas* but always ending up destroying what we wanted to save.

It's a different ballgame now. A Salvadorean water engineer was gunned down in rural Afghanistan a while back even though he worked for Red Cross. UNDP election workers have been held hostage in Afghanistan by another swarm of Islamic fanatics. Development aides are increasingly caught in the middle of political/military conflicts. The stakes are getting higher; more personal risks. At the same time, the world is getting riskier and maybe a few controlled brush fires can cut back superfluous weeds and let the earth spring up again in peace and democracy. That's how the US Forest Service would do it in Montana. Why not in Iraq by cutting out bad weeds like Saddam?

We view ourselves as a tight-knit bunch doing an often dangerous job that few people outside the development brigade appreciate or even understand. This is frustrating when you know that others back home scoff at you as one of the "pin-striped" aid workers who stay in posh hotels (this happens infrequently) or probably a CIA type (the unanswerable charge that goes with the turf – i.e. denial means you are covering up; admission of complicity is satisfying to your critic but also perceived as a lie). If it's becoming more dangerous, at least there are fewer scoffs – CIA types are in and nobody wants to die, even in pin-striped suits.

Perhaps the young are still getting into overseas aid work because a new generation of idealistic, politically correct types have defined the elastic and always elusive term "development"? Maybe so. The "development" firm for which I worked was full of younger, scrubbed types who look like their mums combed their hair before coming to work. Perhaps there are other, more practical reasons. The term "development" is a favourite topic in university international programme lectures, providing hours of intellectual gymnastics and opportunities to produce long-winded definitions. How else could "International Development Studies" masters degree programmes have thrived so well? Often, grads want to do something meaningful for the world, not grubby Peace Corps-type work in some shit hole like Shkoder, Albania. No, we mean big-time policy change, freeing prisoners out of torture cells, settling refugees, organising protests, saving children and so on. Still others believe that development is intangible – an essence that can perhaps only be felt by the initiated: "You know it when you feel it – I am healed – we are developed." Other cautious types want to come up with an exhaustive definition before going any further – as if this would make a difference to how one targets and spends money to help the world's poor. They usually go into accounting.

More modestly, most aid workers simply want to improve things – whether they are working in health, education, water-sewer, environmental protection, public financial management systems, human rights, immigration issues or anti-corruption. Though they couldn't really define it, these poor buggers are really working for "development". Maybe it's not a big enough agenda with so many sufferers around the world. Too technocratic – we really should be doing Johnny Apple-Seed routines disturbing seeds and welfare payments everywhere. Many of the same people often wonder late at night, when they actually go to the field, as the insomniac gas builds up in their stomachs from repeated fare of greasy meals, whether any intended development improvements are actually occurring. They suspect rightly that their efforts will be derailed by some combination of replaced officials, disappearing regimes or shifted budget programme funds from either the donor or the country. Despite these unfortunate realities, most foreign aides, those who often graduate from Peace Corps-type experiences, still keep coming and try to do development. *Don't let the bastards grind you down…*

Jim, let's put it all down in sequence. The prospective aid worker is motivated by one or more of six major reasons to go overseas into development work: first, most candidates have a strong sense of idealism. There seem to be two types of ideals here: (1) spreading the "right values"; and (2) performing ideal good works to save humanity. Both are driven by a crusading spirit, a powerful enthusiasm that drives people away from more suffocating bureaucratic ventures, such as law practice, domestic civil service careers or urban healthcare. What happened to all the nurses, for example? Where is Flo Nightingale when you need her? The premise here is somewhat arrogantly that one has the "right" and "responsible" values of environmental cleanliness (stop the logging and deforestation!); anti-corruption (poverty is no excuse to take bribes – cultures of corruption must be changed!); democracy (transparency is best and civil society should participate in all public decisions!); human rights (accountability, rule of law and due process should prevail!); women's rights (women here deserve the same rights they now have in the US and UK! Genital mutilation is definitely out!) and so on. In many cases, those with these values befriend others with like values, who in turn want to work and learn from more experienced people holding those kinds of near-universal values. No surprise here – and university programmes are excellent breeding grounds for international social change and development. But you have to ask yourself: "What do locals think of we who hold those values?"

I told you once about the Minister of Forestry and Natural Resources in Belize when I had my faculty Fulbright Research Grant to examine forestry in three Central American countries. When I finally gained entry to his office he began wearily with, "You're not another North American social scientist who's going to tell me how to save the forests here, are you?"

I said, "No, actually I don't give a shit what you do with them."

To which he replied, "That's good, now we can talk."

The second kind of idealists are those who simply want to improve people's lives and work quietly to that end in often god-forsaken holes around the world. These are people with good doses of practicality. They combine the best of rational perspectives with the knowledge that enormous irrationalities and cultural differences impede "progress" and that local passions and ecstasies can be triggered by all sorts of things we don't understand. Try shaking hands with someone in a doorway in Kyrgyzstan – that's a major faux pas that would not be intuitively obvious!

I've met committed realist foreign aides in rural parts of Central Asia living much like their wards and they deserve a lot of credit for staying the course – which often takes up their whole professional careers. I recently met a water engineer who spent more than ten years in Armenia trying to ensure that water was delivered safely and efficiently to all Armenians. This is his passion. He is a tough, beaten down, scraggly chain-smoker who will likely die on this job and be unjustly forgotten. These are the kinds of people who have the skills, sensitivities, the realism to cut through sentimental bullshit, and the technical capabilities to design and implement complex systems. They actually help refugees and serve in refugee camps, orphanages, clinics, manage water authorities, schools and so on – bringing a sense that the world cares to their wards. This gives them the reason to continue in what often appears to me as relatively hopeless conditions – those legal and regulatory system design conditions that won't be changed any time soon. How else could they stay motivated and focused? Of course, some aid workers simply do short-term stints and leave – "parachuting in and out", as it is called. But many stay on for months and years in these places, marrying locals, getting new lives. Seeing the happy faces of the locals in their care drives them forward and motivates them to stay. It's paternalistic but it is a necessary motivating factor given the scarcity of Mother or Father Teresas who work for the benefit of the world.

Overall, it is not surprising that many aid workers take a paternalistic stance toward countries, regions, peoples and issues – they are "their" people and the message is just under the surface – "Don't fuck with my people – I know them and you don't." Good works idealism motivates a lot of people to work in US charities and philanthropic causes as well. People who work in social services among the US urban poor are similar, and do their jobs simply and humbly without great fanfare. That they are unnoticed does not diminish their quiet sense of purpose and modest accomplishment.

Not everyone is fitted to serve the poor, even if they think they are and have college degrees to prove it. Some are not fit to be foreign aides because they lack the ideals and basic sensitivities to lesser people and animals. Tolerance of ambiguity, patience and forgiveness are not part of their psychic makeup. You weren't very patient or tolerant, were you Jim? That's probably why you stopped doing this kind of work, but you have to admit that some of the most revealing insights come out of the oddest contexts. You always had that essential quality: an absurdist sense of humour that could make droll connections.

Montana is in many ways a developing country – a beautiful place filled with mostly poor rural types. It was during an interview at Montana State University that I discovered how people and institutions can defeat themselves by getting worked up about minor matters – in this case the behaviour of local bears. I once listened to the farmers in rural Mississippi talk about their wars against beavers in feverish, almost military terms. The damn beavers dammed things up – a genetic problem – and this flooded their crops. They knew these critters deliberately had it in for them and were fighting back. It was the Civil War all over again. Yet there was a certain respect among the earthy rural types for the beavers – they were two groups of living beings fighting it out for survival.

I like to watch animals – they really are human. Why would a squirrel stand up under a car and work at some guy's muffler for over an hour? Why would a fox confidently trot around firing bursts of stealth scent while my dog, livid with anger and confusion, ran ferociously around looking for him? You see, they have to be partly human. But that shouldn't stop us from having some of them for dinner or using their pelts for coats (e.g. nutrias).

In Bozeman, it was the expat doctorates and US Forest Service against the bears. The chairman, Craig McGrath, outfitted to look like a woodsman/cowboy in Montana (PhD, Northwestern), sat at the head of the table (where else?) in the local bar where the department and its then candidate (me) were having after-interview drinks. I should say that this was a normal part of the interview where they watch you to see if booze turns you into a violent maniac or

31

giggling buffoon. Not drinking would be as much of a sin as drinking too much. No excuses – "medical problems, can't drink" etc. – everyone knows the drill. During all this, Chairman Dr Craig was holding forth on the local bear problem. Sure, I enjoy free drinks and maybe I did have too many of them...

In any case, it came out that brown bears were going through the local garbage piles at an alarming rate. Townsfolk would come out for the paper and find a five-hundred-pound bear working their garbage. Imagine the surprise of contract sanitation workers – bears were cutting into their recycling profits. A crisis! My God! These were not the friendly black bears that could be shooed off. (Murmurs of agreement and concern all around – heads thrown vigorously back to drink in the swill.) No, these "damned bears" were coming into town regularly like they owned the place and going though the garbage. If they came in and didn't find enough garbage for their daily meal, they could get pissed and start eating women and children. This could just be the first town to fall to the bears, just like the dominoes in south-east Asia. Fortunately, the USFS had devised a zero-tolerance policy to deal with the problem. Yay, technocrats!

The operation worked like this: the rangers would stake out the town and, through careful coordination of radios and night-vision equipment, they would organise search-and-destroy missions. On observing a bear feeding himself, the ranger would take aim and shoot the fat brown bugger with a dope pellet. The bear could still be a threat, wandering around drunk, possibly damaging private property, falling asleep in someone's front yard. That's right; still cause for alarm. When the bear showed signs he was suitably out of it, the rangers would move in and fasten a bright red tag to one ear, appropriately signed, numbered, and sealed to allow computerised tracking and to prevent tag counterfeiting. The rangers then called in a chopper to fly the five-hundred-pound bear back up into the mountains. Should a tagged bear be caught having another garbage meal in Bozeman, the rangers would shoot to kill, solving the problem at the source. Zero tolerance; no learning curve allowed. Two-step search and destroy. Can the day when the USFS use directed energy laser weapons and active denial technology be far off?

Perhaps as proof that drinking events like this do actually weed out undesirable faculty candidates, I stupidly expressed scepticism that the policy would work. It was my proud vulgarity showing itself just at the wrong time – or the right time: who would really want to work with such a bunch of assholes? The colleagues were visibly upset with my opinion and shifted around in their chairs to face their leader.

"Don't you think the Forest Service knows what they're doing?" the other logger type – PhD Duke – asked.

"Of course they do the best they can," I said, "but imagine if you were a bear. You just had a hearty lunch out of a garbage pail, then after a slight pain in the back, you felt the intoxicating effects of a dope pellet, a real psychedelic experience. During this dreamy state, you could see the valleys below as you flew around in the clouds in a chopper. You were flying like the very birds you watched soaring around you each day in the forest! When you woke up in the deep, snowy mountains from your slumber, you found a pretty red tag on your ear. Maybe you couldn't see it because you don't carry a mirror, but reflection in your favourite fishing pond might stimulate a flash of curiosity. If you were a bear, wouldn't you concentrate hard on what began all this and try to repeat the experience? I mean, from an institutional perspective, shouldn't we consider *actual* incentives and disincentives before we design systems?"

"No, no!" they all growled in unison. "Bears don't think

like that." (Laughter all around.) "You see, they don't learn like us. It's not just mixing up the right kind of response – one part force and two parts diplomacy – you have to kill them or they'll bring in their friends and take over the town!"

My would-be colleagues didn't have much use for ambiguity or lofty concepts like incentives. They would simply wipe out the problem with the scorched earth strategy, something like the Brazilian army in da Cunha's *O Sertao* or *Rebellion in the Backlands*. Here's where we parted company. Maybe some of them should be killed, but there has to be some basic sensitivity – some effort to believe that man is not totally superior, that either rural villagers in some far off place or bears right here in the USA are not totally stupid and uncivilised. A PhD is no guarantee that you will develop this sensitivity – probably the reverse. Mind you, I'm not sure how I would respond if I lived there with five-hundred-pound grizzlies wandering around. Suppose one carried off your wife? (Hmmm, let's see…) I might be a big USFS supporter in a matter of months, but at the time, the rationale seemed wrong.

I suspect that most people in development work have ideals extending far beyond their own self-aggrandisement. Yet, the idealistic motivational strain runs up against two problems – which might be described as "clashes with other ideals". The foreign development aide faces the same kind of dilemmas as a domestic social worker. He or she may view the terrain and figure it's the most backward, shitpot country they've ever seen. Best thing for problems of traditional methods is a strong dose of modernity. This feels good in the field – teaching locals to run accounting systems, water purification plants, irrigation management systems and so on. Any adjustment problems can be dealt with by fixing "incentives" or institutional blockages to motivation. That kind of new institutional economics stuff is easy on paper.

However, on return – particularly to a "development" classroom – one might learn that he or she has actually been part of the neo-imperialist apparatus for keeping the poor down. What we really want, the lecturer might say, is an international system of autarky where locals engage in small, environmentally-sustainable and friendly activities, like gathering nuts, making wooden trinkets from reforested areas protected from evil timber companies and others who would use the cynical cover of "sustained yield management" before chopping the shit out of them for profit. Water management technology can be kept small-scale to prevent dependence on foreign suppliers and to ensure proper local design. All this sounds plausible. One also learns that as a foreign aide, one has been part of the modern-day Kipling imperialist structure. The water manager who has been fighting with corrupt local officials for ten years to deliver water is actually a colonialist-imperialist, and he didn't even know it! Imagine being accused of behaving like Kipling – sipping gin and tonics, flipping coins to grinning natives as they danced around barefoot... One is accused of working in water-sewer, education or health to actually keep hosts in bondage and exploit the almost pure, happy natives via the global capitalist system. The state of nature destroyed by aid. So, no wonder doing the bigger ideals sounds better than cleaning out latrines in rural villages as a Peace Corps volunteer.

This theoretically-driven academic accusation is of course bullshit and frequently levelled by university or think-tank types. They may actually have done a few short-term gigs in the field but are heavily into book-learning – and very select books at that. A US university professor once told me he published an article in a leading journal on public administration in China after spending a total of three days there. He wrote it on the plane back. He got a kick out of this himself: "Me, an expert on China! Ha-ha! That's a good one!"

Although he was quite modest about his lack of real knowledge of the people and its institutions, many students held captive in the lots of classrooms taught by instant experts are not so lucky. Students often hear classroom views on development work by the professor simply lifted from other academics and a few disgruntled types. They may well have been "86ed" from a country or programme for wanting to philosophise more than work – hence the obvious chip on the shoulder. These experts are like the proverbial journalists who wait in the hotel bar for the others to come back from the front so they can learn what to write about.

The other goal of "feeling good about one's work and staying motivated" is related to this. Suppose one recognises the evident dangers of rampant commercialised development and tries to avoid transferring the weaknesses of this system? Many have done this by helping locals to build on the existing system's positive features of their own practices and culture. Why not? While this seems obvious, early agricultural experts from the US would take one look at a system and size it up: "Fucked up – obviously nothing works, let's change the whole thing." (See the classic critique of this kind of practice in *We Don't Know How*[8].) So, foreign aides have really learned over the past forty years that effective transfer of technology depends on recognition of problems and opportunities in existing systems, practices and capacities. One needs to build on them or they will not be used after the aid worker gets back on the plane. Nobody will prepare budgets for the government using the new

---

[8] W. Paddock and E. Paddock (1973), *We Don't Know How, An Independent Audit of What They Call Success in Foreign Assistance* (Ames: Iowa State University Press)

forms; no one will use the new accounting system to track and control budget expenditures.

So, the foreign aide-cum-social worker tries to help the locals adjust to new conditions and respond more effectively to them – blending modernity and local culture. But this can lead to dependency on social workers and the inability of locals to act for themselves and deal with modern complexity – whether they want to or not. Either way, this line of criticism of aid workers (again, typically by spectators, disgruntled field-workers, Monday-morning quarterbacks or theoreticians) often makes the aid worker feel worthless. Admittedly, some of this is healthy and can lead to better field approaches and stronger commitments, but a lot of it is based on jealousy or envy of those who risk all to stay in some hole, actually trying to help while living under the worst of conditions. These are not the conditions endured by academics, or think-tank visitors, or those giving USIA lectures, or even Fulbrighters. They can get on the plane after a few days and trash the world system and its duped aid-workers for perpetuating poverty, ignorance and inequality. Thank God for such visionaries – learned imbeciles would be another way to put it!

A second motive for becoming a foreign aide is travel and adventure. This should be obvious. Let's face it: most jobs permit the thrill of carrying a briefcase, wearing power suits, a lead to specialisation in office politics, strategic manoeuvres, dissimulation and other character-warping activities. This is the kind of office tribalism that most people engage in no matter what level of salary they earn; they simply do it from bigger or smaller offices. Development idealists and good-works people are implicitly bored by this option and often can see beyond the small world of business or government work. A senior consultant with whom I worked in Albania, who had been a US city manager for ten years in two cities, told me he would never go back to domestic work again. He was excited by the thrill of exporting values and systems overseas and working to improve life for municipal citizens. Which would you rather do: prepare and teach the same class to similar crops of bored students and be pecked at by useless deans, or share a glass of Chateau Duvalier 1985 with the biggest drug dealer in Central America as he launches his newly-refurbished jungle steamboat *The New River Queen* in Belize to sail upriver to the mahogany camps? (See book cover for further evidence.) Then write a report about it! Think hard.

We've heard the good news that development work can be exciting. The bad news is that the same pettiness contaminates results here, diverting time and resources from useful work. I mentioned that working at close quarters with the same consultants for long periods of time can also produce the same tribal conflict, the same euphoria of hatred. Goal displacement takes charge – the conflicts become more important than the intended results of your work. This shouldn't happen and the team leader or donor superior should dress down or replace that person. Often it's not so simple.

In Albania, I spent a lot of time fighting with other members of the project on the best way to proceed. It was this possessiveness that took hold – I knew best; so did the others. Fortunately for the continuation of my aid career I was able to release frustration without getting into fisticuffs – a feral solution was a clear possibility in several instances with the same guy. I decided to score a small point one day at an Albanian bakery. I had dropped to this level of imbecility – I saw it as my big chance to humiliate this fat bastard. For consumers, a "bakery" meant a square hole in the outside of a building where one lined up for bread. Bread was sold in blocks (called loaves) that weighed around a quarter-pound and had to be chipped with screwdrivers to loosen them up. With one of these in hand, I faded back.

"Bob," I said, "go out for a pass."

He was a bloated slob. I watched him waddle a few steps backward from where he was standing. I nailed him hard in the chest with a good loaf, the force of which knocked him backward into a large mud puddle. This he hit with a dramatically loud splash. You can't imagine how delicious this childish experience was.

On the receiving end, my boss at IMF spent a lot of time pummelling me with insults of the most subtle and insidious kind – one would not treat a dog this way without risk of being bitten.

"Sir," he would call me with that aloof arrogance, "what are you doing at this meeting? You should be back in your office."

Can't hit guys like that with bread loaves – though I did nail him with a champagne cork from twenty feet at an IMF reception for the office director once. So it happens in aid work, just like any other place.

It has to be said that the same kind of pettiness that causes one to escape to development work also goes on in international work. There's also another dimension – the backlash and jealousy of those who cannot do it against those who can. A Deputy Minister of Agriculture in Costa Rica once asked me, "Ever wonder why there are so many gringo ranchers here?"

I answered vaguely, "Cheap land?"

He said, "No, man. They can't make it in their own country. *They* are the real losers, and here they are showing us how to do cattle ranching!"

I returned from my first IMF mission while still teaching and holding a tenured position at Georgia State University (GSU). I had thought that this experience would benefit at least the department, myself and humanity all in one. My "colleagues" saw it differently. On return, I was handed a two-page reprimand in bold type. The letter was from the University Counsel and focused on my failure to receive permission to work for IMF for a three-week job in the summer. The letter threatened to remove my tenure for cause. While scared, I became a *cause celebre* among others who did international work. It soon transpired that none of them had ever asked permission or filled out any such form. Since all of us were on renewable nine-month contracts, none of us had ever thought of asking for permission to work when we were not technically employed by the university. No one had ever heard of the form! The "colleagues" were simply jealous and were trying to get back at me for the perceived slight of moving ahead of the pack. As one put it so well in the now-famous academic allegory; "You tried to climb out of the lobster trap and the other lobsters tried to pull you back, but they failed and were mad that you escaped! The only way they could deal with that was to pull you back in and try and make life more miserable for you in the trap."

A third motive to get into aid work is to meet interesting and exciting people. Sketches of the amazing people I've met could fill another book.

"What are 'interesting people'? Aren't they everywhere? Or nowhere?" someone might cynically retort.

They are definitely a different breed than the guys I play tennis with on Saturdays from the neighbourhood. And these people are pretty typical Americana.

"Where ya been this time? Oh, Kazakhstan! Is that a fact? Interesting… Hey, Bob, did you hear the score of the Maryland game?"

At the other extreme, in the field you meet all kinds of shipwrecked travellers – people who have been out so long they have no homes. Not sure if these are more "interesting" or just more "pathetic".

A judicial form project in Pakistan was to be evacuated recently due to the spate of killings there in 6/02 and the minor problem of a threat of nuclear war with India over Kashmir. Everyone was gone – the Brits, the Americans – and in came the journalists. All bad signs. But the Asian Development Bank (ADB), not known for its interest in international politics, kept most missions in country. Ours was to stay "until the MOF signed the damn MOU for three hundred million dollars and not before"!

Two Americans working on the ADB judicial reform project pleaded with the country representative in Islamabad to be left in country: they had no place to go! They were part of a fascinating breed of people who no longer had roots or paid taxes anywhere. They usually harbour extreme views, especially about their own countries – lots of Aussies, New Zealanders, Brits and Americans. One or two beers will set them off: "Fucking Blair – we're being overrun with immigrants from here and India! No jobs for good local blokes anymore."

If during one's work he or she can avoid the two types – smug neighbours and shipwrecked expats – the range of other people in the development business is quite fascinating. Many sent overseas have picked up wives and kids (lots of adoptees) and have shuttled between their home countries and others for years. Many, especially the British, it seems, have written about their experiences – e.g. William Boyd on Africa; William Burgess on Asia; Rudyard Kipling on colonial life; Somerset Maugham on the South Pacific; and VS Naipaul on just about everywhere. They describe the really fascinating overseas characters they meet, or imagine they have met, better than anyone.

In some projects, you form a bond with the team that is so deep it chokes you up to leave them. In Kyrghstan, I was thrown together with three other characters for a several-month stint in Jalal-Abad. Just the thought of going to the Ferghana Valley far from any major city, to a place increasingly full of Taliban, gave me the creeps. I have to say, I gave other careers a thought at that juncture, and even made a few phone calls. The risks of going far outweighed the benefits of trying something new.

I was met at the Andijon, Uzbekistan airport, after a flight from Tashkent on a small Yak-40 jet. The two characters who picked me up looked like brother and sister Genghis Khan. The white Lada had a piece of paper taped to the door: "ABT ASSOCIATES ADB PROJECT" – the name of our prime contractor. The two didn't talk much for the two-hour drive, but what they did say sticks in my head. The girl was about to elope with some Russian computer expert on our project to escape an arranged marriage that her parents had set up for her.

"Go for it," I said, without a great deal of enthusiasm.

In Kyrgyzstan, I met the lower rim of the aid business – the ones who stay out for years with EC Tacis, PHARE, DFID and UNDP. For instance, one US guy was not into taking baths or using toilet paper anymore. Shipwrecked types. Why waste trees for such a hypothetical benefit, smelling better for one's colleagues? Another one was an American Marxist who saw the ruined landscapes, villages, factories and clinics and pronounced them exquisitely planned works on the way to socialism, a bright future for them that we had ruined! Where I would see poverty, despair, waste and rotten health and education services, he found planning rationality and the foundation for a golden age.

Working a lot with non-American expats, I'd occasionally run across another American sporting a phoney accent for distinction. I would listen, fascinated by the theatre but curious as to its rationale, then talk in my most common American English to watch the guy cringe. He would quietly drop all linguistic pretences to the eventual amazement of his British, French or New Zealand colleagues. There are people who engage in overseas work to find new identities – just as they had found themselves many times before contemplating their navels or the original intent of the Koran on some mountain in Idaho. Having seen the wrong thing, they were trying to shift into a different gear.

The fourth reason people head overseas is for sexual adventure – or maybe just fantasy. Coming from a broken marriage or relationship, this is the big chance to change and begin a new life – perhaps even a double life: one here and one back home, the mistress or intermittent partner here; the wife and kids at home. It's an opportunity created by familiarity. Development work in countries where people seem to behave predictably and to interact with Westerners fluidly – i.e. Eastern Europe or Latin America – offer intriguing possibilities for people motivated by sexual possibilities. I saw a good example of this in Estonia. Tallinn, full of gorgeous people who are a mixture of Russian, Swedish and Finnish, presented itself as a profound treat for the senses to a man alert and ready as our man Charlie. To say it was the right kind of hell for him, in the George Bernard Shaw sense of a place where the action is, would be an understatement. He spoke the lingo of the born-again Christian, and may have actually adopted the gospel to control his even baser instincts, but his facial expression betrayed him – he had the depraved eyes and mug of a common thug. His slick capacity to persuade in confident, perfectly-modulated tones, got him good jobs like the Chief Financial Officer of a wealthy California city. I knew we were going to have major conflicts once he hit Tallinn. I think he did too – that's why he wanted the job: to let his ape-like, feral impulses and desires loose and to put his controlled Western self in a suspended file for a few years.

And why not? They were all there – the icy heat conveyed by women in these parts – inviting, lustful, hungry, voluptuous, willing beauties – a sexual cornucopia that could drive even the most principled puritan delirious. Charlie had to be cool at first – he simply took the most eager one into his confidence as an *aide-de-camp* to "help" him with his work building a training institute in Tartu. The town, as luck would have it, was quite far from where his wife and two kids were holed up in Tallinn. So, it simply was not safe to race home in the project car at night after a hard day's work. The sly, self-conscious grin she conveyed when she was introduced as his "local assistant" almost produced laughter in those assembled. The outrageous plans of this guy – importing Harleys; his bizarre actions – working the laptop at the pub every night, his past actions – policeman, football player – once bragged that he threw a pizza man out the window after he took the delivery; his suspicions – I was now a spook from the head office there to spy on him; his rather obvious ploys – he found out that AID didn't have clear rules for property disposal after project termination; all these added up to trouble.

On the last point, one month later he notified the police and the development firm for which we worked that after being drugged and robbed by two women (he, a two hundred and twenty-pound former football player!) they took his car keys and car, broke into the project office and stole two computers. Amazing how these things happen. Nothing was done. Two months later, the Tallinn press found out that he had in fact been sleeping with his "assistant" – AKA the Dutch ambassador's wife. The press promptly published accounts and pictures on their front pages, much to the embarrassment of the US embassy and his employer! For him, no more family and not much of a future. As for the computers and equipment, they were never found, but we can bet that they are in use down in Tartu at the "development centre".

He wasn't the most sexually predatory example by any

means. I have worked with Europeans who have several wives in varying states of legality – for example, one in Bulgaria or Macedonia; one back in the UK; one in Albania; one in Charleston; and so on. The work made this all very convenient and one had to envy them for their energy, imagination and the exciting times they were having at middle age with high-potency twenty to twenty-five-year-old women. It certainly motivated them to stay overseas or to move to another country – but certainly not to the boredom of home. The female team leader of our Bulgaria project once asked me, "Do you think these nineteen to twenty-two-year-old women see anything in these drunken, fat foreign consultants other than money and a ticket out of the country some day?"

Not all of the sexual activity was seedy – occasionally the young singles met husbands, wives or girlfriends on our projects. On another USAID-funded Bulgarian project, over a three-year period there were four internal marriages and at least two kids born. In almost every Eastern European project, one or more of the staff ended up overseas with new boy or girlfriend/wife or husband. So the open secret in this business is that the draw of long- and short-term sexual flings or romances on overseas work is very strong.

The fifth reason to do development is to be independent from stifling bureaucracy and hide-bound rules. Sure, there are all kinds of rules in foreign aid, but in the field one has a sense that one is often making them up as one goes along.

"Rule 64: I will work with whomever is in the office today."

I worked in the US at a development firm for a boss who valued the protestant ethics of discipline, hard work, self-denial, goal-direction, responsibility and punctuality. Anarchy, chaos and evasion of duty would not be his favourite values, yet many in the field work from a type of anarchic plan, by indirection, taking several steps back to go forward, thinking out of the box, superficially evading responsibility but actually ingratiating themselves with locals and institutions so that more is accomplished in the end.

"It's amazing what you have done with these cities. How did you get their confidence?" the USAID Chief Technical Officer (CTO) asked.

"We did nothing most of the time except drink, eat and socialise with their families and friends. This led to trust, confidence and the willingness to make changes we recommended during training and technical assistance," I told her.

"You mean you did nothing for several months? Is that shown some place on the work plan?" she asked.

"I don't think so."

Development fieldwork is not for the linear, bureaucratic intellectual. One finds few anal types who never saw a rule they didn't like in this business. They typically flame out from the contradictions of trying to accomplish anything in the chaotic, unplanned environments of most developing countries. Ex-party apparatchiks in Eastern Europe or Central Asia who represent socialist planning and the very box thinking that we want to eliminate, are tough to work with unless one gets to them from a different angle. As the very apotheosis of authoritarian bureaucracy, they like rules and laws and are usually afraid or incapable of working without a narrow regulatory framework. Discretion is the last thing they want as this means responsibility, blame and, under the old system, a possible stint in prison.

Smart college grads and still-thinking adults know that bureaucracies don't think well (whether in the US or Central Asia) and they want to be autonomous helpers of mankind (merging with the idealism rationale above). Despite rule modification in Europe and Latin America, a US Civil Service rule still prohibits staff from taking leaves of absence to work overseas short-term because of conflicts of interest! Bright young public service and international-oriented graduates learn of this, shake their heads and wonder how many more senseless rules will they have to put up with? These potential foreign aides are the classic, modern, racially unbiased, politically correct (PC), culturally sensitive types who don't want to work in large, group-think-prone contexts where risk/reward ratios must be kept in mind at all times and process is the norm. Development work should be different, and this is an important attraction for foreign aides.

The final reason is for status. This rationale fits more for senior foreign aides. There are a lot of real experts in this business – former US city managers of twenty years' experience; people who have managed agricultural development projects in civil wars in two or three countries during their careers; and investment bankers who want to give something back and go places to learn about new cultures and problems so that they can come up with something that just improves lives. These are all pretty unassuming people, and they are the best ones to work with. The status types are in it for the hotels and business-class flights that they believe are their entitlement. "Keep the urchins and beggars away… don't delay my suitcases; I want no hassles at the airports and expect to be picked up at four a.m. and taken to my hotel. I am the instant country expert." The smell of arrogance and hypocrisy starts to get thick with supervisory types in such "soft" areas as: democracy-building; civil society; organisational development; and capacity-building. Many of these activities in the Sixties would have inspired cynical laughter among my fellow students at Berkeley – "Build civil society? How long have you worked for the CIA?"

We were purists then. We knew from our professors the right side of the conflict – we were on the side of the people against repressive regimes, corporate exploitation and threats to human and civil rights. Funny how some of the bad guys have turned out to be the best agents of real change (Bush!) and the ones taking the humanitarian line turned out to be hypocrites and cowards afraid to take a stand for the ideals they preached.

I remember my big discovery while doing my dissertation in Costa Rica that my tennis partner from the embassy was in fact a CIA agent. I was thrilled to the point of paralysis. Didn't know what to do with the information, perhaps warn the local communist party? I told another American, who it turned out was a deep-cover operative for the CIA, which the first guy didn't even know because he was a small-timer, out of the loop. It was Cold War stuff. The Soviets had a big embassy in Costa Rica and the US spent a lot of time using people like this to spy on them. Pretty funny, really.

With the end of the Cold War, we are now free to use these concepts with more reverence, and the false certitude that we can actually apply them with development aid and not just force. Hence the big emphasis of USAID on aid-project strategic objectives and results – e.g. 2.4: more transparent and accountable government institutions – and intermediate objectives – e.g. 2.4.1.2: local government capacity to act. These big-time, macro-political concepts are part of our larger and deeper ideological agenda of exporting political correctness.

"In time of flood, even shit floats," as it is said.

And everywhere we find these instant experts. In Armenia, while with IMF, I was asked to interview the new head of the central bank.

"About what?" I asked.

"Tell him all about monetary policy and the tools the bank can use to stop inflation."

Right, I thought. Knowing nothing about the topic (I am

supposed to set up budget systems, not central banks) except from a book I used in an undergraduate course to teach budgeting – Chapter Three on Fiscal and Monetary Policy – off I went.

"The one-eyed man in the land of the blind is king." So it was with me. But one should try to avoid these situations if possible, or find someone fast who can provide enough substance to get you through. I was lucky. Others, who have the necessary qualities of infinite self-confidence, a high sense of self-approval, and a good read-by-ear personality, can use them to cover the problem of minimal knowledge. Such people positively thrive and have presented all kinds of nonsense to locals. This is really sad. But hey, the experts can add to their CVs and increase their status.

By the way, don't forget to send me your latest CV – we have more work for you. Once an aide, always an aide!

Bethesda, Maryland, 2003

Problems with International Aid

Roger—

Thanks for your latest email and excuse my long reply. It's a week late because there were no phone lines to the hotel. The hotel room was cold last night again and I had to write to keep warm. I gave up when the ink froze in my pen. I'll explain more when I get back next year. I am getting increasingly nervous about this business. With international relations headed over the falls, what better time to take personal stock of where we are headed as foreign aides than now? If I might be permitted a brief rant…

Trade and investment are drying up in the wake of

global fears about terrorism and anti-Western hysteria being whipped up in Asia and the Middle East. Al-queda is going after development workers in garden spots of Western capitalism like Afghanistan and Iraq.

As you know by now, my view has been that the remaining leg on which to keep the global stool upright (besides international institutions such as the UN) is development aid. By contrast, as you know, the public and most US elected leaders view aid as the weakest and perhaps most irrelevant leg. Only US farmers understand the real value of overseas aid – it helps sell their produce from home! The other benefits of aid sound good on paper but in fact are speculative. Many say, such as PT Bauer,[9] that there are no real benefits at all – aid harms the poor because of the siphoning effect of nasty, corrupt regimes that use the funds to buy new homes, cars and shopping trips to London or Washington. But most of the people who say these things have never been poor themselves. Aid can stimulate more corruption, but it still gets the development job done. Remember that corruption still affects many US public works contracts. Aid can also strengthen a nasty local unelected bureaucratic regime within any US local government. We don't stop public works because of these results, do we? Come on!

To clarify what you and I have talked about late into the night over many strong drinks, development aid consists of loans and grants to developing and transitional countries to beef up their various institutional systems. Beefing up economic policy, banking, treasury, budget, procurement, election, education and health systems can help them participate in global markets and maintain governmental

---

[9] PT Bauer and BS Yamey (1983), "Foreign Aid: What is at Stake?" In WS Thompson (editor), *The Third World: Premises of US Foreign Policy* (San Francisco: Institute for Contemporary Studies, 1983)

and economic stability. The assistance can be soft (training and technical assistance, including computerised systems, and salaries) or hard (infrastructure projects such as roads, water-sewer systems and schools). It can also be both, where aid loans pay salaries (recurrent expenses) for capital works (irrigation systems). How aid is accounted for in development budgets, recurrent service budgets and capital budgets is also an important topic because of the interesting possibilities for misuse of funds and corruption that leakages in aid reporting systems provide. I won't bore you with that here.

The kind of trench-digging I'm describing is derived from my work on governmental reform. Often called "governance" to include everything from courts and executive ministries to parliaments, the concept has recently been given more legitimacy as "nation-building". We just started nation-building Iraq now that the Saddam Hussein regime has been deconstructed.

"Nation-building" was a dirty word just twenty years ago when aid "tinkered" with small problems and diplomats and soldiers handled the big problems. In reality, it was often "state-building" or strengthening public sector institutions to govern and deliver services beyond capital cities. Democracy work was done behind the scenes by the CIA, like the creation of the ITT fund in Chile, which was used to destabilise Salvador Allende, and the organisation of "demonstration elections" in Central America. Since Bosnia, Kosovo and Afghanistan, those distinctions are no longer valid. The foreign aid industry consists of aid administrators and technical experts (in USAID, World Bank – locally and at headquarters in Washington), more technical assistance experts (from firms and NGOs) and universities (often summer employment for professors on nine-month contracts relishing the opportunity to get away from the colleagues for a few years).

Through these professional agents in the past, foreign aid would do mechanical kinds of things like train bureaucrats, show farmers how to grow crops, develop extension services to distribute seeds and fertiliser, and install accounting and reporting systems in ministries. We now know there is a structural limitation to aid work. You can't just train away structural (more permanent institutional and cultural) problems caused by repressive dictatorships, especially if they are torturing their own people and developing nuclear weapons to go after a lot of enemies with whom we have been friendly; e.g. Saddam. Can't do it either if we happen to be friendly with the nasty, torturing regime; e.g. Ferdinand Marcos, Manuel Noriega or Anastasio Somoza. These are big structural matters for the policy planners, not for foreign aides or plumbers like us.

In those cases, regime change had to precede the disbursement of development assistance. In recent US instances, the Pentagon is effectively there delivering aid. The US military now disburses development aid to clinics, schools and to build roads. For example the Pentagon technically manages the aid programme in Iraq. Does that mean the rest of us should now wear uniforms? Could you become a Foreign Aide First Class? As countries move beyond the phase of high conflict and social upheaval on a daily basis, the development aid system is expected to replace the military (and the CIA) as agents of reform. Like many other technical consultants, I've been doing the clean-up work on government reform projects in places like Macedonia, Armenia, Albania, Pakistan, Kazakhstan and Kyrgyzstan for the past thirteen years. In those cases, they made their own "transition", sometimes peaceful (Armenia) sometimes not (Bosnia). The strategic idea behind this was to prevent failing states from spawning terrorism and chaos through aid. Strengthening public sector institutions can help impose a just order that can work to alleviate poverty through provision of basic services to their people. In many countries, eighty to ninety percent of the population lack basic services so the need to target right kind of aid is crucial. As a kind of automatic stabiliser, in times of economic and military conflict, aid flows should increase to prevent worse trouble from brewing.

As you know, official development assistance (ODA) is aid administered to promote economic development and welfare. It is "concessional" with a grant element of at least twenty-five percent. Aid flows continue for development and may even increase – partly to assuage guilt over places like Africa, and partly in response to real increases in global poverty. Since 1960, about 1.9 trillion dollars has been transferred in aid from rich countries to poor ones. Studies are conflicting on its effects on poverty, growth, corruption, the environment, health, the size of markets and the efficacy of public sectors. There is also the commonly-cited statistic that the big aid spenders are Norway and Sweden (about 1.2% and 1.0% of GDP) and the US only provides about 0.12% of GDP. This is true, but it ignores the obvious differences in amounts disbursed because of differences in GDP size – the US disburses about $15.8 billion per year in development aid, not including military aid and balance of payments support (FY 2004). Eurocrats and media pundits often forget that in dollar terms, the US remains the world's biggest donor; Norway and Sweden combined disburse less than one billion dollars. It also ignores the fact that the EU only provide an average of 0.33% of their GDP in development aid.[10]

Nowadays the more trendy questions concern effectiveness: where the aid goes; how much political

---

[10] "Europe in the World: Facing Responsibility", *The Economist*, November 23, 2002, pp.21–24; "Net Official Aid", *The Economist*, May 1, 2004, P.104

leverage the aid provides in conflicts (forty-five percent of US aid regularly to Israel and Egypt); and whether small projects from such donors as Sweden (SIDA) and the UK (DFID) are more effective than the large USAID projects. That is, how "smart" is development aid? Aid does provide political leverage, but how much leverage has the US been able to exercise recently over Israel on the Palestinian two-state issue and over Turkey on access of US troops to Iraq? It doesn't work all the time. US aid can be well-targeted. The US has specialised in providing rapid-fire humanitarian aid to a greater extent than Europe. Private and philanthropic aid from the US is also almost four times official US ODA.

There is growing interest in monitoring aid projects to determine if they are effective and well-targeted. This gives the green light to would-be efficiency experts, many of whom have never been out of the US or even visited Washington for more than a summer! Some would say that donors are obsessed with this topic to prove their worth to their handlers. Since USAID has to justify its annual budgets to a relatively risk-averse Congress, they are especially interested in citing measurable results, success stories, and evidence of high performance. This typically produces goal-displacement at the project and country mission office level. Congressionally-induced spinelessness up and down the aid delivery system results in project managers beating up on staff to prove they are doing their jobs to their superiors. Bureaucratic hot-dogs (often young professional types who are on such a fast track you can see their vapour trails) ingratiate upwards and alienate downwards in their perceived hierarchy of life. The ass-kissing moves upward in the chain from those considered flavour of the month by their superiors. For those doing drudge work, or considered not on the fast track of bureaucratic power and success, there are power loops and inside circles that exclude them. Some circles are important (like basic project information needed to plan out the week). Others loops are more petty like who gets invited to power lunches. It's all bullshit, of course, but it is very real.

Do you remember *The Ugly American* by Eugene Burdick? Remember why they were called "ugly"? It's not what you think – early vestiges of the anti-Americanism now sweeping the globe. The "ugly" ones were the drudges in the field trying to implement a simple water pump scheme for poor rural villagers. Obviously, building a well and water delivery system for a mere fourteen thousand dollars to improve poor villager quality of life and strengthen their community and culture, would not be on the minds of the big-project people in the capital city. Fourteen thousand dollars was chicken feed, the kind of money these arrogant and self-approving people would spend to visit Washington for a conference on hunger. Thus, the "beautiful people" were the scrubbed, zealous and inexperienced embassy types and aid efficiency experts in the capital city who spent their time throwing procedural obstacles in the way of the "ugly" development types in the field. The strength of the resultant insurgency and revolution that followed was derived from this value conflict. The conflict between the hard-working, practical but ugly, and the arrogant, cocky, inexperienced but well-fed and handsome Americans working on the aid project in a mythical south-east Asian country! It couldn't possibly have been Vietnam! No way! And it couldn't possibly be Iraq now!

Field project overseers often become obsessed with achieving some kind of measurable result – e.g. better healthcare as the result of training courses for ambulance drivers to improve response times.

They are into scripted mediocrity rather than technical support for professional risk-taking to get real results. How could most of them support this kind of activity? They often lack any recognised technical skills other than "project manage-ment" itself. This is practically a content-free profession, something like that of "leadership specialist", in high demand around the Washington DC area, which allows novices to second-guess expertise in any area you choose – water, sewer, roads, agriculture, health, education or budget-finance reform. Project staff spend a lot of time reporting short-term results that please Congress but have little to do with lasting institutional development. Often spineless cringers, they nevertheless work hard to serve up what their handlers want to hear. Once the project ends, local efforts typically stop. The net effect of pleasing the aid financier is to displace the longer term requirements of front line service delivery with back office support staff needs.

But there's always hope, Roger. Note that the British have moved away from the "control freak" approach. They have less money to waste on big showcase projects that produce short-term measurables. The British Department of International Development (DFID) now takes a hands-off approach – most of the funds for particular countries are not earmarked for particular projects so less time micro-managing them. Unlike USAID project funds that are bid out to mostly US contractors, the British simply add the funds to the country budget with a condition that it try and spend them to benefit the poor. The hope is that by making governments account, manage and spend the money themselves, the money will improve the institutions it passes through.[11] They are betting on the medium-term – that this approach will produce less short-term measurables but more shouldering of responsibility by host governments and more citizen interest in holding their governments accountable.

---

[11] "Aid: Changed by Short, Not Shortchanged", *The Economist*, July 17, 2004, p.57

As you would expect, due largely to the obsession with performance, the design and execution of aid programmes have become rigidly scripted. The film *Casablanca* was reportedly written without an agreed-upon script; the director and producer had to change the ending several times. Nevertheless, it is considered a masterpiece of film, one of the best ever made. Despite the need for the same kind of creativity in producing a film to deliver often complex solutions in diverse contexts and conditions, foreign aid views itself as a simple, scripted affair. Foreign aid should be inventive in finding ways to get funds and know-how to needy beneficiaries. Instead, despite innovatively-written proposals, the administration of aid is a rigidly mechanistic system. It prevents budget and personnel transfers. It displaces programme goals with rule compliance that serve mainly donor interests in Washington, London or Brussels. Aid programmes should be executed by programme experts – technical areas specialists in health, education, water and so on; project administration should be designed around their needs to deliver value for money. It isn't that way now, though at least DFID is experimenting with new ways to do this.

With growing political and economic instability in the world, poor countries are also losing out on trade and investment – and restrictions on their exports from rich countries which are already prohibitive will get worse as the anti-globalisation zealots push for a return to protectionism. Greens with their preference for non-tariff barriers don't help here. Poor countries also lose out because of their kleptocratic regimes, the tin-pot crooks and their bureaucratic cronies who suck all the juices from the body politic and its people. Local bureaucrats and their Byzantine machinery are often the worst cancers on local growth and development. They're the ones who push for and impose rules on all kinds of commerce to increase corruption

57

opportunities – in many ways these regimes profit from the global chaos and get stronger.

Self-serving bureaucrats in poor countries with weak governments make clumsy regulations that force their own citizens to be devious and firms to be irrational (see Nigeria). Their systems stifle initiative and entrepreneurship, and contribute to emigration and the "brain-drain" problem that also plagues poor countries. Some even suggest that incentives for emigration should replace war as the preferred way to deal with renegade regimes in poor countries like Iraq. But even as a joke this idea fails – it would create more terrorism and chaos in a world already on edge.

In contrast with the centralised, heavy-handed and bureaucratic approach to governance which only breeds more corruption, witness the difference in places like Poland. After the transition in 1989, thousands of little kiosks sprang up on sidewalks everywhere to exercise their trading and entrepreneurial skills to try and compensate for loss of their state jobs. The state wisely restrained itself from taxing these budding entrepreneurs, and the benefits of that decision can be seen everywhere today. They would have lost twice – beating up on small entrepreneurs and wasting administrative resources collecting petty cash from paupers. Many of these lucky small entrepreneurs went on to become larger firms that were then justifiably taxed. The newly-created small and medium-sized firms then had the capacity to pay taxes and could proceed to engage in normal tax avoidance behaviour so familiar in the West.

Polish smaller entrepreneurs have either merged or found other work. Some have failed; others have grown in size and stature. The Polish economy boomed, directly absorbing many of the failed entrepreneurs, and providing consumers with incomes to purchase the products of those entrepreneurs who succeeded. Other countries with corrupt, rigid bureaucracies such as Kazakhstan have not learned this lesson. They tax the hell out of small entrepreneurs, harassing them with sudden "control" visits from multiple agencies, which prevents the industrial sector from growing and sustaining the base of economic development. Macedonian tax authorities still force businesses to close up for frequent spot audits that yield very little in new revenues and simply interfere with business operations. The big firms that they seek are clever enough to pay them off or get around the cumbersome rules, so everyone loses.

In any case, not much is spent on development aid world-wide. This is a problem of small aid budgets and excessive bureaucratic complexity that prevents expenditure of what few funds are there. The big issue in Afghanistan now, for instance, is the quality of international reconstruction efforts following the successful demolition of the Taliban regime in 2001. Continued failure to disburse existing commitments for such projects as roads and clinics and to continue this aid for several years could lead to a relapse into chaos and radicalism in this tribal-torn country. The recent lessons of successful rapid-fire aid programmes in Bosnia and Kosovo (i.e. keep the local staff small and independent from the stifling AID bureaucracies with their rigid regulations and protocols; work with Civil Affairs Teams from the US Army) have generally not been followed. Countries destroyed by conflict, invasion, malnutrition and lack of infrastructure need to begin with demonstrable works such as roads, clinics and schools. Often, AID and World Bank bureaucracies act as if Afghanistan was simply a district of Washington and apply the same rules to prevent effective action in the field. All this and now to rebuild Iraq! So far in Iraq, of the eighteen billion dollars appropriated for reconstruction, cumbersome budgetary procurement systems have dispersed only about one billion dollars. This has kept local unemployment high (close to fifty percent) fuelling frustration, lawlessness and terrorism.

It is also well-known that aid funds are often wasted or lost via corruption and mismanagement. That's too bad but won't change soon. It's not a valid reason for stopping development aid. Much of the corruption is caused by local institutional process complexities, like getting a building permit or license to open a business that can require eighty steps in some countries. That's eighty opportunities for bribery. Getting the benefits of aid funds also generates corruption opportunities – like road contracts in the US. EC TACIS and PHARE projects are famous for this, so are many World Bank projects. They give more flexibility to local contracting authorities and suffer more misappropriations. By contrast, USAID projects are tightly controlled from the top, through local missions, and have fewer corruption problems.

Construction and public works projects like roads and dams are always the worst because they require contracting, procurement regulation and construction oversight capacity. Money often flows like water into the wrong hands. Infrastructure projects are regularly blamed for major corruption and other ills. Doling out contracts to political allies and family friends is an old one. More debatable is whether some infrastructure is needed at all. Critics of rural roads projects argue that they facilitate illegal logging, wiping out the forests and bringing indigenous cultures into contact with disease-carrying, rum-swilling outsiders. But absence of good roads clearly increases the costs of imported goods to local villages (the poor pay more than urban residents for the same goods – soap, kerosene and axe handles), and they get less for what they sell (agricultural products like yams, cassava and mangoes). So the issue is not either/or roads, but how to regulate their impact – because the link between poverty and remoteness is real all over the world. In the mid-1970s in Costa Rica, critics of forest policy blamed the government and the donors for building the very roads that allowed illegal logging and deforestation. Nobody stopped to think about the needs of the rural poor – except that they could be handled with happy, indigenous-type activities; again making trinkets and handicrafts.

In practical, regulatory terms, project post-audits need to be strengthened and officials given the authority to stop future projects until missing funds are located. They also need to include the programme impact dimension to ensure that such norms as forest regulations are enforced. This prevents taking the check-out counters out of the grocery store, which encourages customers to rob the place. Of course, every solution leads to new problems. Strengthened audits are no exception. The idea is to redesign controls so that they give more authority to project managers subject to tight ex-post controls. In poor countries, auditors can be bought like anyone else and problems continue.

Aid serves the purpose of getting people and institutions together and improving operations in the medium-term. It is often wasteful, but people and institutions change slowly, even with the famous "right incentives". Some want to deal with the aid problem by granting debt relief. Some countries like Nicaragua pay a hundred and fifty percent of GDP in debt-service payments and have little left over for critical health and education services. Others say that debt relief wouldn't affect much because funds saved would be stolen to line pockets rather than reprogrammed for the poor. It would also encourage reckless future borrowing and create "moral hazard" for creditors, thereby damaging the credit rating of the country and keeping it financially underdeveloped.

Still others say scrap aid and rely on markets. At least this saves on local debt service payments. Experts say that aid inflows to poor countries can do bad things, like appreciate the real exchange rates and weaken export competitiveness. At the same time, structural adjustment programmes (or credits) of the IMF and World Bank typically require policy reforms that include currency devaluation. The only way out of this debt trap is to grow fast and steady – a tall order for many countries led by regimes of questionable integrity or technical interest. Other experts urge reform schemes that integrate all donor activities into distinct funds. Realistically, donors will not get together any time soon. They are in competition to sell loans, like the corner loan shark. Some will always want to "take the lead" because they want professional kudos and even believe that they are best qualified to handle that technical area. On the left, many are confused about aid and seem to have retreated into a kind of smirking isolationism. They don't want "structural reforms" to improve markets and pluralistic institutions. Why? Because they seem to like authoritarian regimes more than US policies and attempts to change regimes. So they are against most development aid as interference with local sovereignty and cultures. How does this help anyone?

In practice, aid has big problems. The big, macro explanations exercise your brain and allow one to imagine big policy changes to make things better. In reality, local institutions are hard to change in the short term. Unions, fractured political coalitions and special interests that receive subsidies or benefits are hard to change for the benefit of the whole country. To change policies and institutions, aid donors need sustained political support. Unfortunately, reform-minded officials whom donors wine and dine after happy agreements often don't last a month in their jobs. There is no sustained personnel continuity needed for top-level support of agreed upon reforms; e.g. eliminating X number of civil service jobs; getting Y number of loss-making state firms off the state budget. To require these kinds of actions via Structural Adjustment Credit (SAC) conditions would naturally be viewed as crass political interference with internal sovereignty.

The lack of local institutional consensus that impedes policy changes has another bad effect for aid: often the aid money isn't spent. Since 1997 in the Dominican Republic, for example, only 6.7% of total approved Inter-American Development Bank aid was disbursed.[12] This means the Government of the Dominican Republic, like many others, does not even take advantage of the borrowed resources that are fully available to it.

Development aid now is often supplied in forms and designs that local officials do not want or need. This is the aid monopoly cartel problem that Easterly[13] writes about extensively. Even in less complicated, more quantifiable areas such as budget reform, much technical assistance is wasted since some of the TA is provided in the form of loans. Seeing this wasted on high-cost internationals who do not deliver on the job or on local sloths generates even more local hostility towards aid.

As you can see, the entire topic of development aid is still contentious both in theory and practice. Lots of absurdities! Lots of problems! Hope I haven't bored you.

Regards.

Bethesda, Maryland, 2003

---

[12] "Dominican Republic: Country Economic Paper 2001" (Washington, DC, Inter-American Development Bank), p.9

[13] William Easterly (2002), "The Cartel of Good Intentions", *Foreign Policy* (July/August)

Dear Jorge—

They were sitting so close to me in the hotel restaurant I couldn't help but hear every word. It may also have been that they were talking to be heard; not an unusual practice in places where you need to be exotic. Why would anyone sit and talk like that in a place like Quetta, Pakistan, as another round of the perpetual border war near the "line of control" was brewing in Kashmir (maybe even nuclear this time)? Why do we call this place "exotic"?

Of course it's exotic: first, Baluchistan Province (of which Quetta is the capital) was basically New Mexico-Arizona – buff-coloured sandstone, adobe-styled buildings with wooden crossbeams sticking out, same desert birds, insects, plants, weather. Was this Nogales, Arizona or Quetta, Pakistan? That cactus, buffalo grass and Russian thistle looked familiar – as did the silver and turquoise jewellery worn by the residents of Quetta. And weren't those meadow larks sitting on that cottonwood tree? The people looked like a combo of Mexican-Navajo and made the same brightly-patterned rugs. We can't do the Mexican restaurant idea after all, though. First, local Islamic fundamentalists torched three movie theatres recently for the crime of showing Western films. Mexican beer just wouldn't fly here. Second, this was a staging area for the raids on the Tora Bora caves during the recent Afghan war to take out the Taliban. The owner of the one local luxury hotel was able to pay off his bank loan by fleecing journalists for every inch of space and towel they used. He even paid off the loan for his Islamabad hotel, which is now finally open for business thanks to the war, so we would have to pay premium prices too! Third, Osama bin Laden likes it here and has been seen here repeatedly – especially after Tora Bora. He probably made it back to the obscure barbeque restaurant I visited last week with our group, led by some local Pakistanis. It was full of long beards, white robes and skull caps sitting in groups at long tables in a dimly lit setting. They quietly and reverently chowed down on scrumptious chicken, juicy beef ribs and excellent pita bread. Hey Osama, pass the salt! Hell, yes, it's exotic!

There they were, two likely strangers getting to know each other over lunch. He was probably Dutch or Finnish, elderly, yellowish skin from prolonged, heavy smoking, something of the cauliflower ears and looks of a man who had drunk through many cold winters in solitary hotel rooms of far-off and uninspiring places. I once stayed in the state hotel in Shkoder, Albania, in winter with no heat, living in what could best be described as a "cave" on the second floor. This might get you into heavy, uncontrolled drinking if stuck there alone (fortunately several of us could be miserable together and this saved our sanity – or perhaps reduced our level of insanity). This man said he was from some UN agency – UNDP, or was it UNCHS? – couldn't hear that acronym – there are so many now in foreign aid – the alphabet soup – that it is hard to keep them straight. Note that this was a big event for me, eavesdropping on a neighbouring table's conversation. Why not? The service was slow and food wasn't any good. The restaurant was a nice diversion from the long hours of work.

She was middle-aged, announced herself as a State Department FSO. Rather well-preserved and casual for a bureaucrat. She said "hi" to me in the hotel now and then, meaning she acknowledged other foreigners. This was a start – many Westerners, especially US women, will flatly deny the existence of other potentially US expats. Only they are there and can know the hopes, needs, aspirations and cultural nuances of the locals. Other expats, especially men, cannot possibly know this and they must be ignored at all costs. Such can-do power-women often wear the Tibetan motif dangly earrings, peasant garb and open-toed sandals. They are people of consequence and their international life validates them at every turn – NGO staff (maybe Oxfam; wait! – remember Al-Queda is an NGO too!); dislike of traditional donors like World Bank or USAID – even though they accept their funding support in every case; Peace Corps experience, and sympathy for all the major causes – HIV/AIDS, anti-GM foods, etc. But this one was different – probably outgrew these kinds of needs. Who knows, her identity was probably based on accomplishment and merit rather than insecurity masked by inflated self-esteem. Does the work cause this grinding cynicism? Or did my cynicism cause me to end up in this Pakistani restaurant as penance?

And now came the countries. He rattled off at least thirty work spots in three continents. She casually rattled off a dozen or so in response. The dizzying list of countries in rapid succession was almost too much to digest.

"Of course we supported community development in Nepal in the 1980s and I worked near the Indian border on our drainage project," he said.

With only the most indirect acknowledgement: "I evaluated rural road maintenance projects in Bangladesh in the 1980s. I found that incentives made all the difference," she added.

"We had to build stakeholder groups that included women as heads of family – that was our incentive system," he said with a dry casualness.

Both experts were into – I should say supported with – money and administrative rank since they were clearly in the supervisory class. They were clearly versed in the major current causes: NGOs; civil society; gender; environment etc. I wondered about the sounds they were making – so predictable as to be almost animal like. They were hitting so many places that they had to run out soon-then what do we talk about? I wondered if they were professional drifters? Were they shipwrecked here temporarily, or did they actually choose this place? Were they also going to plead "no place to go to" if evacuated? Had they learned anything new lately, or was it limited to talking about "lessons learned" without knowing what any of them actually meant? Had they tried anything radical or new other than the latest mod clothing, lifestyles or opinions? Did they have any anchors – any family – or did they just hit countries and rack them up in their memories?

It was summer of 2002, and I was on an Asian Development Bank (ADB) mission to appraise what is called a "devolution support programme". The purpose was to produce an acceptable loan to encourage decentralisation of the existing top-down military structure of General Pervez Musharraf to something like a Western local system in which sub-national officials could raise their own revenue and spend monies in response to citizen needs consistent with national service standards. This would be quite an accomplishment in the centralised caliphate of Pakistan that was really a collection of tribes and formerly autonomous states held together by military force. Over the decades, various leaders had come and gone (Bhutto, Nawaz, Ul Haq etc.) and none had really succeeded in devolving power. More precisely, none had really tried anything that would threaten their central power base. Pakistan is a "low-income economy" with a GNP per capita of only $2230. This is about the level of Nicaragua,

Armenia or Mongolia. Life expectancy is only sixty years, the literacy rate is thirty-eight percent. Only thirty-eight percent of the people have access to healthcare, sixty percent to safe water and thirty percent to sanitation facilities. The infant mortality rate is 90/1000 births – similar to many African countries. So, mixed up a with a potent brew of anti-Western Islamic fundamentalism that threatens daily life, Pakistan is not the typical palm-tree studded, salsa driven developing country.

The day I arrived (5/9/02), twelve Frenchmen had been murdered in Karachi by a car bomb. The next week, India and Pakistan began amassing troops on the Kashmir border and President Vajpayee said that it was time to "teach Pakistan a good lesson".

Son of a bitch! Rotten luck to arrive just when everyone is clearing out and the only ones coming in are either seasoned journalists or wannabees. The girl on the plane with me was from Alabama, there with a film crew that was doing a documentary on the tribal areas and who wore a winter coat because it was going to be forty-two degrees in Islamabad according to the newspaper.

"Shit, it's hot here! What the hell?" she bellowed when the door of the plane was opened on the tarmac. I told her forty-two degrees in centigrade would be about a hundred and five degrees Fahrenheit.

"Shit," she replied.

Both the Pakistani and Indians then proceeded to launch several "test" missiles to intimidate the other side. The Pakistani missiles, which I watched with childish amazement on CNN in the hotel breakfast room, looked something like a cross between toy rockets and old V-2s. The very spectacle of this puerile display scared a lot of people because of the real weaknesses it revealed.

I thought, Now the Indians are sure to attack a country that defends itself with toy rockets!

In the meantime, nearly all foreigners and donor missions had been evacuated by charter or regular air and replaced by teams of international journalists. The ADB mission was headed by a New Zealander and another Australian expat who informed me that they were staying since their embassies didn't really care what they did!

I was intrigued, excited and scared at the same time. At one point, tired of taped messages from the US Embassy, I found a fellow in the hotel lobby wearing a US Embassy t-shirt.

He explained that, "Although I shouldn't be there and was in fact there, I could do what I liked."

As for inside tips on whether there would be a shooting war, he said, "I only read the papers and watch CNN, just like you do." So much for international intelligence!

Such experiences only underscored the absurdity of what was going on and the ridiculousness of wasting any more time on it. I would therefore return to the main business at hand, which was getting the loan memorandum of understanding (or MOU) signed by the ministry of finance (MOF) and our documents ready for the ADB approval process. Nuclear war or not, we were to stay until those tasks were finished, according to our driven team leader.

It made me wonder if I could process this place, pigeon-hole the experience and rattle it off as just another country visited someday like my restaurant neighbours. It's quite easy to forget these experiences if you don't do this for copy – if one is not a professional writer or journalist looking for stories. Most of aid work is compiling reports consistent with scopes of work which allow little time for distractions or local experiences. Still, being in the middle of a potential nuclear war allows for certain distractions…

I heard they caught Sheik Mohammad at a mansion in Rawlpindi, or Pindi as they call it. Turns out the guy was commuting back and forth between Quetta and Karachi on some of the same PIA flights that I took. I'm sure I saw the guy with Osama in the barbeque pit in downtown Quetta. Should I have asked for danger pay?

I'm still in the restaurant waiting for my sandwich and getting nervously impatient. Resist the bad humours – shift into low gear, as in Latin America. No need to rush, let the mind run free. So, what was my dog doing back home? He's a couch and fireplace dog, whose perfect day means lying around waiting for his next meal and then going for a walk. He would be scratching himself now, just up from the morning nap, and heading slowly for his space in a little cove behind the kitchen in expectation of dinner. If home, he and his sidewalk shadow would be bouncing along next to me on his morning walk.

He started right there eleven years ago as a puppy and retreats there whenever anyone shouts or gets into arguments. When I am pissed about something or argue with my youngest kid – a me-clone with the same hot temper – Bennie trots quickly into the back room. It's his safe haven – his anchor. Like most Labradors, he's very sensitive to tone – how people speak to him or around him. He also likes to stare at people who obviously hate or are afraid of dogs. He hangs around and nudges them with his nose until I yell, "Beat it!"

Now my youngest boy was probably replacing another part on his Mustang. Like kids in the 1950s, he would work under his car surrounded by two or three of his lazy teenage pals, cool dudes talking about drag races, the fights they had been in, girls they would like to jump, sweaty, dirty, clothes full of holes. To keep up tribal solidarity, Marty talks to them from under the engine housing or mid-frame of the car. He likes the cool cement of the garage floor and the sense of purpose of working wrenches and tools that only he knows about. They come from his little red tool cart – his organised world, his hideout from chaos, a bit of safe space.

Then there are my grapes in the back yard. I always wanted to have a vineyard just like the people I worked with in Bulgaria and Romania. They make and drink the best unlabelled wine anywhere. Good spirited fun on a hot summer day with friends in the back yard. I want a productive little plot of high-quality vines from which I make rich, deep reddish pinot noir and cabernet wines. We will drink this brew under an arbour on little tables with checkered tablecloths. There is the usual crowd of loud, mean-looking but harmless bumblebees flying around... To be able to conjure an image of maturing grapes, sleeping dog and buzzing bees was my escape – my mental safe haven. Never mind that all eight vines yielded only about fifty grapes. The dog himself(!), deer, raccoons, fox, groundhogs, birds and other forest passersby ate all the rest.

I recalled all this listening to these people because I wondered if they ever turned it off – the civil society crusade, the gender brigades, moving up the scale of countries visited... Was that kind of talk their form of catharsis, their way of relaxing?

Ah, it worked. Here's my sandwich. Now I can read my paper in peace and get back to work...

Stay cool.

Quetta, Pakistan, 2002

V. Joining the Safari

Hey Phil—

How'd I become a foreign aide in the front lines of international development? To paraphrase Elvis, the beat was just so powerful, I tried to do regular work but I couldn't do it. My feet start moving and, I couldn't help it, I just couldn't stand still. I always came back to it from other jobs, like university professorships or brief stints in government service. To quote Homer Simpson: "Boring!" A long string of chance characters reaffirmed this was the right path, this was the profession to have for potentially authentic experiences, self-renewal and genuine defeats that at least have high financial stakes. At the university, eternal, life-long enemies could be made over low-stake issues like teaching schedules and course catalogue descriptions. Here, the battle could be over the best people and approach to win a ten-million-dollar contract – something easily worth fighting about. I've tried the opposite – the risk-averse, careerist conservative places that grind you down and rob you of self-respect. Sure, front offices of development institutions like World Bank and USAID also grind you down and often have the same claustrophobic feel of the university. You get into university teaching for the freedom and status. What freedom? Status with whom – the corner car repair shop won't even take your cheques! The glass is always half-empty in those places; there the man is never satisfied, you perpetually aren't good enough and haven't met standards.

So we get free of our little cage and go into development

aid – it sounds slightly altruistic and is definitely not dull. There are many of you out there who did the same thing and will never go home again, as Thomas Wolfe reminds us. Put another way, development work makes you a misfit for normal jobs!

Best!

Cultural and Behavioural Norms in Costa Rica

Phil—

To continue – I just know you want to hear all this...

I had no concept of "career" beyond permanent university funding, travel and study grants, subsidies, teaching assistantships – and neither did any of my classmates. The University of California was loaded in the 1970s, so why not relieve them of their surplus funds and put them to good use? I did my doctoral thesis in the mid-1970s for two years in Costa Rica financed by an Organisation of American States (OAS) fellowship. At the end of the first year, I had accomplished essentially nothing: probably five hundred sets of tennis with my Uruguayan "boss"; the Resident Representative of OAS. He detested OAS bureaucracy and preferred instead to have lunch and play tennis. The second year focused my attention nicely as I knew that the larger game would soon end: no more OAS money or visa legitimacy. I really didn't want to be tossed out of the country without a finished thesis.

So it was time to move. But that's hard to do in what might be termed cultural molasses. I tried to be sensitive to the local culture, but in reality I often failed at this. In the thesis mill, one had to rush, get things done on time, conduct interviews, mail copies of manuscripts etc. You know that you can't rush anyone in Latin America. To try and do so is a big mistake. Fucking culture! What am I going to do? It got me thinking: is there a difference, for example, between Costa Rican and Guatemalan culture? People from those countries are glad to tell you about the differences in stark terms!

Cultures are those values and attitudes which affect behaviour. There are regional cultures, organisational cultures and national political cultures – all affect behaviour. One should understand the styles, attitudes and rituals that drive behaviour and affect public decisions along a wide range of issues. To answer how culture affects policy decisions, for example, one would need to know how locals treat each other (inter-personal trust and respect or "social capital"). An observant outsider can easily discern this through transactions in the street (formal vs substantive interest in meeting another), restaurants and bars (how do locals treat waiters and unaccompanied women?) and in meetings (how do office colleagues treat each other's mistakes or *faux pas*?).

Americans generalise from their own cultural backgrounds and experience to their aid roles. This is unsurprising as the Dutch, English and Australians do the same thing. It is said that we see the world from the prisms of our own villages. Miss Marple did this effectively to spot criminal types and to distinguish fakes from authentic people. The key perception in aid work might be what kind of village served to develop your mental framework? Was it small town, rural Alabama? Could be interesting if you have insights into the corruption that goes on there and applied them to produce lessons for overseas decentralisation work. But most see only the happy times and the ideal types in their towns, from which they generalise. This can lead to problems –

inability to adjust to the ambiguities of overseas life (e.g. rural Armenia); suspicions of outside snake oil salesmen derived from centuries of rip-offs; invasions and even genocides. Most small US towns don't equip you with this kind of intellectual armament! On the other side, coming from work in rural New Mexico with Navajos equips you just fine to deal with people and tribes in Quetta, Pakistan or Guatemala: same problems, same kinds of local values, and same solutions in most cases.

I was lucky: born on West Side, Manhattan Borough with its constant clash of cultures and classes, and propelled into Costa Rica by a series of fortunate accidents. My summer-school teaching position at Long Beach City College had just been cancelled in the summer of 1972 for lack of enrolment. And so, unemployed, I flew south to visit a friend who was living off a Stanford Law School fellowship.

Costa Rica is famous for its exceptionalism – pluralistic tolerance of differences in opinion; relative forgiveness of political enemies; disciplined governmental restraint from intrusions into the economy; and respect for citizen rights. The place has a large middle class, no real army since 1948, spends most of its annual state budget on health and education, generates massive foreign investments through fiscal incentives and the knowledge that the regime is not corrupt in the usual sense – which means few payments to officials. I found all this out from reading the *Real Guide to Costa Rica* and it had enough magnetic effect to draw me down there.

With 3.4 million people and a GDP per capita of $5850 (meaning it is a "middle-income economy" it has figures similar to Poland, Latvia, Turkey or Thailand), a ninety-five percent literacy rate and life expectancy of seventy-seven years. One hundred percent of the Costa Rican population has access to safe water and ninety-nine percent to sanitation facilities. The infant mortality rate of 13/1000 births is on par with advanced countries like Chile (twelve) and Estonia (fourteen). Costa Rica is a worldwide "green" favourite. In the 1980s, it launched the concept of carbon credits to combat global warming consistent now with the Kyoto Treaty. These are tradable pollution permits that measure reduction in greenhouse gases such as carbon dioxide or CO_2. Costa Rica energetically encourages investment in forests and energy-saving technology. This is astonishing given the fact that in the 1970s when I was there, it had one of the highest rates of deforestation in the world! On the other hand, the roads are either really good or very bad depending on when and where one visits. Scarce state operations and maintenance funds are still used to pay civil servant salaries when the economy (meaning local receipts from tourism, coffee, bananas, beef and the telecoms industry) is not doing well. So the roads go to pot. Nevertheless, these figures stand in stark contrast to the neighbouring toughs with their big, costly and useless armies known historically for beating up their own people. Anastasio Somoza of Nicaragua and "Cara Pina" (Noriega) of Panama fit this mould nicely.

Costa Rican cultural norms are authentic and deeply-held values. They are not the usual smoke-screen and stuff of dreamy tourist writers. Like the rich, according to Scott Fitzgerald, Costa Ricans are different. At the New York Bar in San Jose, Costa Rica, one evening, a fight broke out. What was I doing there? Why wasn't I home writing my thesis? Well, you know I can't miss a good fight or usually avoid being in one. In Costa Rica, fights are quite rare, even in the less well-heeled parts of town – or at least they were in the 1970s. I was there with my Dutch-Guatemalan friend, Hernando, who worked for UNDP, and it was time for an after-work drink. I say "work" loosely as I had no actual schedule other than interviews and trips to libraries. The writing I did at my apartment when there was nothing going on socially (making it easy to see why I did next to nothing the entire first year).

It soon hit me that we were witnessing an actual fight. It wasn't immediately obvious as the music, talk and laughter already shook the walls, and it was hard to see since only dim light filtered through the thick smoke of cigars and weed. The New York Bar was a dark, sleazy place with a bad reputation. I had been there several times and had quiet times with friends. In fact, there could have been an earthquake (tremors occur there on a weekly basis) and no one would have known it. You couldn't really tell when or where it started, but the din was near us at the bar. Two guys were slowly but roughly shoving each other around and making threatening gestures. Would it be the sound of broken glass or the suddenly odd movement of people backward that first alerts you to trouble? One of them landed a punch and the two moved around bumping furniture and surprising couples at tables by sweeping their drinks onto the floor. This only added to the chaos and din of the place.

Hernando was about my size (medium-build) and definitely not a regular on the barroom brawl circuit. He frowned suddenly at me, and with a swift, dashing motion went right up to the large one. He said in his firm, polite tone: "Shame on you, gentlemen! (*Verguenza senores!*) You should not behave like this in a place of decent, innocent people! (*Aca no se debe comprtar asi – en un lugar decente con gente inocentes!*)"

This was quite a risk as they could have easily included him in the fight. In mid-stroke of a nicely-planned punch, the man put down his fist, hunched his shoulders and looked around, almost as if Spock had given him the Vulcan paralysis grip. Hernando was heatedly explaining to him how uncivilised his behaviour was. I could only watch this as a silent film drama – there was far too much din. The guy

77

responded like a scolded dog, staring up passively with his ears drooping as if waiting for a good kick from his master. The scolded one passed by me and several others, saying very politely, "Excuse me (*me perdone!*)" as he and his fight partner squeezed between the upright tables and remaining patrons at the bar on the way out of the front door of the club.

The final story is that they immediately continued the fight in the street and were promptly collared by the police. Proof was there when we emerged an hour later. The two were compressed in the back of what is called a "*perito*" or small doggie wagon operated by the police. Quietly peering out of the little bars in the back like dogs headed for the pound, they perhaps were hoping that someone would feed them some bail.

Costa Ricans are thoughtful and reflective but not passive. Other Latins give them a hard time for not being as macho as they are – e.g. the Mexicans (which works out to something like how the Germans treat the Swiss-Germans). Costa Ricans view pushy behaviour as a puerile waste of time that causes useless wars. This wastes time that could better be spent reading, going to concerts, fucking or working. In short, the defect of Costa Ricans is that, for some reason, they simply want to make love and improve the world. They have no military aspirations or false historical sense of military prowess (such as the French). They have higher standards of civilisation and (not surprisingly) much higher quality of life than their neighbours. For instance, a big problem has always been access to their healthcare system by neighbours who sneak across the Panamanian and Nicaraguan borders for services. *Why* their culture leads to more tolerance, decency and better services is debatable – but it is so. They certainly have no natural resources like Ecuador with its oil. But that has made no difference to wealth in the form of civilised behaviour and social capital (which is perhaps what is really meant by the term "development").

"Culture", which might be defined as the way things are done when no one is looking, is so thick in some places that you can cut it with a knife. Look at extreme cases and the traits become clearer. In Costa Rica, civilisation shines; in places like Saudi Arabia the place and people are artificially contrived, repressed and retrograde on almost every social measure. The women in public consist of large black lumps of robes. Some wear mod disco outfits underneath. Girl watchers, those interested in the unique contours and curves of female bodies, are limited to an array of fantastically sexy hands and heels. The heels are typically nut brown with small white areas in the middle, covered slightly by the upward arch of the lower calf. You can almost lick them they look so tasty. On a more academic scale, inter-personal trust (social capital again) is low, standards of decency are low – "professionals" claw their way up, getting others to do their work and making alliances to acquire more power in the usual game; foreigners are relegated to enclaves (to keep the pure Saudis from being contaminated); and do most of the real labour of the place.

At the same time, many Saudi are ,poor and kept quiescent by their paranoid brand of fundamentalist Islam that has helped the world and the Muslim cause so much the past four years. It is a brand of religion that destroys and does not create – that keeps people down and ignorant rather than allowing them freedom to excel. It is the expression of a people and culture that will never achieve anything except in secret, e.g. inundating the West with odd emails citing Allah. Fundamentalism has been politically useful to the largely corrupt Saudi governing class, but is likely to cost them a social explosion very soon. With the fall of the Hussein regime in Iraq, and the real potential of an oil glut, the Saudi governing class is getting nervous and thinking of buying time with mild political reform (such as the recent municipal elections).

Saudi Arabia is going no place nationally or culturally other than indirectly through gas stations if people keep their SUVs and continue to rely on gas and oil from this region. Costa Rica, despite its much lower per capita income ($5850 v $8740), is at the other end of the civilisation scale. Costa Rica thrives because individual growth and freedom of expression are important to the culture. The weaknesses in Costa Rica are due to lack of resources, lack of institutional systems, or some missing factor (e.g. computer -chip manufacture) that can be easily provided locally or from abroad. Most of these gaps have been plugged so no one really points to lack of resources that can't be generated creatively, e.g. forest bonds; environmental land banks; and fiscal incentives for major private employers like Intel and Phillips. There is, of course, the Spanish heritage of excessive bureaucracy and some of those tendencies can be seen here as well, but at least there is less red-tape and corruption than you would think.

It was nice to start "work" in a place with a future because it gave me the hope that I could contribute to replication of these cultural standards elsewhere in the world. So, off I went into development!

San Jose, Costa Rica, 1976

Travis' Logframe

Gary—

You always thought I was suited for this work – couldn't hold a decent job in the States for more than a few months; liked to read and study; would prefer to help people without doing a lot of physical labour; and rarely considered details. So here I am. Everyone can point to a few key figures who influenced them at key junctures in life. They were their favourite teachers, a patient probation officer, a friend's father or mother, an early employer at the gas station, or an understanding minister, rabbi or priest. Note that in my case, my own father or mother did not figure into it. My father was a nutter – a hobby-mining engineer who filled up our house near Tucson, Arizona, with exotic but essentially worthless rocks. So mining was not even a distant whim for me.

The other people did make a difference. I listened and made course corrections to my life. Once it was my newspaper route supervisor, telling me to keep at it and earn my way out of a whacko household. Another time it as the little league baseball coach, providing us with all the wrong lessons. Coach would show up with a few drinks in him and order the field flooded if we had to play a good team. Several times we saw him crying when we made too many mistakes. "Come on, coach, we'll do better next time!" Fuuuck, what a loser!

Influences who got me into this were people who had good senses of the absurd and droll humour that belied their formal job descriptions. Put another way, they were cynics. Travis King was probably the earliest "development" influence on me. It was a subtle influence – one that took almost a decade to produce strong direction – like a hidden seed, perhaps a benign tumour that grew inside, pushing out the safer but boring alternatives. I saw people rotting away in lots of jobs and wanted to keep moving.

So there was Travis reading a girlie magazine in his USAID office at the Ministry of Agriculture one sunny day in San Jose, Costa Rica, when in I came unannounced. He jumped up and tried to hide the mag but I saw it and we both laughed. That was my introduction to Travis.

The "rural development office" at USAID was hidden in the old Ministry of Agriculture building that rattled a lot during the daily earth tremors. No telling how many earth shakes this place had endured over the years. I went through a few in which, following that short period of helpless twisting and shaking that froze you to your seat for an instant, people ran from their desks toward the stairs and headed out into the street. Nobody paid much attention to them and the Ticos and Ticas had long adjusted to the tremors in style, like a lively new dance number by Los Hicsos to swing to out on the floor. The ministry was on Avenida Dos, a block over from Avenida Central, which had been turned into a pedestrian walkway. The original fast-food joint, "Billy Boy's", was on Avenida Central and served up excellent local-style burgers and milkshakes dating back into the '60s. Avenida Dos featured an actual cow run during the Christmas holidays. Cowboys would run their thundering herds down the wide street, leaving dust and shit in their wake for the unfortunate municipal sanitation crews to clean up.

The AID deal was my last hope as the first-year fellowship from OAS had run out and the second-year extension for good behaviour had not yet been approved by higher-ups in Washington. Despite this minor irritation, I had a rich social life of many distractions there – especially the fantastic array of hot women to chase in order to perfect the more complex Spanish verb tenses. At the end of the first year, I had written a thick set of chapter drafts that could be classified as residual. They didn't lead anywhere. There was no theme and nothing to tie the whole thing into a "thesis", which was the idea in the first place. To keep the academic enterprise going, I needed "bridge financing" for the rent, food and beer. AID was the last and best lead I had. The first year produced mostly false starts on the topic of forestry policy in Costa Rica. Nothing to show for that first year except an incredible social life and hundreds of sets of tennis, many with my Uruguayan boss at OAS. But the party was over. It was time to move. I energetically explained my innovative idea to Travis behind his big desk full of girlie magazines.

"We create jobs and income for the poor farmers by giving them contracts to grow pulpwood for the new pulp mill that is going in. Let's think out of the box: AID could help here by subsidising any potential company losses from their non-performance or bad weather with loan guarantees. No, this isn't the banana company in Guatemala," I said to head off the obvious objection. "Here we are financing the poor!" with a little tap on his desk for emphasis.

Not very original I have to admit in retrospect – there was an exact replica of my project idea in the Philippines called PICOP and financed by World Bank, but I didn't know that. It sounded good at the time and Travis gave me six weeks to work out a proposal for AID financing. I was covered.

Travis had that alert, electric grin at all times that let you know he was switched on. He'd never tell you the idea was pure bullshit – he'd simply look away in to the distance and hiss through his teeth to let you know he wasn't convinced. He was from a small Texas ranching family, an earthy, agricultural type who liked pithy idiom. His words were refreshing, good fun and almost like learning a new language on top of Spanish. Travis was a tough guy down under – had survived in Vietnam when all of his small party had been killed while trapped in a shed. The VC gunned down the others but he was hidden under the floorboards and escaped. Later he was blown up by a grenade and had a metal plate in his head that didn't show at all. His head looked OK to me.

"Why don't you get hitched to her?" he had said suddenly one day after I came back from lunch with my then flame. There's a thought. Never occurred to me until he said it.

"That mare's going to find another stud if you don't get on her." So I took the hint twenty-eight years ago and am still married to the same mare.

Travis and I didn't always see eye to eye. I hadn't put my small, unsolicited proposal in the right AID format. I couldn't just ask for funding – everything had to be documented in a pro-forma and justified logically. In 1977, that format was called the Logframe. What was that? That he would show me in the "war room". The AID rural development office had a room with a little table divided like a miniature football field into four quarters called inputs, outputs, results and risks. It looked something like this:

INPUTS:	OUTPUTS:	RESULTS:	RISKS:
$$	Thick reports	Reports circulated	Reports not finished on time and thus not circulated

I was to break down my proposal into ideas and write them on little pieces of paper. I did that and he pushed them decisively around with a long wooden stick into the right boxes. We argued about missing ideas on pieces of paper and about which box they should be in – e.g. outputs vs results. I burst out laughing.

"Come on, Travis! You're a grown man. Let me just write a proposal my way." I was obviously new to this game!

That's when I saw the gritty, professional side to him.

"If you don't want to play the game, fuck ya, just fuck ya."

So I settled down and played the game to ensure his approval and my bridge financing. In January 2000, twenty-five years later sitting in a freezing Kiev apartment doing a Logframe for the British aid organisation (DFID), I reflected on the long, probably circular path, to that task. I had to laugh at the absurdity of it all. There was red-faced

Travis bellowing, "Fuck ya if you don't want to play the game, just fuck ya". So there I was still playing the aid game years later!

Logframes went out of style at USAID in the 1980s. They were picked up by other donors such as British DFID and the Asian Development Bank (ADB). In sum, they are paper justifications for programmes and projects that satisfy bureaucratic needs for certainty where none usually exist. Why not? Project risks do entail little things like regime changes, revolutions, crop failures, revenue collapses and banking system failures. But despite the obvious risk, so what? What chances of a revolution next year (thirty percent) and what should we do about it (change the work plan, or evacuate and then change the work plan)? In most countries, despite elaborate work plans, activity scripts, and management to-do lists, our host governments really have no big plans other than their own meetings – often with other donors to hustle more money. Nevertheless, results frameworks are still the preferred framework or mechanism for conducting aid business. You must use them to bid for work: donors justify award decisions on how well proposals tie activities to them; donors then monitor and evaluate results on the basis of the results frameworks. The evaluation score goes into contractor or consultant file for future performance reference. The obvious problem with measuring what cannot really be measured (e.g. attributing the influence of the project on changes in local laws) is goal displacement. Most of the time overseas is typically spent by project teams doing things to achieve performance measures, often at the expense of doing the chance, informal things that can mean more to systems' sustainability than all the logframes in the world. The latter should be avoided as unprogrammed, wasteful time. The idea of spending a day drinking in a pub with local finance department counterparts would be considered corruption and incompetence, despite its obvious payoffs in better working relations and productivity later!

The comparative perspective often brings objects into focus. Travis may not have been the best rural development officer or professional influence on me – until you met his successor. This guy had lost his balls (*cojones*) years ago and was the classic risk-averse bureaucrat. One might expect this from agriculture types – farmers were often risk-averse because they became possessive about the main asset – land. But Travis was a rural farmer type and he loved risks. The reason for small farmer risk-aversion, obviously, is that they had everything to lose. Paradoxically, short-term risk-aversion screened out potentially new ideas that could lower medium-term financial risks for farmers. AID was supposed to be there for that purpose – to come up with methods and systems to lower aversion to risks, and to promote agricultural development. When the subsequently spectacular successes of this country are considered, the lack of enthusiasm encountered for my forestry ideas by this guy boggles the mind. Costa Rica and the concept of green forestry and agricultural diversification are almost synonymous. But they weren't then. Lots of scientific types were filling local heads with advice on why new things could not be done.

Travis' successor, Jim, showed his stuff one day in Turrialba. I had organised a meeting at the nursery of a person with whom I was working. I say "working" loosely – he provided advanced knowledge and I eagerly absorbed it. Craig was a Swiss-trained US forester who had been in the country for years, trying out new agro-based ways to generate small farmer income. He had demonstrated through numerous pilot projects the virtue of integrating production with coffee, bees and shade trees; pine tree plantations with toy factories and fence-post markets; tilapia fish ponds with small rural restaurants; and later the big one – for which Costa Rica is now famous: macadamia. He was using a new bio-forestry technique that would push pine growth yields into the stratosphere, called *microryaze*. The idea was that small nursery seedlings of pine would be fitted with mushrooms at their roots. At the age of about two months, the mushrooms would rot and bust open, sending spores into the roots. The thrill of getting spored would turn the pine needles brown for a short time, giving the seedling the appearance of near-death. It was like an after-sex experience. For, after a brief period of exhaustion, the tree would explode and grow like hell. "Bring on the next spore," the tree might exclaim!

Jim, Travis and I arrived at the nursery in Turrialba before Craig. Since the 1940s, Turrialba had been home to a lot of tropical agriculture research sponsored by OAS. As luck would have it, Farmer Jim spotted the brown seedlings.

"This means a poorly-run nursery. Not getting enough iron and water," he said. "I saw the same thing in Liberia in 1965."

Looking sceptically at me through his thick goggles, he said sadly. "You don't seriously expect AID to support this kind of nonsense do you?"

Travis looked off into space and hissed through his teeth – far too respectful to say anything that would contradict his successor. At this point, we hear sloshing in the mud. It's Craig moving quickly towards us, his shined cordovan shoes full of fresh mud, and signature red hair shoots protruding from his large, shiny head, most of which was bald. He moved aggressively up, smiling confidently and shaking hands all around.

"Sorry for the delay. We had a problem with some angry bees on a pilot farm."

"Craig," I said, "Jim is concerned that the seedlings are sick and may die."

"They are in a way," he said to Jim, "but they're being re-born as the most powerful, fastest-growing pine trees on earth. It's almost a miracle and not surprising that you would make that observation. But be careful of appearances in the tropics!"

He proceeded to smoothly and politely demolish the guy's observation, quickly and efficiently producing growth figures from other parts of his nursery using the same technique.

Jim was obviously miffed but couldn't show that he was an out-of-date fuddy-duddy. He didn't say much after that. Craig showed us around the nursery and we all headed for lunch. I now knew what Travis had meant when he said: "Watch out for Jim. He doesn't listen." At a local restaurant, we were served silverware in plastic covers for sanitary purposes. As Jim started to rip his open, I told him not to.

"It's the local custom. You eat with the plastic on."

"That's right," Craig said, and stabbed a piece of tilapia fish with the sharp end of his plastic bag. Travis burst out laughing.

When my little bridge contract ended, I didn't go back to the Rural Development Office. After all, Travis had gone.

Sorry to be so serious about all this.

San Jose, Costa Rica, 1977

Selling Aid to Pakistan: The ADB in Action

Dear Mike—

You know I always liked doing field interviews, writing analyses and giving gratuitous advice. This was my idea of the good life as a foreign aide on safari. This was fun and mostly successful work. Sometimes an official would erupt unexpectedly and it took time through translators (in Eastern Europe) to sort out how I'd managed to piss the guy off. Always picking up dos and don'ts from daily work. For example, in discussions with ministry of finance people, I learned never use a basket case for comparison with an obviously more developed place – e.g. a budget sub-system in Bulgaria with one in Nigeria. I don't understand Bulgarian, but I do understand a fist violently pounded on the table accompanied by loud, angry, red-faced bursts of exclamation. He said something like, "Idiot! Why do we have to take this crap from morons?"

Aid work is a rapid-fire, quick-learning environment. Quick results are demanded in the right form. No treatises, no major intellectual breakthroughs required, and no extensions of deadlines. Later, I moved on to writing proposals, based on refinement of the initial scientific method picked up from my mentor Travis – I could now skilfully move logical pieces of paper around a special table.

Like most people, I'd read the usual books trashing development assistance as mere "aid capitalism" for selling projects to shady characters in corrupt ministries. None of this prepared me for the rather demeaning experience of actually peddling aid projects in the field. I'd said these kinds of things myself in academic treatises designed specifically for getting tenure. But it didn't really happen that way – did it?

It's quite different when it all happens to you. As a member of a technical appraisal mission, I worked several times for a "task manager" who often had a big stake in getting the project written up positively with more potential benefits than risks, and getting the country government representative to sign off on it – even if it was only a technical assistance grant. It could always lead to a loan later, which means you have successfully generated cash for your employer (the "donor"). Think of generating cash from the likes of Honduras or Nicaragua with debt burdens of more than a hundred and fifty percent of GDP! Most of the revenue from each banana sold goes abroad to debt service. But there I was in Pakistan helping to "sell" a 1.3 million dollar grant – which should have been something like selling German beer; not a big problem.

You still have to know how and where to sell. Believe it or not, some people detest German beer! Much of the task revolves around personal and tribal politics that may be centred in particular government ministries, e.g. education or health. Some ministries have open accounts with specific donors; multilateral (e.g. World Bank), regional (e.g. ADB – Asian Development Bank) or bilateral (e.g. Japan or the Dutch). I frequently got these relationships and the alphabet soup confused (e.g. SACs or structural adjustment credits and CASs or country assistance strategies). Often, I left meetings without a clear understanding of what had happened. In exotic settings such as Pakistan, colonial architecture in Lahore with palm trees and excellent tea, it was all like trying to sort out a disturbing dream.

"How will I take notes at that meeting which I can't find without my notebook? I can't remember where the meeting will be but know the time. I also lost my notebook someplace."

I dreamt one night in Quetta that one of the Pakistani team members, a nice, quiet accountant who looked something like bin Laden, had arrived at my house in suburban Maryland. Now, what was Furquan the accountant from Islamabad doing at my house in Potomac, MD? Why, he was listening to my explanation of how municipal regulations required cutting up trash wood into smaller pieces. What else? The sheer oddity of these juxtaposed places, people and ideas left me in a state of blissful amusement and cold perplexity.

So I am here at the ministry in Islamabad today. It is not a dream or a book that I am reading. In front of me a high Ministry of Finance official wearing the traditional long white robe, is pleading with our mission leader. His little hands are folded tightly in front of him and he has tears in his eyes. Caught me off guard. We used to whine about teaching early Monday-Wednesday-Friday courses or Saturday classes, but we didn't sob and throw tantrums. In life, real men don't cry.

Much of the aid business works at this arcane level – lots of peculiar abbreviations and informal understandings. But unlike university faculty business, they involve lots of money. It took me three meetings to figure out what was going on here. In the first, it transpired that in his last visit our mission chief had promised the man $150,000 for a study of civil service reforms of pay and grading systems that (a) had already been done by several other donors, (b) could not possibly make a difference since so much money (including golden handshake provision for those sacked) would be required to do the job right, and (c) would clearly cut into the paltry 1.3 million dollar sum we had for the larger planned decentralisation project. I learned quickly that what sounded like a lot of money would not go very far at all. In academia, a forty thousand dollar grant to me was worth a fortune – summer off, graduate assistants, and class or two off during the year! In development assistance, one million dollars would be quickly gobbled up in high overheads, expensive equipment, lots of travel and loaded-rate salaries. Not much left over to do anything by that formula.

Nevertheless, we weren't going to piss away a hundred and fifty thousand dollars on a worthless study that would lead nowhere. That part made perfect sense to me – more for him was less for us. In the second meeting, I took up our case, protested and actually got a hearing. The MOF guy pleaded with me to let him have the funds. The third member of the team backed me on this. He also hinted to me that the guy had already received funds from a World

Bank grant (and maybe other sources too) to do the same thing! So back we went to the guy's office. The team leader explained the full situation to him. The man reacted with bitter surprise and wept openly.

"Marshuk, I can explain everything. The World Bank grant was different. You promised me. What of my staff? Where will they go?"

I felt like I needed a long shower to wash off the grime. This must be the tip of the aid iceberg – handing out grant and loan money for programmatically useless purposes, perhaps in exchange for something else later? Later the task manager said to me, "I feel very bad for him. Can't we give him something?"

I stood my ground, said it was a waste, and added something with a grand gesture like, "We need to stand tough."

Then an idea hit me. Why not use the institutional weaknesses of this place (over-centralisation and authoritarianism) as a strength – how about that for a lesson learned? We tell him that he can have the money if General Nariz, head of the military dictatorship euphemism known as the National Reconstruction Bureau, says it is OK. Marshuk did this and, predictably, the guy turned white and looked down quietly at his hands.

"That won't be necessary." We left his office and never discussed the matter again. Power lives!

A commonly cited weakness of all foreign aid is lack of accountability for project results in reducing poverty and stimulating development. Task managers' professional advancement is based on having project loan and grant MOUs signed. They basically sell loans. Rarely are evaluations based on actual loan or grant performance because that person has likely been transferred in the two to three-year period following MOU approval. The spectacle of a power-hungry task manager running around selling his projects for formal or informal favours is not unknown in the business. It makes an already morally ambiguous aid business even more pathetic. How low can you go?

Sincerely,

Islamabad, Pakistan, 2000

The Albanian Superman

Dear Gary—

I should say it was a telling introduction to the country. This guy gave new meaning to the term "sleazy official", though others came close right there in Vlore, Albania. These were the happy times of 1995–1996 when Albania was considered to be the maverick reformer of south-eastern Europe. The "transition" had occurred in 1991–1992, during which the nation had trashed itself in a fit of fury and ecstasy at being released from Enver Hoxja's deathly grip. On arrival in 1995, I found the place picking itself up with Sali Berisha in charge. He was the World Bank's "wonder boy", a strong supporter of Polish "big bang" economic policies that were creating fast local growth. In Poland it really happened.

The orthodox model and neo-classical economics were the way to go. Policy cause led to economic effect – in Poland the chain of causation worked. A few pulls of this and that lever (floating the currency, fixing the banking system, cutting tax rates, widening the base and cutting massive public expenditure wastage by selling off state bakeries, warehouses, soap factories, grocery stores and other communist enterprises), and the place took off! In Albania, the economy was largely built on the sand of the pyramid schemes and "hot" capital or money that flowed in and out fast to weakly regulated local financial institutions and corrupt officials – buccaneer capitalism at its finest.

We were to report to the State Secretary for Local Government in the Ministry of Interior. Odd place to report – you might think of the US Interior Ministry that handles mining and grazing leases. In the communist system (and Hoxja's was the "pure" form we should remember), cities were part of the central government/party apparatus. Since there was always the danger that one of them would do something crazy like break away or demand freedom, they were tightly linked into the state security apparatus – the Albanian KGB (known as sigurimi) represented by the Ministry of Interior.

We sat across the large table from Ferdinand Poni himself. He was a squatty, pear-shaped official with a sly, drooling grin and greasy black hair, shoulder length. To his left was his luscious brunette "assistant", who occasionally caressed his hair, much like Leni did with her employer, and also Joseph K's lawyer, Dr Huld in Kafka's *Trial*. When this wasn't enough encouragement for him to continue, she would wink at him in approval. Naturally, a lot of his macho show was to impress her – it took about two minutes to figure this out. I was impressed with her smooth, ivory-skinned arms, shoulders and neck and imagined how they would feel during a heavy massage – the other option was to watch Poni grin and drool...

Using translators in some places can be a problem. It is a big one where the intent of the locals is to give orders for you to follow. On our side were the usual platitudes about democracy, transparent government and accountability that would make everything happy and wonderful. Not sure how this was translated. The response was strange. Poni drooled openly, saliva dropping to the table in long, clear globs – just like a fucking dog. His malevolent grin nicely complemented his pugnacious stare at us. Not the kind of disrespectful bite-the-hand response you'd expect from an aid recipient. You might want some gratitude, some indication of support for us, the experts, and our worthy, universal goals. Instead, he began a list of needs: repairs of city hall; new computers; trips to Brussels for unnamed purposes (certainly not to take his girlfriend shopping). This wasn't going to be easy!

Meanwhile, Albania was the Team Leader's first assignment in a tough place. Tough – meaning hard to get basic things done. Nothing really worked outside of Tirana – phones, heat or electricity. Robert couldn't even get through to his sick wife in the US on the old state phone system from Tirana. He threatened to quit several times for reasons like this. When he found out that part of his new job would be to repair, clean and paint city halls, he announced he was quitting again. Who wouldn't? I took him down the street to see a colleague from the firm who was Team Leader on a World Bank irrigation project. That calmed him down a bit, but it was clear that something had to give at this end.

The break came when we spent the night in one of Enver Hoxja's luxury pads in Vlore. Hoxja built himself strategic sprawling palaces at key places around the country – on the Adriatic Sea (here), in the mountains, overlooking Lake Ohrid (Pogradec) – it was the least he could do for himself. We were put up at his beach pad by officials from Vlore city. The central government technically still owned and ran the place and local officials had to get their permission to put their guests up there. I could tell Poni was up to something – he had frequent whispering and nodding sessions with the officials and it was clear they concerned us. The translator told us what they were saying. Their facial expressions belied the words, which were in effect: "We will talk with AID and have these clowns replaced with people who will do the physical work we want, give us the computers and Brussels trips like we asked for."

Hoxja's beach resort had everything but heat. The water bottles we filled with hot water at the restaurant became freezing cold around three a.m. The room they put us up in was enormous, with heavy dark furniture and thick curtains – probably Mrs Hoxja's place. We each had gigantic beds. They were freezing and the sheets were like cardboard. Robert snored so loud from the other side of the room that I could only chatter and curl up in a ball. I stopped his snoring by hitting him with a shoe – not a bad desperation shot. He popped up, looked around, then fell back into quiet repose.

The next morning our driver, George, told us he had heard the officials scheming that they were going to get rid of us and tell AID that they wanted a new, more pliant crew that would do what they wanted. With this warning, I went to AID and told the woman running the mission. She understood fully and called a meeting in Poni's office at Ministry of Interior. He sat literally on a throne above the rest of us and the mission director. It was the big showdown – the grand power play. He would risk all to get rid of us. AID would bend to his will. Just like old times when Interior security forces jailed people on appearances and rumours – up to thirty-five percent of the population was in jail during Enver Hoxja's reign; another ten percent in "exile villages" where they would be isolated for one to two years until they learned the value of loyalty to the great benefactor.

Only it didn't go as planned. Poni led off with a statement of Interior Ministry objectives and described how other donors (e.g. EC Phare) fit into the picture. They were expected to provide study trips, computers, maintenance work around city halls, and quiet obedience in the back of his office at Interior. We would have to do the same as part of our programme (stated through the translator).

I could almost hear Robert packing his suitcase. In this case, I would be right behind him! The AID director, a kindly, shy woman with quiet determination (and therefore extremely effective), got up and simply restated our terms of reference. She noted that AID offered its local government assistance as a grant which they could accept or reject at any time. If they wanted something else besides our TOR we could not provide it under this project. She also noted that under grants, AID could not provide equipment or un-budgeted labour such as painting buildings by the Team Leader. Then she sat down and we all waited in silence for Poni's response.

This threw him off balance. It took him a while to get his act together. He looked surprised and beaten, less cocksure of himself. He tried to smile and look gracious. It was clear that he did not want to be blamed for losing an AID grant because he had been caught being greedy. She had called his bluff and now he was backing down. Interesting how people who only play power games can shift from being the bully to obsequious victim in but a few scenes…

Another curious lesson: Poni later became our biggest supporter! He apparently respected that we had (albeit unintentionally) won a power game that we weren't even playing. From his side, he took it out on the EC Phare team that had been corralled in his office – intercepting more of their calls, demanded more computers and so on. But otherwise he got all his local government advice from us and even showed up at times in our office – at which point we always invited him, his cell phone and girlfriend for a drink. Had it not been for the 1997 civil war over the pyramid schemes and subsequent election results which led to his replacement, we were on course to achieve wonders in local government decentralisation by total accident!

Despite being a busted country, Albania was full of magic and wonder. There were major geographic surprises – mountains rolling down onto beaches, flatland vineyards, fruit orchards, and olives everywhere! Tremendous potential! I ran on overdrive to try and soak it all in. The people all looked like us – a nice Greek-Italian blend. They were Mediterranean types – from the Illyrians of thousands of years ago – not Slavs and not exactly Greeks: as with most people around here, a delightful mixture of different ethnic groups.

One afternoon we visited our local government finance office in Vlore and found no one there. Time for a drive with George in his faithful truck and Willi the ubiquitous "Inspector". Willi was right out of an Italian Fascist drama of the 1930s. He wore a white trenchcoat that contrasted nicely with his olive-coloured skin and shiny, Brillianteened black hair, worn of course in a '50s DA style – shabby gentile. He was an important prefect official with police powers accorded "inspectors" or "controllers". That is, he could do virtually anything and receive bribes or payments in return for his appropriate regulatory response – which he would decide because he was in charge. Here comes Willi now, walking erectly upright, little feet moving quickly along under his trenchcoat like a wind-up soldier. Flashing the politician's smile, he strolled forward, waving here and there to people in the street and to others cheering him on from their windows. He fondled the lusty women who came near him – all with good cheer and Italian gusto. Only he wasn't Italian and the cheering throngs were in his head.

He directed George to a farm about ten miles inland from Vlore, which was on the Adriatic Coast. This should not be confused with Dubrovnik up coast in Croatia, which is a classic seaside resort. Vlore is a criminal den where nearly everyone wears a gun and locals try to look friendly without really succeeding! This was at least a refreshing authenticity! People in the West try to look tough, like '50s-styled "cats" and hoods a là Gene Vincent, but sanitised with their gym-bred muscles and designer motorcycle jackets. The hoods are real here and all look like John Belushi – who is in fact from Korce. In contrast with Copacabana or Miami Beach, however, the beaches in Vlore feature cows wandering around in search of food, rusty steel spikes still protruding from the sands, cement pilings and old pillboxes and bunkers scattered about to prevent the invasions that Hoxja feared would come from all directions. Local fishermen are also authentic machos. They have efficiently learned to use dynamite to blow up their daily catch, but often blow themselves up in the process – a good example of how efficiency many not lead to effectiveness!

We left Vlore and headed up into the hills, which smoothed out into lush, open countryside. A lot of the land was still divided up into the large rectangular plots of collective farms where most rural people worked and lived. There was no private land ownership under Hohja's hard-line communist regime. He even saw Tito and the Yugoslavs as capitalist sell-outs! The old state farms had not yet been divided up into private plots by Berisha.

Bunkers dotted open fields facing in all directions. They were of two sizes: the big ones were on the beach had been converted into restaurants; smaller ones nestled around a mother pillbox in the middle of the cement brood. Officers would stay in the large one and direct operations; enlistees would occupy the little ones. They had been ordered to shoot enemies and also fleeing colleagues who might pass in front of their bunker. It was a fun time under Hoxja.

We drove down a bumpy dirt road and came to a large walled farm – dirty brown brick walls with turrets on each corner like a prison – the walls surrounded probably about a hundred acres. It was a state tomato farm and processing plant. Why not? The state ran laundries, groceries, hotels and bakeries; it could do tomatoes too. Since there was no big market for tomatoes anymore (anyone can grow tomatoes in their yards and make tomato paste), the place was for sale.

Willi, ever the entrepreneur, had apparently told George to give me a tour while he would visit a friend in a nearby farmhouse. We let him off and proceeded through the gate into the plant. Not much to see – old machinery from China circa 1960 – rusty old pipes and tubes going every which way, including over the road, and hundreds of mostly broken little windows. Depressing would be an understatement. I tried to ask basic questions about production and profits. George suddenly changed his expression and looking around – said it was a set-up: "Willi wants you to buy this and I would share the funds with him."

"Where would we get the funds, George? From the project budget?"

"Willi thinks all Americans are rich and can simply arrange for the cash payment. But you know that you wouldn't really be buying anything. No one at this stage can figure out who owns the place – the city, the relatives of former workers, the central government, or a state enterprise. You would be buying big trouble."

It was a fantasy scheme – right out of the March Hare and the Mad Hatter's tea party. Rule 42 – everyone who pays for a state tomato plant gets nothing! I thanked him as always for looking out for me. He was a real trooper. We looked out for each other. Once we planned to go to Ohrid in Macedonia for the weekend in his truck. Just before leaving I could see he was nervous and stressed.

"What's the problem, George? Don't want to leave the luxury of Albania for Ohrid?" (Ohrid was one of the finest lakeside resorts in Europe.)

"I can't do it."

"Do what?"

"Drive my truck over the border."

"Why not?"

"Well, I don't really have title to it. You see, many vehicles in this country have been obtained illegally."

"OK, George, not a problem. You pick us up on Sunday at the Albanian side of the border."

So there was always some scam and people like George

were essential to pierce them – he knew them all because he had been part of most of them! Tiring of this particular scam, I said we should pick up Willi at the farm. Who was his friend? That became quickly obvious – I saw Willi run by the open window chasing a vivacious, full-bodied blonde girl of about twenty. The family was away, and even if they had been home they were probably afraid that the little inspector could abuse his powers. They would know that he could make it hard for them if they interfered with his chasing of their daughter. So around they went – back and forth. Couldn't see the details, but Willi was obviously having fun. You had to soak all this in – can't say I've ever had to wait on someone like this before. George was getting bored and started the engine, thinking this would hurry him along. But the truck had actually been stuck all along where we'd parked – in a kind of mud ditch it turned out. George hadn't noticed. We tried several methods – rocking the truck with his gears, me pushing from the back then from the front: nothing doing.

This all seemed quite normal for an afternoon soap opera. The anxieties of being stuck in the mud out in the country; Willi chasing a farm girl around in front of the window as in Li'l Abner; George cursing his rotten luck; I'm in my usual state of contradictory emotions. Nice to have a break from real work, but also would like to get back to it. Strange to be so far from home in such an odd place – next to an Albanian state tomato-paste factory. The characters and their Li'l Abner garb should also be noted. These people looked quite normal. All of them could be doing the same things in rural US without attracting Immigration and Naturalisation Service (INS) attention. In other places, such as Armenia, everyone looks exotically different – not like us at all. Hence any photos you take in Armenia reveal an almost Hollywood casting quality – sharp-featured faces; excessively luscious women; brightly-coloured clothes or all black leather; dozens of different hand holds of cigarettes at dinner; old Russian soldiers in great coats holding little pig-tailed girls' hands in subway stations etc. These human elements were unique and I had never seen sights of such intensity before.

In Albania, people were deceptively normal looking. There's another John Belushi type! So, as George cursed and I reflected on things, along the road came another regular-looking guy. He was slightly taller than me, about six foot three and two hundred pounds. Not overly large but bigger than George or me. He wore farmhand-type clothes – large baggy pants and a plaid shirt. Hailing him and going through the usual hearty handshake greeting with strangers, George explained our predicament to him. I almost ignored all this since this was simply one man and we were going to need at least a truck and chain to get this thing out of the ditch. They talked for a while and I saw him wrench his body forward like a jack-knife, hammer the truck with both hands outstretched, and abruptly thrust the truck forward out of its hole! The sound of his hands hitting the truck made a loud thud – like a controlled car wreck. George shook his hand again and off he went down the road. Now all we had to do was get Willi out of the farmer's daughter's bedroom!

I asked George, "Who was that masked man? Does he eat the local state farm tomatoes for breakfast?" He just shrugged as if supermen like this lived all over the place beyond cities like Vlore.

Son of a bitch!

Vlore, Albania, 1996

The Urchins of Tirana

Bill—

As we all know, there is a certain kind of pampered international consultant that gives the rest a bad name. Some of these fit the description of Theroux's "agents of virtue" or "virtue activists". But the more problematic types are the arrogant, pampered sissies who expect to be treated like royalty. I'm convinced now that this is the main reason USAID is so suspicious of international circuit freeloaders. Over the years, I've met a few and you can often size them up quickly by their attitudes towards beggars and street urchins. Might be a good litmus test to get into development work altogether!

"Look at those appalling people! Christ, what a zoo! Get away from me, you little scum!"

In places like Tirana, Jalal-Abad, Tashkent and most of the third world, urchins and beggars are everywhere. Often these are gypsies who literally pull at your clothes in the markets. When you give them something, their friends see this and join in the tugging. They haven't learned the fine art of begging yet. Like much else in the development business, it's a trade off between helping some beggars a bit, not helping others, trying to please all of them, or shooing them all off. It's triage time. The refined consultant types will get angry and threaten the little urchins, who then scamper back a few steps in surprised retreat before advancing again. The scenes bring to mind the cruelty of the painter Titorelli in Kafka's *Trial*. Remember how the pervert artist lived in his roof-top den which dozens of little urchins ("brats" as he called them) would suddenly visit and taunt him? He kept an ice pick handy to poke at their eyes and faces, which kept them alert and at bay! Some aid consultants seem to have adopted his methods!

I must admit, the onslaught can be fierce and scary. With one-legged teenagers on wooden platforms chasing you around the streets, others screaming as they tug at you, some even going for your wallet as they beg, it can be unnerving and even embarrassing. I've seen local proprietors in Albania and Bulgaria kick and punch them, telling them that previous dictators would never have stood for such unmannerly behaviour. In reality lot of the begging consists of well-organised rackets. A head pimp or manager controls a team of boys and girls which he protects in exchange for a percentage of their takings. To prime the pump a bit, he dresses them up in Dickensian rags, orphan pauper garb, complete with bent stove-pipe hats, ragged black coats with sleeves that drag on the ground, and soot daubed on their faces.

Of course there were few beggars in Hoxja's Albania because most people were in jail and the economy jerked along with printed money and international project hand-outs like the Chinese steel mill in Elbasan. Think of it – jail all the poor as a solution to poverty! This represented only a small part of the Great Benefactor's policy genius. It was different in those days before the "transition" or system collapse.

I tried a different tack in Albania, the lessons of which have served me well. As in many transitional and develop-ing countries, there are a wealth of small bills in circulation. One-lek notes are small and virtually worthless, so I always packed one pocket full of them to be handed out to every urchin I saw in a two-block radius from the hotel. It helped beyond that radius too. Unless they were gypsies, they would remember you paid and leave you alone. They even knew that you would occasionally give them surprising extra amounts during your walks around town. This built up a base of political capital that came in handy.

One day, as I walked along the main boulevard near the Palace of Culture in Tirana, up from Skanderburg Square, I was suddenly confronted by a punk-looking tough who shouted and made threatening gestures – they were clearly demands, though I couldn't understand them. He held out his hand and made the other into a fist. I wasn't really scared. I could always run. It was daytime and on a main street. Still, I expected some kind of feral solution to the whole thing and was prepared to fight – for what? My little pocketful of leks? It was the principle, I reasoned – no beggar will take from me unless I want to give it to him. While I was turning over the tactics of the situation in my mind, suddenly the man fell backwards and was thrown to the ground. Over him stood none other than the shoe-shine boy from across the street whom I had occasionally paid to shine my shoes. He had come to my rescue! Punk-man ran off and the shoe-shine boy motioned that I could now pass without fear. I didn't give him anything – that would have been offensive, but I had my shoes shined again the next day and tipped him a few thousand leks for obvious reasons...

Regards,

Tirana, Albania, 1996

Staying Politically Correct in Nepal

Terry—

Anthropologists call it "joking behaviour". Their longshoremen or prisoner subjects suddenly engage in raw tribal brawls and revert to animal behaviour. Professionals in the health field let off steam by laughing at their wards – the elderly, infirm, the crippled of all types. To hear this kind of raw, cruel talk smacks of prejudice, cultural insensitivity, domination and exploitation, all of which are against the modern social grain. It sounds terribly "insensitive" to the PC police and they would be suitably "outraged". Unfortunately, most of these people have never worked in intense field situations for long periods so are clueless – they may have studied them, they may have done some supervision from a distance, but daily interaction with these unfortunate people they have not done. However, the self-appointed experts can judge – it is their right and specialty.

Still, there is the other extreme – where one blows off too much steam. These are the experts who *do* work in the social services business but have developed a genuine contempt for their wards. They have a lot of experience and technical know-how. They basically hate the poor, the backward, the corrupt, the unclean, incompetent people with whom they have to work overseas. These are the ones who should be targets of the PC police, but they usually miss them and go after the committed ones who are honestly tired of overwork and let the odd remark slip.

Frank and I worked together in Nepal a few years ago. He was a Brit who had lived in Australia and married an Irish woman while stationed in Belfast with the British Army, then became an American to get him a proper home in suburban Virginia (where he should have stayed to begin with). He spoke with a heavily-accented and gruff lisp, which, combined with a deep cynicism and biting sarcasm, alerted you to be ready for excellent Oscar Wilde-type wit and wisdom. Of all people, he might have said, "I can sympathise with anything except human suffering" (from *The Picture of Dorian Gray*).

Frank had that attractive stiff-upper-lip style and an unassuming bloke-of-the-people manner. Once asked at a party how he liked cats, he replied: "Not too much, but then I've never had one cooked just right either." It was this way of dividing listeners into amused adherents and horrified leave-takers that made him an original. Definitely not PC; he rightly didn't give a shit what anyone thought!

Work with him in Nepal was interesting since I had never been to that part of Asia before and didn't know what to expect. I had arrived for my part of the World Bank mission about a week after they were well into it. As anyone can tell you after a long flight like that (Washington–Frankfurt–Karachi–Kathmandu) you arrive in a very discombobulated state and are not sure whether to eat or sleep. I find that the only solution in such circumstances is to have three to four beers and go to bed. That seems to sort out the next day fine. So after meeting the rest of the team at dinner on the first evening at the hotel Soltee Oberoi that's exactly what I did.

The plan was to meet at breakfast and get moving on how we would accomplish the TOR as a team with multiple specialties. I came into the breakfast room and spotted Frank sitting by himself, looking around nervously and finishing his breakfast cigarette.

"How's it going Frank?" (A normally innocuous greeting that should require only a nod.)

He replied, "Well bloody awful, that's how!"

Christ, the guy must have had a rough night! I thought.

I returned with a bowl of cereal and began probing his reply as cautiously as I could. Seemed to be a bit explosive, and I wasn't sure just what would piss him off most.

"Tom has no brain," he said. "There: I've said it and shouldn't have." I thought of Spock's brain stolen from him and how he led the operation to put it back. Closer to home, I soon learned that what Frank said was true.

Over the course of the mission with Frank, I can say I've never laughed so hard, which, of course, got me into serious trouble. Remember when as a kid you tried not to laugh and ended up pissing in your pants anyway? The next day Frank was back at his spot, this time waving his arms wildly not at me but at one of the waiters.

"It's a rat, you bloody fools! There he is!" he shouted. Sure enough, a rat lumbered down the aisle and under a table, followed by a rag-tag team of waiters who recklessly chased him around between tables. Since the waiters were grinning it was clear that this was not an unusual event. Just another rat! Nevertheless, some of their glee may have been from nervousness – chasing rats around the restaurant of Kathmandu's five-star hotel couldn't be good advertising in any culture. Directing operations from his seat, perhaps as he did during military skirmishes in Belfast, Frank shouted, "No, over here – there he goes!" To which the waiters reversed course and ran in a line in the other direction.

Technically Frank knew his stuff. He developed an entire model for down-sizing the civil service based on position, pay, body count and grading data that he gathered with a passion. He wanted to cut their bureaucracy back: "Useless corrupt buggers!" as he put it.

In fact, he often wanted to cut into and put down Nepal itself. It was here that the question arose in my mind – at least about how suited he was for development work – despite having a lot more experience than most people.

"If they'd stop shitting in their own food, they'd have fewer health problems," he said once. As insensitive as that sounds, in fact it was largely true. Many would shit and piss in the streets downtown. Is it this kind of natural, indigenous behaviour that gives rise to SARS now? The Nepalese bureaucracy was impenetrable, with tribes and castes so rigid that formal rules bore little relationship to what actually happened internally. Externally, nothing would happen unless someone paid a bribe – no decision, no license and so on. Even though Frank had a point, why keep working in a place that you felt was hopeless? I couldn't do it – you won't find me going back to Saudi Arabia or Nepal. I have nothing to offer them.

The big day came and we accompanied Tom, the mission chief, into the deputy minister's office for an explanation of our civil service reform plan. This should have been straight forward except for small indications that things were not what they seemed (back to Riggs "prismatic society"[14] again). We had recommended sacking forty thousand civil servants and the Nepali authorities quickly agreed. We had recommended that copy machines be put in ministry offices so that citizens would not have to spend two to three days in Kathmandu to get documents copied to fulfil bureaucratic requirements.

"What? That'll not be possible!" the deputy minister said gravely.

No problem sacking forty thousand people, though! How would that happen to meet World Bank conditions for the next structural adjustment loan? One way, of course, would be to retain ghost workers (paid no-shows) who were not registered in the accounting and payroll system and could not be tracked against the establishment roster. The bigger problem for Tom was that loans or grants were being provided by their regional competitor, the Asian Development Bank (ADB). ADB was offering them a loan to do civil service reform without any prior requirement to sack staff. Tom's career was suddenly in jeopardy if he couldn't beat ADB.

It was clear that Tom (and we) needed to sell the public sector downsizing plan badly. Tom had an idea. He had been with the World Bank for ten years and knew how it operated. A good way to get the point across was to use an

---

[14] Fred Riggs (1964), *Administration in Developing Countries: The Theory of Prismatic Society* (Boston: Houghton Mifflin)

analogy. What better one in this case than the coral reef rehabilitation project in Malawi? Civil service reform – coral reefs, they were obviously the same kind of thing in his mind. Nepali officials, in a landlocked country, should also see the connection very clearly.

Frank sat next to me, in his usual form. His face positively exuded cynical mischief. Written all over it was: "What does the dumb fuck have to say to them today?"

Frank continued, quietly scoffing at Tom's presentation and making wry comments that somehow he either ignored or couldn't hear. I thought of Connolly's Theory of Permanent Adolescence. Some of us were condemned to relive our school-boy days until we dropped dead. In boarding school days, I had to hold my laughter back several times, even as I pissed in my pants. The penalty then for bursting out in uncontrolled laughter and coughing was a slap in the face or whack with the ruler, perhaps some kind of hole-digging later.

Here, a peal of inappropriate laughter could lead to serious consequences: no more short-term contracts with the World Bank and possible unemployment for a time. I had to hold it back. I felt some tears running down my cheeks and kept my head deliberately in my notebook to avert my eyes from Frank's cruel, cynical, grinning reaction to Tom. That would be the end of it!

Of course his whole analogy was bullshit. Tom told the puzzled deputy minister that the plan for coral reef rehab was detailed on perforated paper that could be detached as the project was implemented, just like it could be for civil service reform.

"That's right, you fucking idiot, civil service and coral reefs! Same thing!" Frank hissed through his teeth.

My forehead almost stuck to my notebook. I could feel my pants getting wet and warm. Tom was saying to the deputy that, "Of course, the civil service reform project would take longer than reef rehabilitation" – an attempt at light humour.

That brought the house down – all of us roared with a sudden thunderclap of laughter – Frank, the two other mission members and I laughed suspiciously for at least a minute, releasing it all in one burst. We coughed in spasms and sputtered, wiping tears away. Then we laughed for several minutes more! I was saved even though my pants were soaked.

You have to wonder, though, what motivation other than money and business-class air seats someone like Frank had to stay in development work – not that those motives are necessarily wrong, but there should be other compensating benefits, such as the knowledge that you have made things slightly better. If you're pissed off at the locals because they are corrupt, incompetent, weird, filthy and stupid, then maybe another line of work might be in your interest. This is the opposite problem of one who sees things local through a lens of fairyland cheerfulness – potential converts to the religions of the West; politically correct; environmentally sustainable; small is beautiful development (Tom's problem). At least the latter can say that he/she is following the donor's lingo and goals and that astonishing benefits can happen. Pure cynics like Frank don't really care.

After an unforgettable mission experience like this, I occasionally wonder where Frank ended up. What happens to a guy like that? Does he walk around until he runs out of money, or does he patrol the streets and hang around the coffee shops of 19th Street NW (one of many "development hookers") waiting to accidentally run into someone who can send him on another World Bank mission?

I saw him by accident a few years ago as I was leaving one of the cavernous World Bank buildings around that area. He was walking with David Stearman, a Canadian colleague of mine. David was often moody but interesting to talk to and to work with overseas. I caught up to them and joined in their conversation. They were talking about a recent African mission from which David had just returned. It transpired quickly that David's World Bank friend had just committed suicide on the mission. According to David he was at a conference in Kenya and, shortly before the lunch break, had excused himself, gone to the men's room and hung himself. As I was trying to recover from the shock of hearing this and to think of something soothing to say to David, Frank piped up in his grinning, throaty, powerful voice: "Must have been a bloody awful meeting then, no?"

"Come on, Frank, it was David's friend," I said.

"Did he carry a rope around in his briefcase for just such occasions?" he said, with a merry grin.

David and Frank just walked on in silence. I saw them to the corner and said goodbye. Haven't seen either of them since.

Stay tuned!

Kathmandu, Nepal, 1993

Tropical Brawls

"These things happen in Mexico," he said soothingly. "Don't forget you're dealing with a different kind of people from Americans."

"I don't forget it! How can I forget it, when you're getting just as shiftless as they are!"

Patrica Highsmith, *The Car*

Dear Jorge—

I have to remember the intoxicating times we had last summer in Berkeley before I got my fellowship and drove down here with that luscious sexpot who wanted some adventure on her way to Peru. It was a journey right out of Robert Stone's *Flag for Sunrise*. So, all the thoughts come back. What a fantastic life that was – state-subsidised learning and sex.

I even drank tea then, and a hot tea in the fog can often stimulate unexpected memories. Or was it simply the perpetually dreary weather that made me remember? I was sitting in my favourite restaurant in Berkeley last fall when one of those peculiar events occurred that bring back the old memories – and a few unpleasant reflections. It was cold and foggy outside the window, and it was always great to sit in a cosy place without a lot of noise inside – the canned elevator music or the odd radio that the proprietor forgot about playing static and country and western before you complain and have it killed. It wasn't music – it was the murder of silence. As you used to point out, sometimes it's the contrast of a place that conjures up opposite reflections. You cower in a freezing hotel room – you think about last summer on a tropical beach. You work in a dry place, you need a drink worse than ever before – hundreds, you think. I was sitting in the "famous" Berkeley Anchor Restaurant on a cold, foggy evening in December having tea and trying to read a few pages of a new detective novel.

I always felt that Berkeley in the fall was itself a maze of the unexpected. Beyond the colourful local scene, which is often a caricature of the far-out place it just has to be for authenticity – to make that statement – the frigid winds and grey streets belie the outsider image of California as one palm-studded beach. The café was typical Berkeley;

driftwood on the walls, dramatic art on the ceiling and floors, all soothed by soft new-wave music. Steam condensed on the plate-glass windows from the cold outside giving the place a cosy, hermetic feel to it. It was a Monday night. Not too full. The wooden tables were placed about at random and covered with heavy Guatemalan knit mats consistent with the multi-cultural feel. At the corner table was a group of leathered-up types drinking beer. Maybe they were lathered up too! At another table there was an elderly, distinguished-looking group that featured a bearded man holding court – talking in a loud, deep-toned, crackly voice used for lecturing to his students – while the others at the table nodded affirmation. At yet another table, two women were arguing. One had the fixed, shrewish smile of one on the attack. The other shook her large mop of curly hair and seemed near tears. And it was only Monday!

The rest of the scraggly, mountaineer types in the Anchor sat quietly at their tables writing poetry or just enjoying a good high. You remember that I used to write stories (or try to), and know a bit about the life. I even had a sinecure then, a tenured slot until I fell down the professional black hole and was "released from duty", as they say. After a few years of getting the head back together, you recall that I started up again as freshman English teacher at nearby Contra Costa College just to keep me off the streets. It was all a matter of self-control, you see, and I knew I could do it. You couldn't tell from the surface of things. I was cool and collected and talked a good game. Did you notice that my hands shook a bit? The giveaway used to be my fingernails, always bitten to the quick. This was a symptom of the underlying turmoil and character imbalance. My front teeth had little cracks in them from biting the nails, so I achieved balance: longer nails and better teeth – a small price to pay for inner strength regained!

The atmosphere at the Anchor was a thick serenity, the kind you could cut with a knife – people sitting at separate tables, the place exuding an earnest, European-style chumminess. Here, the Paris bistro atmosphere of Alan Furst's WWII French resistance novels come to mind. It was serene until a rotund, pimply-faced man with red hair in white jeans erupted at one table, suddenly waving his arms in the air like a madman, smashing what appeared to be his teacup and actually pointing the rest at the waiter, who was apparently attending him! His face was boiling red to match his pimples, squeezing his hollow, closely-set eyes even closer together. With veins popping from his thickish neck, he focused his mind on aiming the sharp little porcelain stump at the waiter as if this would make him beg for mercy. Nobody in the Anchor paid much attention. Probably another ex-faculty member down on his luck, I figured. His threats and howls seemed more of a plea for understanding: "Short-change me like this, you mother-fucker, and I kill you!"

The hulking waiter took it all in from a few feet back, forearms folded so that his biceps bulged like coiled springs ready for action. Like combat signals from some prehistoric lizard, he flexed them a few times to warn the man not to go too far. At the same time, it was pretty clear that the two of them knew each other. The guy was probably a regular customer. Sitting behind the big man's table, it was apparent that the waiter was a dead-ringer for Gene Vincent (be-bopa-lu-la) in the '50s rocker mould – greasy hair slicked back to contrast with his stained white jacket, the beaming, muscular, self-confident grin (remember Jack Palance in *Shane*?). The waiter had a powerful stare that pierced through you, sparkling and reflecting inner reserves of power. "Gene" was probably from some place like Minsk where '50s rocker-types are now a dime a dozen. He said a few mechanically sturdy words in a thick accent to let the guy know his limits: "You hold it, you, or I cut off your balls!"

It was another little altercation, nothing serious, nothing for me to get involved in. I thought of fights I had seen in the tropics, far different from cold, damp places like Berkeley. What made them different? I didn't have much street experience and had only read about brawls in adventure books. Like you, I had been beaten up during and after school by the local bullies, but the only thing I learned from those humiliations was that I should have been bigger and stronger. I got into fist fights as a kid often does, on the spur of the moment – the lack of self-control again.

"What did you call me, fucker?" the wiry, rat-faced kid would say out of the blue.

The obvious answer was "nothing", since you didn't know he existed, but you couldn't just back down. That would be a cowardly way out, and pleading ignorance only works in court, not on the street. So I'd come up with a line from a recent Brando film like "You scum-sucking pig!" This produced the predictable whack to the head, which was always like hitting a tree in a car, a buzzing sound in my ears and a salty taste of blood in the mouth. I'd get in a few half-hearted punches for self-respect, but nothing really driven by the fiery, medieval rage needed for a good fight. I couldn't even get mad in these circumstances. It was another almost amusing misunderstanding. Why hate someone you might work with in the biology lab next year? But this analytic paralysis led to some severe beatings and I decided to get reasonable as a survival mechanism. As for why people like me fight (fought, I should say) it was situational, nothing more. Despite what the cerebral types say, I think that poor people in poor countries really do the same thing, I reflected, meaning that like the Coronel's Lady and Sister O'Grady, we are all amazingly similar.

I may have told you about my pals from Baltimore who were never real enemies but fought all the time anyway.

They started and ended as friends – maybe even better friends because of the intervening physical trials. So, why did they fight in the first place? I figured it was some combo of macho-flexing, posturing, impatience, frustration, misunderstanding, release and recreation. Nothing more. Others saw something more profound at work, naturally: class-conflict, social deprivation and poverty and an underlying radical ideological motivation – which, in my view, was just bullshit!

The detached, cerebral perspective on fighting was certainly alive among the tropical upper classes. I had worked briefly with a guy in Ecuador who after a hard day's work fancied shooting at people who got in the way of his car with a large .38 pistol he carried in his expensive leather briefcase. He admitted all this to me after a number of stiff pisco sours. Prior to this admission, he came off as just another condescending, paternalistic egghead who lived in his hill estate and observed the poor as one would a colony of ants. As a lawyer, he was rich-country cultured and sported his degree from the Sorbonne. He displayed a kind of dutiful pity for the working poor and their old street jalopies that got in his way. To him they were simply dumb brutes driving junk around.

"They should be forced to wear seatbelts and meet emission standards like civilised people," he once remarked as we walked back to the office.

"What if they can't afford to?"

"Then they should ride the bus like their compatriots."

He gave hefty tips to old ladies and street beggars and he was sensitive to the poor as long as they behaved themselves; begging quietly, gratefully, and out of the view of finer folk. In his view, the lot of them should be treated with a firm hand and handled like stray dogs – with a few warning shots and a kick. As a parliamentarian, he had once winged an opponent with his .38 on the floor of chambers: "I only made him dance – just a few shots, no harm there."

His opponent had challenged his manhood – a major cultural offence around here ("*Usted es un maricon!*").

Another time he had hit an opponent (of an important parliamentary bill he was introducing) five times in the face before being restrained by his colleagues.

"Yes, yes. I should have hit him only once, but this was authentic, civilised conflict among real men," he explained. I often thought about that. Was that less absurd than it sounded?

Looking around at the earthy, chic surroundings of the Berkeley Anchor, I thought of the restaurants in the poor country tropics and how deceptive they really were. They hid the underlying violence of the barrios and shacks populated by hoards of sick and half-dressed kids. The restaurants typically lit pretty strings of soft coloured lights amidst their palm trees, which blew around in the warmth and comfort of the tropical breezes. The lights were almost surreal – some of them were bottle green, like old-time Christmas-tree lights, painting the darkness.

And my mind turned to our old colleague, Bob Slaton, who had often dined at a place here also called the Anchor, AKA *La Ancla*. You recall that the place was in Tegucigalpa, Honduras, where he frequently worked on aid projects as a water engineer. I learned that Slaton had recently died in a car accident in Rwanda while doing another of his foreign aid missions to save the world.

So what was he doing sitting across the table from me grinning? I had seen him several times since his death. He had passed by without noticing me; getting into a car – always at a distance. But here he was. I knew it wasn't an hallucination because my head was back together now, the doctor had said so several times. Still, it could have been a simple maladjustment to grief, like the self-help books said. Maybe it was a virtual Bob, and I missed him more than I knew. Or maybe he was coming to get me to join him.

There he was, large as life. Slaton took a drag of his cigarette and flicked the ashes under the table. "You're talking about my old asshole boss, aren't you? Carlo, AKA Dr Carlo Roncarlo, and 'the name that went on forever' who shot at people while commuting to work to make laws that others should obey? Shit like that made me really respect the guy. It was like working for an overgrown insect, a bee."

"Who, Bob? The Ecuadorian was your boss? And why was he like a bee?" I asked.

Slaton eyed me with that mocking look that hinted I didn't get it. "Sure: he had a bushy yellow beard and wavy long hair; his eyes protruded from all this and moved in slime from side to side behind his coke-bottle glasses… just like a fucking insect! Gave me the creeps when he stared at you with those giant, unblinking eyes for really long times!

"And Roncarlo dressed like a pimp – sharkskin suits that looked like they were pasted on his torso. He was cultured, if that's the word – had a doctorate in law with a few years' practice in Buenos Aires, in, as we know [again the mocking look] the home of the most arrogant people in Latin America. The point is that I didn't like him talking down to me from commanding heights with his little studied courtesy routine. He was a cold fish," said Slaton.

"So you couldn't deal with him like all your other bosses? You ended up on the street again?" I asked Slaton.

Somehow Slaton had gotten inside my head and was comparing the Ecuadorian to Roncarlo. I didn't have any use for Roncarlo. Fact is that I hadn't really liked Slaton either. He was a crude bastard, an embarrassment if you happened to be out with the "right kind of people". When we were growing up together in the projects ("estates", as they say in the UK, which sounds better than public housing) I saved him from drowning in one of the city's rotten neighbourhood pools that were really death traps. He had drowned and came back to life after I gave him mouth to mouth – a new thing back in the 1950s – so he puked and came back to continue his future of world drifting.

Slaton stared in that hard, absent way towards me, his eyes reflected a sleepy cunning – maybe he didn't know I was there. Maybe he didn't remember who I was. It was the look of cruel curiosity, of a man about to commit a murder after having thought deeply about how to do it.

"You don't know the half of it. Roncarlo was superficially solicitous, asking little things like: 'Did you have a good weekend?' You knew it was bullshit and a prelude to something unpleasant from the defiant and contemptuous smile that would stretch across his pock-marked face during disagreements and heated discussions. He ran the office like someone who had once read a minute manager book!"

Slaton, like me, was a cynic and liked to mimic people down to their voice and gestures: "Are you certain about that, senor? I don't know that at all…" implying that if he didn't know it, it couldn't be so, since he knew it all. To round out the imitation, Slaton waved his little hand around suavely, underscoring his statement as the authority figure in control.

Slaton then closed it with, "Of course the asshole didn't know it – that or anything else!"

Now the memories are really coming back in force! I had known Slaton from high school days – "Hey, Coolness!" we called him. Not too ambitious, he was always ready to joke and tell amazing stories rather than work. He had a real tattoo on his arm and drove a '55 Chevrolet that regularly featured a crowd of kids looking under the hood during lunch-time in the pot-holed parking lot of the school.

Slaton was himself an "authentic fighter". In a drunken melee with some Okies (i.e. students from University of Oklahoma) in Anaheim, he had been kicked in the eye while down, following an awkward stumble and a fall.

Later, the Okie came around to see how he was and Slaton gave him a beer. He had spent his college summers selling popcorn at Disneyland which permitted him to polish his technical skills in the areas of chasing women, hitching rides on sailboats and finding wild parties, while others of his school class worked behind desks in banks, investment houses or congressional offices.

"Hell no, I'm no fighter – I'm a lover," Slaton had replied, and this was the truth. He had an effortless, magnetic charm with the most luscious of women that I could never understand or, of course, emulate.

Slaton told me, "I always wanted to pop Roncarlo one day and walk out of the job. Why not? Rational opposition to gratuitous violence also permitted rational exceptions." Slaton looked at me with that intense stare as if I had already heard what he said and should make some intelligent reply now. "What if I maimed the guy and had to work in another office with him someday? What if I got a black eye and had to face the humiliation of merry glances and jibes at the office?"

I remembered at least one reason why I liked Slaton: he agreed with me on the big matters like why we fight! In play as in physical combat, Slaton's intentions were a mixture of friendship and competition, a display of skill, and if someone got hurt magnanimity would prevail – something to laugh about with the injured one later. All this meant he liked clear rules of the game and to avoid at all costs any kind of drunken brawls with toughs who sported broken bottles and knives. Slaton was actually quite sensitive and could even be poetic when he wanted to.

"You should know that I once spent an evening looking through the erotic curves of my beer glass filled with golden, bubbling liquid flesh, in Teguc during a warm evening in November 1987," Slaton told me. "And you would be pleased to hear that the effect of the strings of clear coloured bulbs and neon lights behind the palm-covered bar was surreal, almost magical. And I asked myself, 'How could I have possibly put up with those conditions?'" He said this with that malicious grin on his powerful and expressive face that I remembered so well. "I didn't get paid enough to save that place!"

A certain type of girl liked his low-rider look, the weathered, pock-marked pineapple-like face covered partially by the cheap wrap-around shades he wore, even indoors. True he wasn't young – forty-ish. But his off-hand dress style, particularly his astonishing plaid waistcoats, really turned them on. The coat he had on at my table in the Berkeley Anchor extended almost down to his knees and was covered with large brown and orange plaids. It was a style you might find during a grey winter worn by low-level clerks in northern English mill towns. He had taken it off and underneath was a wrinkled white shirt with sleeves rolled up above his elbows. He really was an odd type, a real American foreigner – a foreigner here, and everywhere else as well!

"Unlike the slick, greasy pimp Carlo, I believe I understood the locals," he told me, "and at least the ladies respected me," he added with his wry grin again. "The rest of them had their funny ways, but I'll tell you what, you didn't have to bribe them twice!"

Slaton was not a profound thinker and had no strategic view of life or the world. Anyone who spoke more than a few multi-syllabled words around him got the "amazing bullshit!" stare from him. Most people didn't even know he was onto them – which made it even more funny when they went on. The anti-intellectual strain in him made him self-conscious around glib, erudite types whom he resented. The bullshit alarm would sound regularly and he was on guard.

Like me, Slaton was from an inner-city neighbourhood of Baltimore. He had that earthy quality picked up from the characters with whom he had grown up as sometime allies and enemies in the constant struggle for turf. He still had a scar at the back of his neck – from a botched stitching job done by a quack doctor in a nearby community clinic. He had been hit by a badly thrown rock by one of his own gang members aiming at an opposing gang in front of them.

"A brilliant shot!" as he maliciously described it afterwards. "I can laugh about it now. Sometimes I used to amuse myself after work watching the daily rock throw in Palestine between opposing tribes on the Ancla's CNN cable," he said suddenly. "Always wondered how many of them actually connected. They looked so bad. You know that their aim must be simply awful. Maybe it was the rocks. They'd all been thrown so many times that you couldn't really aim them. On the other hand, how many of *peleteros de la calle* from that region ever even made it into the major leagues? But they couldn't be any worse than the bastard who gave me this scar. You remember it, right?"

"Sure, Bob. What are you without your scar?"

His scar bothered him. He held within him a mixture of shame, anger, resentment, and the will to get even for his defect. He could tell when people had been staring at him, too ashamed to ask where it came from. The scar was also his badge, part of his cultural portfolio along with the tattoo – his constant reminder of where he came from and why the musing of intellectuals, the wordy and pompous, irritated him. He had been around talking heads full of abstractions, framing theoretical options and unanswerable questions too long. He had spent four long years learning about revolution from people who had never tossed a good rock or changed any institution off paper, and three more years learning how to politely screw people as a clever lawyer, all at the nearby breeding ground for social change: University of California, Berkeley.

"I nearly got a few scars one evening in Teguc. Carlo

wouldn't have been around – he was probably licking boots and kissing rings at an embassy party."

"I don't remember you telling me about that one, Bob. Not making it up, are you?"

"Get fucked, will you? Can I have some of your water? My throat's dry. Thanks."

Curiously, his hand touched his throat and it seemed to pass into his neck, as if it wasn't there. Either it wasn't, or I wasn't there listening and watching all this. Slaton stared hard at me and smiled knowingly after taking a swig. "That's better."

The relative silence of his little restaurant table had been suddenly shattered by the sound of a bottle skidding by and breaking at his feet, thrown probably from the outdoor patio Licoreria a few feet away from him next door. The bottle hit, smashed and parts slid toward a few girls at the next table who let out a chorus of shrieks.

"Nothing unusual in the sound of bottles busting on pavement," said Slaton. "I was used to glass breaking – bottles dropping from hands, falling off tables, chucked from passing cars, and the crunch of glass being stepped on. But in this quiet old neighbourhood it didn't fit. You got the sensation of an unexpectedly large wave approaching a line of surfers and spilling them like driftwood into the air. The noise was a signal that something was swelling up, maybe the ninth wave (remember Eugene Burdick's Ninth Wave?) to use an old surfing metaphor."

He took a drag of his cigarette and I assumed the role, as I often did around him, of dutiful listener of another fantastic tale.

"The area was filled with enormous royal palms and those carnivorous tropical hardwood trees, their roots mightily buckling the pavement everywhere. As the huge higueron trees swayed in the soft tropical breeze, it seemed to be the same old quiet place. The deceptive serenity of the tropics." Slaton suddenly asked me, "Ever read Robert Kaplan? He once said that: 'even if poverty and perceived inequality vanished tomorrow, and the rough places in the road to development were smoothed over, human depravity and outrage would continue. There is a certain unredemptive and darkly evil violence that pervades the world no matter how hard we efficiency experts try to eliminate it.'"

As if in response to Kaplan's insight, halfway through my third beer Slaton saw the main fight start. It came into view, segment after segment, like a groaning, thudding wave, heralded by a piling-up of chairs and tables, flying bottles and broken glass. Slaton was in an analytical mood, the spectator taking it all in. The fight was an anthology of all the techniques – punching, kicking, jagged bottles into faces…

It was the sounds that alerted him. Four guys got up quickly and moved deftly around one of the larger patio tables facing each other, kicking their stools back almost in unison. A tribal warm-up dance. You could smell their sweaty aftershave lotion as they moved, hinting that this might not be their full-time profession.

"I could see saliva drooling from the shorter bearded fat guy's mouth. He was working himself up, foaming, rolling his eyes around, groaning and panting wildly like a dog to scare the other three. With his pony-tail flapping around, he quickly dispatched the table aside so that they now all faced each other. It reminded me of a scene from Paul Simon's *Capeman*, you know – the Puerto Ricans up on the stage dancing in unison, a deadly gang dance with razor-sharp knives flashing. No knives here yet, just fists, flying tables and a few bottles. But the casting was similar. Pony-tail man reminded me of the bully Luke from my old Baltimore neighbourhood. He picked on me until I surprised him one day with repeated, quick jabs to his stomach. This put me in a category with him as street equal.

"There was also a darker, short kid in a long t-shirt and the standard reversed baseball cap. He swept a mug off one of the nearby tables that exploded with a muffled sound, shattering more glass around the patio. He looked like William, my black friend with whom I used to shop-lift after school. Taller and more muscular, pony-tail man had had enough preliminaries and, swinging downwards, connected with the neck of the short fat guy, who in turn promptly grabbed him by the beard and punched rapidly at his stomach. Nothing unusual here, fighting anywhere seems to contain the same cast of characters. It just depends on how big the fight is. The short guy had real class, kicking high like a ballet dancer to ward off the others.

"Being in the line of fire, I was scared," Slaton admitted, "but I stayed close, interested really in what made them keep on trying to destroy each other for apparently no reason."

"Sure you did. You were just afraid to leave. Wasn't it all a waste of time?"

Slaton shot back, "You always liked the higher pleasures, didn't you? Like grading English papers and going to faculty meetings. This was like a dream. Few of them were connecting. They kicked high, jumped over tables and mostly stirred up the air with their wild swings. As they got into their stride, more bottles flew around, more tables were shoved aside and more punches were thrown. But among the coloured lights and dark shadows, it was like a pantomime comedy, a puppet show for kids, with only the shouting, swearing, grunting and groaning giving the scene its violent cast.

"Their brown, shiny flesh gleamed like boot polish in the street lamp and neon sign of the outdoor pub. The four moved around rhythmically, swinging and kicking as if dancing to the beat of a merenguero Johnny Ventura cut – like the one that played on the radio from the little caged office in the middle of the patio. A choreographed fight. And sometimes there would be a crack, like the sound of an ash bat hitting a good solid double to left, as one of them connected. At one point, the shirtless guy's body arched backwards and he fell on a table and rolled over a chair with a lot of noise. He was all twisted but up instantly and back with a punch of his own, rejoining the fray and sending his wild fists into his fat colleague's bearded jaw."

"What about the people in the middle of all this? Did they just watch?" I asked.

"They were fascinated by the live combat drama, but on edge, ready to run for it if things got out of hand. I'm sure I once told you about the Managua bar in the tough barrio where I found at least four separate fights going on simultaneously. The people there just sat around idly nursing their drinks. What's the problem? Just a little altercation to beat the heat and to relieve the boredom?"

Slaton said the people in Teguc were less interested in being unwilling participants. It appeared that the "licoreria four" were getting more focused with their shots, like loosened-up tennis players. They were taking time with their punches and connecting more solidly now. The sound of a fist hitting a jaw was the same anywhere – a muffled whack followed by a short groan and the emission of a loud oath between gritted teeth.

"*Puta cornudo!*"

The one in the white shirt and slacks threw a bottle over the head of his shorter adversary with the long t-shirt, narrowly missing several nearby tables. The gleaming missile flew in an arc and disappeared without a sound in the darkness behind the pub office and beer dispensary.

The pace stepped up. Couples began to scramble away from the melee, some giggling, others gravely looking back over their shoulders, like scolded dogs. As if part of the evening work plan, the waiters and manager quietly walked backwards into the office, swinging the iron gate shut and locking themselves in. They could start on the accounts early tonight! The rapidity with which they did this could only have meant that brawls happened here all the time. They looked out from behind the bars like recently caged animals, their white paws holding onto the bars in wonder and amazement. They would wait until the fight blew over, as they did regularly when violent cloudbursts hit this barrio, pounding the palms with the sound of war drums, and all would scatter.

"While his waiters watched the melee from inside the cage," Slaton continued, "the rotund manager got on the phone and called the police, in large part because the brawl was taking too long. Enough was enough, even here. The man, quite reasonably, wanted the game to end before it scared off his customers. But it continued. The skinny one shoved one of the metal tables aside and, as it rolled towards me, I moved aside and let it pass into the street. The shirtless man was hit in the stomach by the fat one, fell backwards over another table, and hit the pavement groaning. Angry shouts of, *'Mierde!' 'Puta!'* and *'Tu madre!'* spiced the air for authenticity.

"You should've been there," said Slaton. "The brawl would have made a great beer commercial for Salva Vida – 'It's worth fighting for' they could sing to a salsa beat, pausing briefly for one last swig and a swing before being carted off to the police station, beaten to a pulp but smiling through their missing teeth in the back of the perito wagon.

"The human cloudburst was already dying down. Fewer tables were rolling around and no more bottles were smashing the pavement. The four were taking wild swings and staggering around – swaggering forward, glancing about victoriously as if they were brave, great conquerors of important adversaries. The boys were getting tired now and could barely even shout.

"This is where it got interesting," Slaton noted. "The bearded fat one had paused in mid-punch like a still-shot, and began talking to the others now, holding up his arm, a signal that as friends they should re-unite. Language was being used again. Shouts were replaced with modulated sentences: '*Guardarse y paramos para un ratito. Tomamos un poco y platicamos no?*' – 'Let's have another drink and talk about this'...'*No lo hizo en serio!*' – 'He didn't mean it' – a probable reference to a 'dis' or some kind of insult tossed out by one of them that kicked off the whole affair. The bare-chested one tried to hold two others apart – the out-of-place guy with the slacks on and the muscular, bare-chested guy with the pony-tail. They were locked together and still it happened; a wild swing at the air by one of them trying to break free of the embrace of the other three – to show off hidden reserves of power and resistance."

"How do these things happen to you, Slaton? Weren't you afraid?"

"Listen," he said with a grin and a long drag on his cigarette, "the melee was slowing down. The small guy with the t-shirt turned over a table and chair and sat down. In a nice sweeping gesture, the other three followed suit. I shit you not! At this moment, up drives a small black Lada with several cops inside. This was the classic local police car, with a blue light taped onto the roof to impress motorists. On cue, all four doors opened quietly and out jump the proud, well-decorated but lightly-armed police. They surrounded the table cautiously, ready for any pugnacious response to their presence. The police looked like Mexican motorcycle cops, sporting little caps with leather straps over the top, and lots of shoulder and waist belts and badges to give them the appropriate air of authority. But they had been to this kind of thing before and were cool.

"The 'licoreria four' looked up, surprised, as if they had been there at the table all along, and began laughing and joking with the police. The fat bearded guy even offered one of the police his drink. The four drunks got up with their arms around each other in a gesture of brotherly love, and could be seen explaining things emphatically to the police. One of the police took notes on his little pad while another cop actually took a quick nip from the proffered drink. All this took place in a scene of destruction, broken glass, overturned tables, and a manager in his little cage not about to come out and press charges. 'No, nothing to do with these people! All the destruction is just a coincidence!' A short time later, the police looked around with hard stares at the grinning bystanders and drove off.

"As I prepared to make a run for my pension, the manager and waiter opened their cage door and emerged to survey the damage. At this moment, the fat bearded one reached across the table and punched the short scraggly guy on the cheek. All of them jumped up and proceeded to have a go at it again. Half-time was officially over. The short scraggly guy punched the fat man and pulled his pony-tail. A few more shouts penetrated the air, waking any of the remaining dogs that had slept through the first half. This time the manager and waiters got involved and shouted at them – wagging their fingers at them to impart shame while shoving them a few times for emphasis.

"Then the action stopped for good. The four stopped fighting and now listened in silence to the sober ones. It was sinking in that these people could banish them permanently from the licoreria – a fate worse than jail. They hung their heads in shame, nodding together in understanding as the manager and waiter cursed at them. *'Verguenza senores!'* could be heard. The slack-shirt man got up from the table and walked off, returning in a beaten up old mini-car. To sounds of amused chuckling and chatter from the remaining patrons hiding behind overturned tables, the other three got in the car and all four of them drove off together!

"Can you picture all this happening here?"

"All what? Fights happen here all the time."

"No, man! The reconciliation. This place is too stiff, too civilised and up-tight, am I right?"

"Could be…"

"But the real point of all this was how Roncarlo dealt with it."

I was still not on Slaton's wave-length. "Roncarlo? What did he have to do with all this? What do you mean?"

"At work the next day, I really got into a nice blow-by-blow account of the fight scene with the Honduran staff, who were really interested and amused. I actually thought Roncarlo would like to hear about it. Why not? An Argentinean, he had been rumoured to be a Montenero guerrilla in his spare time. He had worked abroad on projects like these for over twenty-five years, it was said, to keep him out of Buenos Aires and the possibility of sudden arrest. At his age of around fifty, he remained energetic and could drink and dance all night with the right crowd. He might even lighten up if he thought there was some personal advantage to it and if he wasn't such a distantly arrogant class snob.

"So I told the fucker: 'Carlo, this was good. One guy went over the table after he was hit. Another guy left the ground after he was punched in the stomach. A third guy was hit by a flying bottle and had to bandage up his head after the melee. Fantastic! Carlo, you should have been there!'

"The calculating, stealthy bee eyes stared in disbelief, oscillating back and forth like a diesel mars light combing the tracks ahead. After a lengthy pause, he said, 'Do you like to watch people suffer, Slaton?'

"'Of course, Carlo, I love suffering! And suppose they weren't? How do you know they were suffering Carlo?'

"He flashed a quick, contemptuous grin and made a

giggling sound to destroy the ridiculous proposition of his untutored opponent. 'Only an outsider like yourself could possibly suggest that they were not suffering. They were poor and fought because they were miserable. In other contexts, they would revolt and fight in armies against aggressors and imperialists. They were miserable and the better classes have an obligation to either help them reason their way out of disputes like humans instead of dumb brutes, or lead them into battle. We have laws against physical violence like this, that's why we need many good lawyers.'"

"'But who were they? Couldn't they have been lawyers themselves out for a little exercise? We used to cavort and fight as well, and go home friends – just like the four guys I described. Are you reading too much into your own rituals? Perhaps the fight was nothing more than a good row.'"

"That's how I would see it," I interrupted.

"In polite silence, Roncarlo observed me speaking, with his famously studied courtesy, as he moved around his office, puttering with papers and making notes on other matters.

"The guy was thinking, 'I can't deal with this barbarian'!" Slaton said.

"Were you coming up with those questions just to piss him off?"

"No man, it was true. Real fights between real people have nothing to do with political abstractions. They probably went home, drank some more beer together and watched TV.

"Roncarlo was so good at dressing up disrespect with a smile. If I could do that, I could really have gone places," Slaton added.

It was clear that the whole topic of brawling didn't interest Roncarlo, despite its commonplace occurrence in Honduras. Why it didn't was not clear to Slaton. Perhaps such matters were beneath him, simply bad habits of the lower orders. Roncarlo, of course, didn't go to football games and was opposed to baseball in principle. Baseball, as we all know, is a capitalist mechanism to exploit local players (or tempt them financially away from the revolution!) even though Castro played it – but not well enough to get a ticket out to the majors. To someone like Roncarlo, Slaton's fight scene would fall into the juvenile category of souping up a carburettor of his 1955 Chevrolet. The topic was alien.

Judgmental silence implied that Slaton was missing something. As a foreigner he couldn't know the complex social reality of what he had seen. It wasn't just a superficial fight in an outdoor pub. How could he have been so dense! It was part of a deeper struggle for freedom and rights in an unjust capitalist society. Roncarlo had explained to him that such behaviour was actually a residual of changing social relations that would disappear with further changes in ownership of the means of production.

"What did you say to him?"

"I don't want it to sound like I disliked the bastard. He wasn't a bad guy otherwise, even though he was a flaming asshole and a snob most of the time. He did have a certain elegance to him that I respected, and every now and then we even agreed on things. He was also technically competent, which counts for a lot with me. I gave him a little slap on the back and said, 'Sure Jorge, any day now these little barroom brawls will take on a deeper social meaning and be replaced by party cell meetings.'

"Of course, Roncarlo had no use for me socially, but he needed my services to do the technical water job I was hired for. Water, not *waiter*! I used to tell him when he wanted me to get him coffee – that's what I do! We did have meals together. After I told him about the brawl, we left the office and headed to a restaurant for lunch. Not the *Ancla*, obviously! Roncarlo's style was that he would talk from a little scribbled piece of paper and I would listen to monologues on such exciting dinner topics as next week's work plan, his current programme and the political complexity of Jorge's position amidst the swift and unpredictable currents of the government. His tone always made it clear that all of this would be incomprehensible to dolts like me. Roncarlo liked to draw power vectors on napkins, revealing high conceptual abilities, but really wasting a lot of paper. I knew all this could change tomorrow, which meant more vectors, napkins and wasted trees. It was literally a rolling plan – rolled on successive napkins.

"As we left the restaurant, a little half-dressed boy of around ten approached us and pointed to my shoes. Sure enough, I had stepped in dogshit, requiring a quick, professional shine from the lad and his silent partner in the bushes. I knew the drill and laughed. Roncarlo swiftly cut through the little ruse by indicating to me that the shit was, in fact, on top of the shoe. This meant obviously that one kid had tossed it on from out of view, generating demand, while the other would offer the service to be supplied instantly. I wanted to give them a tip for their ingenuity as well as get a shine. I also knew the security value of paying off urchins in a two-block radius of where I worked or stayed, because these kids could become your allies against other toughs and it cost me next to nothing.

"Roncarlo lunged forward and tried to kick the boy like a football, but he moved swiftly to avoid his foot. Like the red-necked guy at the counter here a few minutes ago, Roncarlo was frustrated and his action was also way out of proportion to the 'offence', if that is the right word.

"In an almost predictable response to the kick, the kid moved forward quickly and slashed Roncarlo's leg with his handy knife, then faded imperceptibly into crowded streets with his partner hauling the little shine box behind him. Roncarlo didn't know what had happened, and only reacted with a wounded howl a few minutes after they had fled the scene. His pant leg became dark and the blood flowed thickly and red.

"'Little barbarian *putas!*' Roncarlo yelled through gritted teeth."

"Did he provide another seminar on the meaning of getting stabbed by an urchin?" I asked Slaton.

I recalled Slaton's words on this from an earlier tale of his. It was at points like these in his overseas work that Slaton felt his street learning was closer to reality than Roncarlo's vaunted social class theories, which only reminded him of his university profs. The fight and the knifing signified nothing more than a blow-off of steam or sexual energy related to some common insult; it happened all the time. To the intellectual, steeped in paradigms, evolutionary schemes and structural contradictions, fighting and knifing was evidence of acute backwardness and depravity caused by some combo of capitalism and corrupt police. In Roncarlo's intellectually pinched view of things, the brawl was more than the simple product of free-time, high spirits and immaturity. Roncarlo was the old sage. It was a symptom of something structural and deep. Old caciques like Roncarlo were amicable and fun, always touching, providing, directing, joking, hugging, kissing and singing to keep up the spirit and maintain control. At the same time, Slaton had said, people like him were aggressively paternalistic – they would control your every move if they could.

Back at the office, Slaton watched Roncarlo furrow his mighty brow. He was going to accompany the drags on his cigarette now with something really deep. Slaton picked up the story again.

"Roncarlo said, 'You know, those children are actually a residual of imperialist depravity. Popular materialist culture produces such behaviour and it cannot continue,' he said angrily as he put a new bandage on his leg.

"By this he meant that their kind had to be stomped out by some kind of apparatus which he or his kind would control. At the same time, the good street urchins who obeyed and were grateful for his handouts were to be treated tolerantly and wisely by men such as Roncarlo, those destined to lead them out of this miserable condition... and shit like that," as Slaton described it so elegantly.

I was having trouble following Slaton. His words seemed weak, as if the volume was dropping and he were receding. When he spoke he seemed to me to be speaking through a long tube from a great distance away. But he was still there, not moving except for his mouth. I looked over at Gene to give me the check so I could wrap this up. I looked back and Bob was not there. He was gone. Was he ever there? This gave me a chill. I must be in really bad shape. I'm sure it wasn't the tea! I needed to get home and ponder this one. Why did he keep turning up at a distance? Why was he across the table this time? It was pretty obvious, and I knew. My time too was coming, and I could then listen to non-stop Slaton stories in the world beyond, out there somewhere...

The Anchor was almost empty, as it should be around midnight. I had been there for hours. The women had stopped arguing and left the place. The leathernecks ran out of beer and had slipped out quietly. Gene stood by the register, staring into space with his tough, worried look, ready for anything, even at this hour.

Tegucigalpa, Honduras, 1980

Community Rat-Beating in Pakistan

William—

Remember in the fifth grade when you visited my house? You knew that I used to raise white mice, and you liked to visit them. Long-time pals like you recall that I had hundreds of mice in cages all around the house, running in wheels, eating lettuce or drinking water as they do to pass the time. Without telling me, my parents decided to reduce the crowding. They contacted the University of Arizona Psychology Department, which made weekly calls when I was away at school to retrieve some of them for experiments... So I liked white mice.

Now rats are a different story. City rats running around garbage pales, in alleys and around city parks, give me the willies. New Yorkers seem to have adapted and don't really mind the millions of rats experts estimate to live in that city. I always like rat stories and they produce an almost intoxicating high when I hear the details. In Vietnam, the government recently banned snake and cat sales because this habit (or local culinary taste) had increased the number of rats which, in turn, damaged crops. Now the population is eating rats instead, putting locals directly in competition with the snakes and cats for food. The good news is that fewer rats means more snails, a new market opportunity...

These are some of the memories conjured up during a recent trip to Pakistan, where I was sent to assist the government in allocating more power to district villages and towns where treatment of rats had a long history. We were in Bhutto's palace, seated in a room with the signature long table so that the leader could talk and the attendees could listen. Since the real team leader had not arrived yet, I was moved up to sit next to the general on one side of the table and across from his star aide, Daniyal. The air conditioner was turned up high and roared ahead, inducing more daydreaming and distraction. Were countries like this more focused before air conditioning?

I was listening to our man Daniyal Saleem expound tightly and thoughtfully on how the real Pakistani villagers treated rats. It was obvious how he got elected to parliament – he was a real populist showman! Wearing his white robe, he clearly commanded respect from our team of Pakistani consultants. He also conjured up fear in his wake.

"I'm not going to waste my time with questions like that since it means you aren't up on the topic of municipal finance in this country," he told one man, who promptly shrunk six inches in stature. Fear came into his eyes as if there could be more problems later.

Daniyal was both the central mouthpiece and the key advisor to General Nariz (retired), head of the infamous "National Reconstruction Bureau" which represented the quasi-civilian side of the military government of General Pevez Musharraf. We should also note that in 2003, Daniyal was appointed head of NRB and the retired general re-retired. Daniyal had a very Western side to him, having received undergraduate and graduate degrees from Boston University and having a mother from North Dakota. So socially he was a regular American guy – told great jokes. But that's another story. As a quasi-American he had to reassure his followers that he was sensitive to local concerns – not simply a mindless Westerner who cow-towed to expat consultants. It was a delicate balancing act, not unlike that of Pevez Musharraf himself. In the nineteenth century, anti-colonialism arguments against the British system were always a local vote-getter and crowd pleaser. (As the US becomes more entwined in Pakistani politics, in a few years the British may become the good guys and let's see what happens to us!)

Daniyal was providing us with background for implementation of our "fiscal decentralisation" project financed by the ADB. The project supported the new government policy with expatriate consultants, a local sub-contractor firm from Islamabad, and funds for training. He was superb – no notes, all from the head – lucid, organised and forceful. Tea and biscuits all around, served to us as always in our places at the long dark mahogany table. This was the life! Air conditioner on full-blast so it was freezing inside and scorching outside (forty-five centigrade or a hundred and fifteen Fahrenheit). The air conditioner droned on. Daniyal drew his pictures on the flipchart which we all copied like dutiful schoolboys (there were no girls around here – since Benizar Bhutto was forced out).

Now he dissected the fiscal transfer (or central government grant) formulae proposals and argued for use of performance criteria. Here he wanted the most advanced formula from the UK and US to motivate local government managers to do the right technical things (e.g. mobilise their own revenues to finance services) and encourage the right kinds of social results for a modern Muslim state (e.g. reward schools that increased girls' school enrolment). His diagrams were all balloons and arrows – the stock-in-trade of public sector training and capacity-building work. Whoa! Starting to doze off again! Can't do that – might ask me some technical point – respectful references to me as "Dr Guess" meant I had to appear attentive.

Daniyal knew the deepest historical roots and why proposed systems would or would not be consistent with that cultural history. This was sheer genius – how many government officials could do this – and at his age (around twenty-seven)? This guy could be President someday and Pakistan would be so lucky. Here he was raising the question of how we could create a local community electoral system where none had really existed before. He emphasised that, under the old imposed colonial system, villages and districts were all part of the provincial structure which the new Devolution Programme was trying to change.

In his mind, historically a "cooperative spirit" existed at the village level that dated back five thousand years. This could be learned from legends recounting village behaviour when flooding occurred. Floods frequently came to rural villages, which mostly lacked drainage ditches, sewers or river flood bank control systems. They had no systems of planning or financing local public works, other than provincial largess. Provincial funds somehow would not materialise despite promises and the rats would swim into town in the floodwaters. In his version of Pakistani history, villages would spontaneously organise out of a community sense of duty and beat up the invading hoards of rats with sticks. Here, I could picture a Richard Scarry kind of place, every villager had a label – assistant rat beater, cadet rat-beater, senior rat-beater and so on – all part of a community army that simply knew what to do because they were local, had community culture and felt good about themselves. It was no longer a struggle for self-preservation or family survival in a state of nature. No, turf considerations were set aside, and all gathered up clubs and beat the shit out of the rats. He explained this as if it had happened yesterday; and it was a positive thing – communities fighting rats. I appreciated how this view coincided nicely with the NGO anthropological view of development – bottom-up, community initiated, small-scale and egalitarian.

So what happened to this spirit? Almost predictably, nineteenth century British-appointed Delimitation Officers fractionalised the villages by drawing arbitrary lines between them for administrative control purposes. Now the floods grow worse each year, more are homeless, disease spreads, people are drowned and the rats run wild because there is no community spirit. It is every villager for himself. Brother fights brother over village elections because they are set against each other by an unjust electoral system. Corruption is merely decentralised because there is no spirit to energise the local system and keep it pure. This example woke me up. Don't hear this kind of thing often anymore. It was perfectly magic for the group! In one masterful stroke, Daniyal painted a historical picture of the golden days, took an excellent jab at the former colonial masters, and justified the organic nature of villages/districts under the new NRB programme on which we were advising. The Citizen Community Boards proposed by NRB would serve as the foundation of a new community spirit! They would contribute funds; they would find their own funds for projects they needed – not corrupt politicians. They would even by law get a percentage of the local development budget for their projects. Union Councils and villages would be integrated back into the structure and community would function again! Too bad our own policy advisers can't paint such colourful pictures for their programmes!

Over to you.

Islamabad, Pakistan, 2001

Washington: Inside the IMF

Dear Ted—

Outsiders have varying perceptions of aid workers. When we return to stateside, many of our "neighbours" believe that all of us work for the CIA and that's that. Why else would we travel to places with unpronounceable names all the time?

"I know you work for the CIA," a really dense professor once told me during an interview at Seton Hall University. "How else could you know all those people in Central America?" Seeing that I was unable to think of anything to say in response, he went on: "That's not necessarily a bad thing. I had some good friends who worked for the CIA."

The thing that troubled him more during my interview was not that I worked for the CIA but that I was a Nazi. I hadn't slept well at the Motel 6 in South Orange, New Jersey, they had put me up in the night before. The room was too hot and more than compensated for the wintry conditions outside in this really miserable-looking rust-belt place. You needed to be sharp for university interviews, but my brain was sticking to the inside of my head – going very slow today. Mouth–brain coordination was also not in place – producing inappropriate comments and overall a bad game. His last remark, though, did focus me a bit and bring out a note of protest.

"Now why am I a Nazi?" I asked wearily. He had a chilling smile that flashed victoriously as his large mouth seemed to generate words from a sideways chewing motion like a goat chewing its cud. Try it sometime – very hard to do both at once. Only stork-type birds can do this, angling their heads as they obliquely check around for insects.

"You mentioned that you had a grant to do a TV programme and didn't know anything technical about cameras, shots or filming."

"Yes, that's right." Even bigger smile combined with a sad look of concern.

"You also mentioned that you would delegate this task to a technician."

"Yes, that's right." Time for the clincher.

"Well?"

"That's just what the Nazis did."

"What? Hire cameramen?"

"No, delegate the dirty work of gassing Jews to lower officials who could say they were just following orders."

These are the kinds of off-the-wall remarks you have to be able to deal with during interviews. You can't just laugh at them, or tell them to "get fucked" or threaten them with a growl and a spring. That wouldn't do. Unfortunately, I had no clue on how to deal with the situation. I did describe the event to a good friend of mine who was also Jewish and he thought it was really rich. But he also got upset and said that people who misused the holocaust experience like that were more suspect than those who flat out rejected the whole idea. All this mileage from the story of a TV grant!

The best reaction you can get from others about aid work is indifference. You want them to treat you as a normal member of the community.

"Where you been the last two months? Haven't seen you around the neighbourhood?"

"I've been in Kyrgyzstan working on a social services project."

My Saturday morning tennis partner blinked a few times, produced a swift smile and turned to his friend. "Hey Bill, you watch the Georgetown game last night?"

In fact, after working in a hall of mirrors like the International Monetary Fund (IMF), you can understand the combination of suspicion and indifference received from outsiders! My first mission on arrival at IMF was to Myanmar. Not wanting to appear stupid, I indicated that I had always wanted to visit Africa.

"It's not in Africa. Here it is on the map – used to be called Burma," they said jovially.

I had worked with Mr Prem on mission in Ecuador and he seemed no stranger than the rest of us – certainly less weird than most on my university faculty. A normal day in Quito, Ecuador, was to work with my Ecuadorian partner, Ernesto, at the Ministry of Finance interviewing different officials about public expenditure control matters. We did this during the days and then would step out in the evenings to engage in jollification with Ernesto's former colleagues from that very same Ministry and other state enterprises. We were on orders to appear at Mr Prem's hotel room by five each morning. He didn't drink, dance or eat meat. We did all three but had to repent by five and appear for purification at that hour. This worked out fine since we came in from the evening's festivities around three or four and could swing by his room.

There he would sit, incense burning in the corner, praying with his sari on. The silence was all very fine with us. My ears were still ringing from the salsa music and the head pounding from excessive booze. Ernesto knew very little English, and staring alertly at Mr Prem (eyes literally bulging out so far as to touch the inside of his sunglasses – which he wore indoors) would say at appropriate intervals, "You are very right, sir."

Mr Prem would continue talking about himself, his books, his aspirations in life, on this mission, and his accomplishments throughout the world in improving public expenditure management. One night, Mr Prem had a dream that, through the mist of a thick forest, he heard his father crying for help. The next day I received a message for him to call India. On return, he told us that his father was dying and that he would leave immediately. So all in all, an OK bloke in the field.

Now in his office turf it was a different story. His large office instantly revealed his mental architecture – most offices do. Upon entry to the palace, you were to sit in front of and below his large desk. He would stand behind the desk and his lectern. From here he would deliver the word. The style – top-down, authoritarian, hierarchical, formalistic and impersonal – was all very foreign and colonial to me. It gave me the creeps to go in there. I had thought university deans and civil service officials were pompous. Nothing like this!

"Are you in the habit of causing trouble, sir?" he once inquired obliquely as he poured himself a glass of water from a sidebar pitcher. How do you answer that one, I wondered?

"Not at all (Your lordship? Your honour? Your nothingness!)…"

"Because you sent this memo to the director asking for a day's leave of absence from the office."

"Right, as you know I'm commuting from Atlanta until I get settled in and sometimes the schedules don't jibe precisely. As I mentioned, I need next Friday off and wanted to square it with the front office."

"Sir, you cannot simply make up your own procedures," he said in that bouncy, deep tone accompanied by rolling movements of the head for emphasis.

"No, right."

"We have procedures here and the director of the office cannot be bothered by such petty matters as a day's leave for staff."

"Right."

A few days later, he called me into his office to announce that I would be working on a research project when not on mission. A draft would be expected within three months of a paper on the determinants of good public expenditure management in Africa. I was to do a comparative study and identify the main institutional mechanisms that facilitated or impeded good results, and make recommendations accordingly. I was to situate myself in the IMF basement archives for a month or so and read the Policy Framework Paper and Article 4 files on each country for my data. I would also have access to the Fund-Bank library which had plenty of materials on Africa. The assignment was a bit of a shock since I had only read two books on Africa in my life – *Tropical Gangsters* (Robert Klitgaard's comic masterpiece of how aid should not be done) and *Mr Johnson* (Joyce Carey's brilliant sketch of colonial administrators attempting to apply first-world controls to a road construction project with predictable results). But neither of these were going to help here!

"Very good, sir," I said, to indicate that I was getting the respectful linguistic patterns of the office down pat. "I wonder if I might ask a favour, though…"

"Sir?"

This was getting easy. "Yes, would it be possible to perform this study precisely as you outlined it, but covering Latin America?"

"I'm sorry, what did you say?"

"Applied to Latin America where I have about fifteen years' experience and could get a lot of primary data and information as well."

"Sir, I thought I made myself clear. If you have any further questions as you proceed with the work on Africa, please notify me through my secretary, Yoki."

Shit! I thought. Not looking good at all and only the first month! Wonder how long this job will last?

One of my university colleagues told me you had to show up drunk or harass secretaries repeatedly to get fired by IMF. It may be easier than they said. But I persisted. First, the guys in my unit gave me all the names of all the African countries – since I could only name three or four of them besides South Africa. Each day I went down and read their files. The files contained IMF Board deliberations and source documents of the fiscal management problems these places had experienced over a ten-year period (1981–'91). It was quite fascinating and often amusing reading. Most of these places were basket cases that had been threatened, cajoled, arm-twisted, to meet conditions allowed to blame IMF for their poverty problems, and punished in some cases with no programme – i.e. no more fresh cash to pay off past loans. But in all cases, the Board relented and the soft loan money would again flow into the country.

As for expenditure control issues, different mechanisms and so on – not much here. I then moved to ordering Aide Memoirs and World Bank Public Expenditure Reviews. These also were interesting and I learned a great deal about African public financial management. The diversity of problems and response mechanisms were also documented and this made it easier to write that part of the report. Now came the part where I was to come up with what determined how and why these places responded like they did and what effects they had on fiscal problems (e.g. major budget deficits, inflation, debt arrears, over-committed budgets and untraceable expenditures, especially in salaries and projects). Why did cash limits work in Somalia in 1994 but not in Congo in 1996? Try and answer that one without reference to flabby notions of "political will" or better "leadership!"

As required, I turned in a draft to him. A few weeks later when he had read it, I made an appointment and went to discuss with him what I had tried to do. Sitting below his severe gaze in front of his lectern, I explained that, "The determinants isolated were: political structure; degree of democracy; demography; geography; income distribution; and levels of education/health. There could be others but these seemed like the main ones cited in the literature."

He made a sour expression, pinched up his face like a dried almond. "Sir, I see what you have done. But I don't see that you've discussed the most obvious influence on expenditure management."

"No? What would that be?"

"Race."

Once again I was in one of these increasingly frequent situations where I wasn't sure how to respond. What was he getting at? Was it some American bias – maybe thinking of race as blacks and whites?

"Race? Not sure I follow you…"

"It should be quite simple," he added icily and impliedly, "for someone as simple as you." He pulled some skin on his left forearm as a demo. "I am black and you are white."

"Right. Nevertheless, there's a thing that confuses me, and you might help me with it, and that is that there are clearly major differences in expenditure management performance among these countries."

"So?"

"To explain racial differences on expenditure management we need a variable, some variation."

"And?"

"I'm certainly no expert on Africa, but it appears to me that race is not really a variable there. I mean, aren't they all black? If they are, except in places like South Africa that you wanted me to exclude from the sample, how can we use race for any kind of explanation?"

Apparently he hadn't thought of this and it threw him. I sensed some confusion, followed by a quick rebound, as the sub-continental need to control inferiors, perhaps racial inferiors such as myself, reasserted itself.

"I am not happy with your work on this. Come back to me when you have something I can read and understand."

Life at the IMF was not fun in a professional sense but I worked with some extremely talented people. The Australians and New Zealanders liked yo-yo and paper airplane contests. I learned a lot of new yo-yo tricks and new ways to make better planes. They also liked to show they could bowl paper wads better than I could throw baseball-style into the trash can across the room. Many of our non-travel days in the office were devoted to these three main activities. I got back into yo-yoing and learned how to finally do a decent paper airplane. I did hold my own against the bowlers.

We should not leave the reader with the impression that IMF is populated solely with nasty Indian manager-types. My introduction to IMF was from the office occupant next door, who one morning knocked on my door, entered and introduced himself. He had that strained look that comes just before you make a serious announcement, often notification of some behaviour on your part that will need adjustment. He gave that look and announced, "I'd like to tell you how happy I am to have someone next door who swears."

Naturally, we became the best of friends and I can attribute my short tenure there (two years) to palling around with wild, uncultured types such as Cramer. I had asked my wife and two boys (seven and nine) to join us at an old Italian restaurant (La Roma) that no longer exists in the Cleveland Park area of Washington that folded after about fifty years in the late Nineties. I told my wife that the former Inland Revenue Commissioner for Australia would join us – the idea was to impress her with the fine quality people I worked with – no longer some asshole Associate Professor who wrote obscure articles and taught peculiar classes – someone who actually worked with people, albeit through numbers.

The restaurant had excellent paper napkins, the kind that could be made into paper airplanes by a skilled engineer. Cramer was just the man and soon planes were swooping here and there among the guests. One landed several tables over in the ice cream of a startled couple and stuck there. Over came the elderly lady and I could see my wife red-faced and trying to stop the whole thing. Our boys were also giving it a shot and did manage a few short flights. At least they mastered the design which has helped them at college. I expected the woman to launch into a tirade. Instead, as owner of the place, she complemented us on our planes and flying skills.

There are many with authority problems at the Fund, mostly Aussies and Kiwis. This keeps the place from becoming totally constipated in formality. The fund is run by French, Germans, Brits and Indians. There are a few odd Americans like me, and most have authority problems but repress them. Those with such problems may stay because they have narrow technical specialties. Most head to the

World Bank where the working culture is much more laid back and speaking out is not usually penalised in fund style, with silent outrage. Try explaining this kind of place to your neighbours!

Regards,

Washington DC, 1991

Fun and Games in Saudi Arabia

Dear Jim—

There are times in one's career when you know you've hit bottom. Last January, I ended up in a Ukrainian railway car leaving from Kiev station late at night in the snow, sitting there on a little bunk with no heat or light, near a woman who simply stared at me in the dark. I had finally hit bottom and believed that it was the end of the line for me. If I had had a cell phone, I would have called someone and quit. How I would have gotten home from there in less than two days is not clear. At least I knew where I stood with things – this was just the shits.

Now in Saudi Arabia, there was more of a lag effect. The cumulative effects of just how bad the place was took a few days to sink in. It has been sinking in further with time. Now I can say with bold clarity that this is by far the shittiest place I've ever been. With the operating premise barred, let's take it from the top. No need to try and be objective about this for the editors. The experience did raise Mickelwait's Question (Don Mickelwait was a founder of DAI thirty-five years ago and remains a moral guide to even those of us who have departed from the firm): "Why are you in this business?" Had that been my assigned country, I could not have answered it.

Luckily it wasn't. My short-term job was with World Bank to prepare and teach seminars on key topics of public expenditure management, including particular items such as operations and maintenance of capital facilities, and measurement of subsidies. Substituting capital for current expenditures is a familiar game in these parts: the government borrows cheap for facilities, uses the savings to pay salaries and lets the facility go to pot by not budgeting maintenance expenses. The "poor" government then applies for more capital funds (a loan or credit) to replace (prematurely of course) the facility. Urban bus systems do that in the US to replace rolling stock that need current maintenance. Capital transfers work nicely to relieve any hard budget constraints. This kind of sequence is made routine in most places by governmental transfer rules that do not prohibit it. My job was to prepare training materials, develop a few cases and exercises, and give part of a week-long course at the Institute of Public Administration in Riyadh. It is expected that locals, in these situation, will help out by getting you a country budget that you can refer to for form and structure purposes, and possibly a few figures indicating trends for illustrative purposes.

Here it was different right away. We were assigned a handler, a "professor" from the Institute of Public Admin-istration. Imagine the typical government service training academy – barracks architecture, cheap cafeteria and so on. This one was like a Marriott, ten storeys high with an indoor pool and gym. Lots of space in which the be-sheeted students and professors could mingle quietly. A serene and ever helpful "professor" was in charge of us. When not praying to Allah, the twenty-five-year-old official of IPA with a Master's degree from some minor US college was to assist us. His assistance included censoring the materials we wrote. I had included a few paragraphs in the facts of a case on budget subsidies about imported sheep on their way from Australia committing suicide on board. I also spiced up the character names to include Al-Hacker from "Yes Minister" – these kinds of things had to go. But his literal mind only carried him as far as his confused need to command infidels like us would take him. I had prepared a case dealing with the costs of snow removal which I had just converted to sand removal. He never caught this. It might have been an insult to this snoop – but technically the case was correct; sand and snow behaved very much the same way, producing drifts, rusting out machinery and ruining roads. As for the state budget, he assured us that that was secret and we couldn't see it. He was also in charge of the keys and to prevent theft of audio-visual machines and other equipment from the IPA, he would retain the key at all times.

The "professor" had about the same physical qualities as Bin Laden – tall, serene, gaunt, pious. Probably masturbated a lot too. The prof was easily riled up by challenges to his authority and became especially prickly on questions of honour. He prayed a lot and always asked to be excused to pray someplace. Maybe he wanted to kill us and had to repent of this evil thought every fifteen minutes. At the same time, he showed us pictures of his "real" self with no sheet on – the cool dude wearing big jewels with slicked back hair and expensive shades. Had a luscious chick with him in Manila too, nothing like the local broads who weren't cosmopolitan enough for him. Did we want to go to the camel races?

"Fuckenay, shit yes!"

Off we went in his new BMW at about a hundred miles an hour on the freeway (all cars drove that fast – it was the only thrill there other than prayer and eating as far as I could tell). Bad luck. A vicious sandstorm was in progress that harmed the eyes of the camels – people could always wear shades but the camels couldn't. Why not get them shades, I thought. Possibly a new Middle Eastern product for the market – designer shades for camels. Probably would be prohibited by the Mullahs…

It was getting to be fun already. In class, I couldn't run the electronic boards unless permission was granted to use the key. The boards were cool in that I could fill several of them up with lists and diagrams before class and then use them to guide discussion – this was pre-Power Point (or at least my use of it). Therefore I couldn't really run the class unless the "professor" gave me the key. Why must he keep the key? Theft. To fully understand how absurd this was, it needs to be recognised that each Friday at Chop-Chop Square in downtown Riyadh, they hold public mutilations and executions for thieves and murderers.

"Do you like horror shows?" he inquired. I thought of a good horror movie. Might just do it to relieve the boredom – maybe Bela Lugosi.

"Yes, but I didn't know you had movie theatres here?"

"No, of course we don't. Allah forbids them. I mean watching the Friday executions."

Whoa baby! "No thanks, we should be getting back to work."

This comment seemed to pique him a bit. He looked at us suspiciously and added, "We are a civilised country like the US, you know."

"Of course you are. I wonder if your courts are administered by religious or civil authorities?"

"Our judges are trained at the Sorbonne. They are every bit as qualified as American and British judges."

"Of course they are," I said, unconvinced by anything this asshole said.

At the IPA, the "professor" demanded my key after the first morning break. I told him this procedure was slowing me up in that I always had to worry if I could find him, so I was going to keep the key until the course was over.

"You must give me the key," he said bluntly.

"I can't do that."

"Then I must inform the Director of your insubordination."

"Do what you have to, but why is the key so important to you? You only keep it. I actually have to use it."

"It is a security matter. If you lose the key, it is my responsibility. If thieves got the key and stole our equipment, I would be in trouble."

"You're saying that even with the public spectacle of weekly mutilations, thieves would still brave it and come in this building to steal equipment?"

"That's right," he said, "we can't take a chance." He looked at me with even more suspicion and hostility.

"Can't imagine them taking the risk of losing an arm or head for an A-V machine."

"You aren't Muslim and you aren't from here."

I know I should have given him the key. I was working short-term for World Bank and any bad reports on me could cost me my next short-term job if not all of them. But why not egg the arrogant little bastard on? After all, he was clearly a prick.

Other than the fun work at IPA, Riyadh had a lot to offer for recreation. For example, if you were into golf (not me!), you could play on the buff-coloured desert course using red golf balls, portable astro-turf grass rugs and black oiled "greens". The nineteenth hole pub with the guys was most fun, with non-alcoholic beer from Heineken and Guinness. And let's not forget the women.

"What are those, Malcolm?"

"Those are women," he replied. Two five-foot black lumps passed us with tiny slits for the eyes. They looked like a shoal of tadpoles or guppies out of water. They were, in fact, heavily laden "women" in their stylish chadors or burkas – this year's fashion I was told – which something like the fashion fifteen hundred years ago. I turned around and really checked them out as best I could. No tits, hips or legs showing. No skin of course.

"Wait, Malcolm, check the ankles!" They were a luscious mixture of caramel and white flowing down erotically into shoes that produced squeaks from the leather soles, conjuring up instant images of lusty bed noises during a hot night of sex. I was getting a hard-on just thinking about it.

"Can't stand it, Malcolm. Let's get out of here!"

With no booze, no women, no dogs to pet and no entertainment possibilities like movies, we were left with food as the main source of excitement. It was the Friday holiday so that evening after golf we ate at an outdoor place that served excellent lamb shish and veggies. Can't complain at all about the food.

There go the horns, it's time for prayers again and the waiters lock up the doors, leaving us outside at our table. The mosques send out pitiful wails from old loudspeakers. Usually they are tapes but sometimes the Mullahs wail out the prayers aloud. To an outsider like me, the sound is a clunky form of murdering silence; it is the plaints of a sick cow bellowing into the wind; more appropriately now, it sounds a lot like an air-raid siren. It is reactionary, medieval and chilling. Not music at all. Why was this different from the singing at Ejiamatsin in Armenia – the fourth century chorus and organ? Because that was uplifting, soulful, forgiving, touching to the soul, the songs of many generations praying to God almighty. What does God think when he hears this? Is this sound beautiful, uplifting, spiritual? Or is it more of a retching sound, like a sick animal puking?

Where is the aesthetic and cosmic element in any of this? I thought, as the truck pulled up and a group of robed bearded ones shouted and waved their fists in our direction.

Thinking they might just be some of our fun-loving students from the IPA, we waved back. This gesture seemed to anger them and whip them up to a greater pitch. They had jumped from their white truck and were heading towards us.

We were not sure what to make of all this. They did seem angry that we were eating dinner. Did they want a bite?

"Drop it! Drop it!" we heard from behind us. I turned and saw the waiter running towards us from the sliding glass doors. "Drop it!" he yelled.

"Drop what?"

"The food! Now!"

Both of us held our hands up at the table and dropped the food into our dishes. My bread bounced onto the floor. The bearded ones were the religious police, checking up on violators during prayers. They caught us red-handed as it were. A heated discussion was going on between the waiter, who obviously saw this as partly a religious issue and partly a problem of lost business. What would it do to business if the foreign ones were hauled in? The police wanted to haul us in as a lesson to all foreign infidels. Luckily the waiter won. He got a big tip that evening, I can tell you that.

How bad is this place? Johnny Carson probably would have said something like: "It's so bad that the female parts on the oil wells wear tiny burkas!"

First, American consumers like oil so Saudi Arabia has been our number one economic and political partner in this region. This is rapidly changing in the wake of Iraq, like an earthquake, as we shift from here to places like Qatar. Excellent move! Culturally, there cannot be a country anywhere more alien to us and our social-political values than Saudi Arabia. By contrast, Myanmar is simple thugocracy, going through the normal routines of beating up its own people. There are lots of those places. This place is the right-wing of an already aggressive religion that keeps its people ignorant, controlled and manipulated through the Mullah apparatus and dispensation of goodies from the cities to rural areas. Despite all its wealth, many Saudis are in fact very poor and services do not reach the smaller towns. They are also ignorant and filled with a simple religious message – obey the Mullahs and hate the infidels that cause all your problems. Saudi Arabia is an ultra-centralised theocracy where the chosen ones are very serious hypocrites. How serious? That's what the causeways to Bahrain and Qatar are for – pleasure and women for the chosen ones to let off steam from the hard week of lying around on couches and drinking tea. Most of the technical and manual labour is done by foreigners – who are resented for doing their work and taking pay for it. Hence our job at IPA and the wish to control us through the key!

Women have not been a problem for the Saudi system until recently. They received education in non-macho topics like accounting and computers. They were kept home and got fat with the other ladies on daily teas and cakes. Marriages have been arranged and, as my Pakistani friends tell me, men often get bored with their fat wives, leading to trips across the causeway – or in Pakistan to seedier sections of Karachi or Islamabad. Not that cheating on arranged brides who become fat and cow-like under Islam should be condemned as distinctive from other hypocritical practices in the West – e.g. abstinent priests who are also sexual predators for a start! The difference in Saudi Arabia is that those without political influence, education or position that try these things in the country are regularly whipped, beaten and mutilated as punishment. The "chosen ones" (the wider royal family, for example) indulge and allow their unlucky compatriots who are caught to be beaten and whipped. Without pressing the point too harshly, this isn't just dishonourable – it is the system of a coward – not just in sex and pleasure, but education, rights and governance. Severe moral prohibition systems breed all kinds of individual perverts and corrupt institutional systems set up to get around these harsh rules – whether run by fundamentalist Baptists in rural Alabama or by mullahs here in Riyadh.

Wish you were here!

Riyadh, Saudi Arabia, 1992

VI. Dangers
Field Work in Belize

Mary—

I found just the place for you! I even saw you yesterday in Belmopan when you were eighteen years old again. Actually, she was not from Baltimore like you but from Wales. You really need to de-pressurise and lay back for a while before plotting out your next job, boyfriend, base of operations, and overall life trajectory. Belize is not known for its intense pace and this just might work for you. I have worked here several times in the past fifteen years and always come away wondering how the place survives. It is a small British protectorate in Central America of about two hundred and fifty thousand people. They speak English, Spanish, Creole and Maya. The one radio station features people who can, incredibly, talk all four languages during their shows! Its main industry is tourism from the US. It's also a nice place to trans-ship drugs and other hot items. Guatemala went to war with the UK in the 1960s to protect its claim that Belize (or British Honduras as it was known) was simply another province of Guatemala and not part of the British Commonwealth. The UK got them to back down with their Harriers and jungle troops but maps of Guatemala include it as a province to this day. Belmopan is the capital – the pace is even slower there. A few years ago, I interviewed a deputy minister of planning in his Belmopan office while his assistant slept nearby in a large easy chair. Large buzzing flies entered and exited his mouth, and still he didn't wake up. He was obviously used to it.

My base for interviews in country was Mom's International Triangle guest house in Belize City. My trips between Honduras, Costa Rica and Belize were financed by a Fulbright grant to do comparative research on the different forestry policies of all three countries – they actually represented three quite distinct approaches to forestry development: fiscal incentives (Costa Rica); mercantilism (Belize); and state ownership and control of the forests (Honduras). I mean, it wasn't that I just wanted to visit all three places (which I did), there was actually a good rationale. The research required surveys and Belize is not the place to do rural surveys of sawmills. Nobody answers the phone and officials either sleep the heat away in their offices or at home. That makes it tough to get around.

I had been stood up on interviews several times and had to return to the guest house empty handed each night. That put an edge on the day and put me into foul moods more than once! What a fucking waste of time! Mornings began with a hearty breakfast of Johnny Cakes and coffee. Following the day's fiascos, I would return for dinner. Where else could you sit down and instantly be joined by random Rastafarians out for free handouts and dinner? It was also wise not to tell them to bugger off. Two joined me one evening and it can be said that they were easily ninety percent thug and ten percent spiritual peace. I'm quite certain that they had plans to mug me and given their size, their success was a distinct possibility. So I definitely paid for their meals – they even received a tip from me to cover their time eating a free meal! Unlike urchins in Eastern Europe or other parts of the world, I cannot say with any confidence that these people could be bought off. I think they would mug you after paying for their dinner. Life for them was a random sequence of opportunities to survive.

So things were moving along slowly. I couldn't even get a copy of the state budget – not because it was secret as in

Saudi Arabia but because not enough had been printed. So I had to go through a garbage pale at the Her Majesty's Government Printing Office in Belmopan to get one – last year's edition and pretty beat up – the revenue section had been somehow dipped in motor oil! (Did this mean financially they were in the black? No chance!) Getting desperate, I met with a colleague at the Belize Institute of Management. This was an AID-funded operation intended to stimulate private sector activity through training and technical assistance activities. At one meeting with a colleague at the hotel next door, we discussed business for almost an hour before realising that no one had asked us if we wanted to order anything exotic – such as coffee. The positive spread effect of the Institute and the project in other words was zero! No chance of any entrepreneurial energy or motivation contaminating this place! Although in the Tropics, it was in permanent deep freeze.

As a solution to my problem of interview failure, my colleague had suggested visiting a sawmill in Orange Walk Town and gave me the number of the manager. Using his phone, I contacted the guy and set up an appointment. I then made the three-hour trip by bus the next day and met his driver at the bus station. The bus was the usual Central American run, an old rickety affair that stopped in front of this or that tree all the way up – to let people return to their shacks after shopping in the city. It looked something like the buses for sale in souvenir shops – suitcases and fruit on the roof, brightly-coloured red and yellow names and designs all over it, e.g. *"Mi Dona Maria"*, and pasajeros compressed into it almost to the bursting point. A poor guy in front of me with long blonde hair was reading poetry to a ravishing, shapely brunette who looked out the window in boredom. He was really getting into it (sounded like Byron but couldn't be sure) and he started weeping at one point. Her response was to look around at me in embarrassment.

She apparently was looking for more action than poetry, or at least this kind of poet – would have preferred a more Oscar Wild-ish type I'm sure. Ah but, buses like this do stimulate the romantic impulses. Remember Bunuel's *Mexican Busride* film? The back of the bus became an open field and the other passengers played guitars and sang while the protagonist rolled around on top of the buxom maiden he had been fantasising about during the ride!

Finally, we arrived in Orange Walk Town near the Mexican border and I was in business!

At the large sawmill I met the owner, Joe Lonsdale, at his office. I went through the questions with him and he thoughtfully responded to each one of them. About an hour later we all went to a nearby restaurant for lunch. There he painted in expansive terms his plans for a new pulp mill to be towed in from Costa Rica by boat, which would open up new markets and generate more jobs for locals. We then adjourned to his mill for a tour. The mahogany was piled up about three storeys in large clumps awaiting their turn at the mill. Some of the logs must have weighed a ton. They were golden brown and looked almost good enough to eat! The logs were either floated down the river or brought in by truck. At the riverfront was a dead-ringer for the *African Queen*. The function of this boat was to provide supplies, equipment and personnel to the mahogany camp up river. It had just received a new hull and was about to be launched. Joe's accountant, a swarthy black guy in a white shirt and tie, smashed a champagne bottle on the hull and down it went on its rollers and into the river with a loud splash. We then shared the other bottle of Chateau Duvalier (1986) right there in the jungle (see cover). I was beginning to see how the poet on the bus got overwhelmed with uncontrollable rushes of emotion. I too was getting fired up by even limited research success after so many failures.

At the Friday night party in the USAID compound that

night, I sought out the State Department guy who was handling the Fulbright programme there to tell him of my success. I'd approached similar types in other countries to fill them in on my doings. Their usual response was to look vaguely at you with their glassy, fish-like eyes. They transmitted signals of nervous impatience, meaning that they hoped you would stop soon. This one, Nathan, was quite different. The guy didn't seem like such a bad egg. I had met him on arrival earlier that summer. He had told me about his stint teaching English at an African university where the chairman died from a snake bite to his ass while taking a shit in a nearby outhouse. I always remembered that story and envied him, wishing that some of my university departments had outhouses too. Here he gave a surprisingly uptight response.

"What? You interviewed Joe Lonsdale! Jesus!" He starts looking around, finds someone and motions energetically to him to come over. "Listen to this, Bob."

I recounted my story less proudly than before, sensing some kind of bureaucratic problem with these people, now wearing their official State Department armour.

"What were you thinking? You had no permission to travel there. Any idea what happened there today?"

"Only that I had an interview and it went well."

"Bob (Top Duck) White was gunned down in Orange Walk Town the same time you were there."

Fucking White Duck – must be a joke. "I didn't do it, guys, honest! Check my briefcase. Only Fulbright surveys."

"Funny as hell."

"Who's Duckman?"

"He's a right-wing radio talkshow guy from Daytona Beach, Florida, who is also a gun nut. Always brags on his shows that he carries four or five guns on him and would shoot anyone for anything – because it's his constitutional right."

"So how'd he get shot?"

"Obviously someone he knew. The place is crawling with drugs and thugs. Even some of the Mennonites pack rods and are into drugs."

At this I burst out laughing. "Come on, Nathan, you don't believe that hysterical kind of shit, do you? You'd be investigating everyone; nuns, priests. I saw a lot of Mennonites running around in their wool suits in hundred degree weather selling chairs and tables. Didn't look dangerous to me."

"That's because you don't know what's going on here. Some of them may have even gunned Top Duck down. More to the point—" he waved his finger in my face threateningly "—you had no business at Lonsdale's sawmill."

"Why not? He's part of my survey sample."

"We've been investigating the guy and his operations for some time."

"Come on, you think he is a thug too?"

"He's the biggest drug dealer in Central America by far."

I couldn't stand it. I burst out laughing again.

"Alright fucker, you're *persona non grata*. We're shipping you back to Costa Rica to finish your work there."

"You can't do that. That's up to the Fulbright programme people."

"I run the programme here, you're out."

"Come on, Nathan, you're just too lazy to do the paperwork if I get shot, right?"

"That's right."

"What makes you think Lonsdale is a drug dealer?"

"What makes you think he isn't? Where's the money coming from to finance his big ideas?"

"From mahogany sales."

Both of them smirked. "You're supposed to be the expert. You should know that world mahogany prices have dropped."

"Savings, then."

"There's no banking system here, and where would he get savings?"

"Efficiencies."

"Now it's my turn to laugh. That's all bullshit and you know it," said Nathan proudly. "Want to know where his funds are coming from? His kid was an honours grad at Georgia Tech, inventing a microscopic drill for his senior project. He developed this and uses it to inject the mahogany with cocaine, trans-ships it up to Mexico and into the US. Presto! Savings!" He slapped my back and roared with laughter.

That had me stumped. Lonsdale had fooled me.

"It's OK. Now you just tell us next time you have a bright idea for an interview. If you need someone legitimate to talk with, let me know."

"So I can stay?"

"Have a beer on us."

Thus ended my last working trip to Belize. I went down there later on a boon-doggle to appraise skin-diving shop business opportunities for a bored Atlanta housewife. But that was a waste of time. At least I got an article published on the forestry work.

Hang in there!

Belize City, Belize, 1988

World-Class Hotels

One of the risks of overseas work lies in the hotel accommodation. Many of these places are unbelievable shit holes. On longer-term project work you can qualify for an apartment. These are usually quite good (i.e. heat, phones, hot water, inside security). So much for the luxury travel motive for getting into overseas development work! Donor appraisal missions treat you individually quite well. Such organisations as World Bank, Asian Development Bank and so on wine and dine you in style – but they also work you to death in exchange! Once you win a project from one of these organisations, the party is over. Projects are won by bidding firms with the richest combination of cost and technical efficiency scores on their proposals. This usually means squeezing staff, putting them up in dives, minimising daily *per diem* rates, coach-class travel and so on. Other places exist where it wouldn't matter what *per diem* rates are available, there simply aren't any decent places to stay!

The State Hotel in Shkoder, Albania, would be one of the very worst, for example. Albania felt guilty after forty years of an ultra-communist police state that locked up thirty-five percent of the population on political crimes, so the government instituted a restitution programme that gave ex-political prisoners some kind of facility to manage or work in such as a hospital, hotel or restaurant. You might think that the hotel service is really bad and the place is run like a prison. In Albania this can actually be true! The workers are all former inmates who learned their hotel management and culinary arts skills from watching how efficiently Albanian prisons were operated. That explains why our manager in Shkoder would stand around in dark corners smoking and chatting quietly with his small staff. The rooms that were left after part of the cement structure gave way in the back and fell into the vacant lot were like caves. Mine had a toilet with no seat, one small forty-watt light bulb and a broken shower. Only the electricity worked and this powered my portable heater (ten dollars in the market) which I brought with me on all trips. The catch is the heater only worked when there was power.

My partner on this mission was in a better room but it faced the street. The location became problematic one night when rocks were flung through his window, breaking the glass and creating a major racket. While it was probably a random event (i.e. drunks heading home), he was frightened to death that someone was in his room and proceeded to unload his portable mace gun in the emptiness. Naturally this burned his own face and made it difficult for him to get back to sleep. So we all looked like shit each morning, exchanging incredible tales of the night before.

In Yerevan, Armenia, at the famous Razdan Hotel, I tried to sleep amidst sounds of machine guns and dogs barking outside the window. It wasn't every night, but just enough so I wouldn't forget. I heard short bursts of machine-gun fire while in bed. Not a problem. I was told this was all between rival mafias in the woods below the hotel. Wouldn't affect us or anybody we knew. The dogs were a bit worse. Dozens of them would bark all night, probably hungry and riled up by one of them in heat, people shouting at them or some combination of all three. I thought one night, "HBTD" the University of Georgia slogan "how 'bout them dogs? How about them fucking dogs?" That night a machine-gun burst went off in the alley and there was much less barking. One of the mafia apparently didn't like the noise either.

Most of the action was at night. One day, I saw some of these dogs up close. It is now known that the "transition" displaced many people and their dogs had been abandoned *en masse*. Why people would abandon their dogs after having them around for so long was not clear. The dogs had, predictably, returned to pack status and roamed the streets behind a number of alpha males which then directed packs of them against adults and children. They had killed many people and some of them spread diseases like rabies in cities of the former Soviet Union. Municipalities responded with squads of trucks armed with long plier-like tongs. They were amazingly effective at surprising sleeping dogs, lifting them into the air and tossing them into the back of the truck. Naturally, this approach didn't work on moving dogs!

I was crossing a street in Yerevan alone one day to find a kiosk to buy some beer for my room fridge. As luck would have it, a pack of large dogs came between me and the curve where I was headed. They were moving ahead in front of me to my left, luckily. I was not walking directly toward them or vice versa or it would have likely been curtains. I stopped. They stopped. The alpha male stared at me and trotted a few steps in my direction. He didn't look too serious but I stayed put. He wasn't intent on anything in particular which was a good sign to me. After a minute or so, he headed back to his pack and the rest of them followed. I let them go by and continued ahead, noticing only later that I had pissed in my pants.

In at least one case, I deliberately stayed at a dump because it had other qualities. I'm talking about the Plaza Naco Hotel in Santo Domingo, Dominican Republic. In Fodor's *Guide to Baseball*, the Plaza Naco is mentioned as the main housing for all expat baseball players. The real centre of the baseball universe is the Dominican Republic which (now that most Cubans have already defected) is now the major supplier of major league baseball players. Juan Marichal was Minister of Public Works when I worked there on our Inter-American Development Bank project. Sammy Sosa and Pedro Martinez could be seen in the hotel lobby on occasion, coming to see their agents or managers. One or more of the Alou brothers could always be seen around town. Here you met the players on their way up (out of college), on their way down (nine to ten years, nine to ten teams), trying to stabilise their careers (recovering from injuries) as well as the scouts and managers. The Plaza Naco hotel is close to the stadium (Quisqueya). Baseball is a lively affair here, much livelier than in the US. Instead of the sad droning of funereal organ music between innings, games feature fleshy sex-pots in hotpants dancing on top of the dugouts, often between batters as well as innings! They dance to the loud beat of a band sitting a few rows back (the DR is also a salsa and meringue capital – with merenguero Johnny Ventura still around as mayor of Santo Domingo). All this is good news for baseball fans.

The bad news is the condition of the closest hotel: Plaza Naco. Even in the best of times (pre 9/11), the place was a dump. It has a nice lobby and a small pool, but the food is disgusting for breakfast (twenty-five dollars, included) or any other meal. Breakfast typically featured tropical enigmas like no bananas in a place where there are banana trees growing wild in front of the hotel. Often no bread either for some reason. During a stay back in 2000, I noticed one of the elevators didn't work and was in the process of being repaired. In a ten-storey hotel this could mean long waits and crowds. Again not a big problem for me given the opportunity to chat with ballplayers and other interesting tourists. Need we mention the women in this place? They can only have been cloned or created that dream-perfect in a lab someplace, proving that Dominicans created cloning to satisfy their voracious sexual appetites that the rest of us can only envy and imagine from where such appetites come. Recently, I was explaining to an IADB friend there that I was staying at the Plaza Naco. His expression became serious. He was trying to think of something.

"That's the place! The famous missed ten-storey swan dive," he smiled broadly.

"What? Jesus!"

"Yes, I'm sure. The elevator was being repaired and something went wrong with the electrical system and the shaft caught fire."

"And?"

"Smoke was bad and forced evacuation of the upper

floors. The worst hit was the office of an IADB-financed health project on the tenth floor. One woman became hysterical from smoke inhalation and believed in that instant of panic that she could save herself by leaping out of the window and hitting the pool ten floors below. She missed. But it didn't matter as the pool was only four feet deep."

"Christ!'

This time (post 9/11), the place was even more seedy: the emails didn't work; TV cable malfunctioned; the bar was being fixed and was closed; the air conditioning was either freezing at thirty degrees or off, meaning humidity and heat. The food and service was still awful. Not good. But we bear our crosses and I wasn't there much anyway, day or night. For the price (ninety dollars a day), the service and overall quality was clearly outrageous.

In these situations, it's always useful to find someone worse off than yourself. That provides perspective and calms you down. I ran into a Chilean several times who was there for a conference of Latin American health ministers. He was quietly recounting to a staff member in the elevator how nothing at all worked in his room. Not even the phone. I asked him about it and he told me a few more things that were broken. Clearly he was used to this treatment and didn't get excited or make threats, so I was impressed and always greeted the guy when I could. To this he would smile weakly and shrug, as if to say, "My sentence here will never end!"

On my last morning there, I was in the breakfast room having whatever was available that day – a few pieces of old bread and sugared-up orange juice. The tea was OK. Suddenly, the ceiling collapsed right in front of me and a huge wave of water sloshed over two or three tables. Water was everywhere – could be from someone's toilet, shower – or both. Fortunately, no one was sitting at the tables. In back of them was my Chilean friend with his colleagues at another table. He was staring passively at the event, taking a draw on his cigarette and contemplating the whole mess quietly. Didn't even shrug this time as if to say, "So what else is new?" No question about it, the place was a dangerous dump. I've got to find a better place as close to the stadium on my next trip…

Best regards,

> Shkoder, Albania, Yerevan, Armenia and Santo
> Domingo, Dominican Republic, 1990s

Paranoid Fantasies

"What you cannot cure, you must endure."

Proverb fashioned by our Pakistani project assistant who later quit and fled Islamabad for Karachi after 9/11

Intrigues happen to other people. In real life, the closest you get to them is a Ken Follett thriller. Occasionally, one meets a security type, looking over his shoulder and playing G-man. Mostly, it's just the need to feel important and hunted – if not wanted. These types thrive on intrigue and secrecy, even though most of it is in their heads. I knew a kid once who played cop, wore a uniform and drove around looking for speeders and other offenders. I was actually with him once when we pulled someone over. The guy could actually make a siren noise that carried for blocks. The poor woman he pulled over in his old Ford was terrified and my colleague let her off with a warning. It wasn't just a prank as I saw it. He actually believed he was an authority figure and probably moved on to big-time counter-terrorism later – or maybe just criminal impersonation.

As the line between civilian and military development aid blurs (e.g. civil affairs projects in Afghanistan, Kosovo and Iraq), the risks of development work increase. Our team leader in Albania explained the CIA's plan for survival and evacuation to me in late 1996. He had been issued a yellow Motorola radio from the US Embassy and was breathlessly telling us what we should do and how to do it when the shooting started in the coming civil war of 1997.

"Come on Robert," I said gleefully, "grow up." That pissed him off and he wouldn't talk to me anymore that day. But he got the last laugh. Sure enough, the shooting started in 1997 in Tirana. In other cities, like Vlore, places turned into wild-west settings with everyone shooting. The country divided up into five small, competing regions based on opposing tribal loyalties. The Vlore region was cut off from Tirana. Near the Greek border in Korce where our driver and his family lived, George shot at bandits trying to steal his truck for several hours. One of his friends was shot and killed in the shoot-out. So the shit really did hit the fan and the radio came in handy for urban guerrilla warfare after all.

It is a fact that most hotel rooms are bugged and that computer programmes are used that regularly filter emails for key words. I've always imagined that my hotel room was bugged, but it never mattered because I only used my room to sleep in, quietly work in, play my portable tape recorder, and swear occasionally when work wasn't going well. However, email filtering turned out to be a bigger problem.

In Pakistan three years ago, I indirectly worked for the military organisation that ran the country called euphemistically the "National Reconstruction Bureau". Authoritarian regimes like to market themselves with crude irony, like Orwellian peace for war, truth for lies and slavery for freedom. The US military presented its "Shock and Awe" show in Iraq! The Burmese junta calls itself the "State Law and Order Reconstruction Committee" (SLORC), a chilling name to try and obtain legitimacy from the world for what is simply a group of thugs in imported uniforms. In Pakistan, the NRB included the ISS, the Inter-Services Security unit that used to be filled with Taliban types to undermine Indian efforts in Kashmir and the Soviet and later Western efforts in Afghanistan. Now parts of NRB are there to snoop on mainly internal enemies of the military state.

Our project, financed by the ADB, required the services of a driver. Our driver was not only a blockhead, but simply didn't know how to drive a car. I'm sure he had never driven before. This was evident in his habit of regularly running traffic lights, driving on all sides of the road across clearly-painted lanes, actually running over a bicyclist and narrowly missing large trucks head on in several instances. Since fatal accidents are a normal part of the foreign aide's world, I was not about to let this bastard kill us off for nothing. So I fired him. Two days later, as if by magic, he was back at the wheel. I protested and ordered him off again. I was later told by our assistant, Ali, that the driver in fact worked for General Sharif and couldn't be fired. I told him, "OK, fine, he's a spy. Now find us a spy who can drive."

Nevertheless, our driver stayed put behind the wheel. Every trip was an ordeal as we shouted orders and words of caution from the back seat. He continued to drive and made every effort to improve. I started praising the guy – the same guy I used to curse at for putting us at risk. He got better and I finally congratulated him on learning to drive so well at our expense. In the beginning, I'm certain, he had never held a steering wheel in his hands. As for his spying, we used to test him out. He may have understood some English, but he certainly couldn't speak it. I wondered what his reports to the General would sound like?

"Do you have the plans for the rocket, Helmut?" I said to our team leader suddenly. The driver leaned way back in his seat to take this all in. John played along.

"I have them in my briefcase. I will leave it in our office at NRB tonight and we can discuss the plans tomorrow." It was playing with fire but it broke up the monotony of daily interviews and reports that could be measured in bulk rather than practical utility.

The bigger problem turned out to be email filter. The ISS used a filter to track subversive emails and link them to local miscreants. Such filters are regularly used to filter out spam and filthy words. That can develop into conflict over (a) what is filthy, and (b) if it is filthy, is it still necessary for normal work? For example:

> Larry,
>
> I fully endorse the attempt to reduce SPAM! Good useful job, but can you please take "fuck" and "screw" off the forbidden list? I do not have the impression that these are words that are accurate identifiers of SPAM. (I certainly have never received any SPAM with these words in them.) I will be happy to keep sending you words that seem to be interfering with my receipt of professional e-mails.
>
> Thanks

In Islamabad, Paul was the head of the local UNDP governance office. He was weird guy with a plaster of Paris hairdo – possibly a wig. He wore a black glove for use with his custom oak pool stick at the UNDP club. Not a bad show for someone who couldn't play pool that well. Paul was one of those characters you meet whom you realise, after a few conversations, must have been in the same room with you dozens of times over the past fifteen years in many countries, but still you never met. You figure out later that you never met for a reason – the guy was a spook.

Ear stuck to the cell phone, reeking of self-importance, Paul was always wired into his emails to stay in the loop. He was a sexual curiosity as well. I got the sense that he was a slimy, predatory kind of pervert – the kind odious even to the most liberal and progressive among us. The idea surfaced that he was doing the UN's good works mainly to facilitate his sexual appetites (one of the reasons mentioned above for getting into development work). How do I know all this? When invited to the large UN mansion they gave him for housing in the most fashionable area of Islamabad (Blue Area), the place was always filled with younger lackeys – all boys and effeminate young men there to lap up his every word. Of course, it could all be my imagination.

It was time to get an invite back to the UNDP club. The other mission members were headed out for the evening and because of the Stage 3 Alert – from the suicide bombings of the French in Karachi in late May, the church bombing in Islamabad in March, and the threat of nuclear war with India over Kashmir now in June – I wasn't allowed to go out alone. Might not have come back – meaning big legal and insurance problems for ADB and the possibility that the others on the mission would have to pick up my end of the work. Still, I needed to get out of the fucking hotel – luxury or not, it was driving me nuts – an air-conditioned nightmare full of ship-wrecked foreigners, journalists and tinsel-town wedding parties. Time for a quick email first, then onto the task of getting out of here. The mission included two Marxist, feminist Pakistani women who, needless to say, were not welcomed by the government officials we visited. For some reason, in this still hide-bound Islamic republic they didn't want to be lectured on women's rights. Pakistan is definitely not a theocracy but women's rights were not on the agenda. The effect of the ladies ranting at local government officials was, quite obviously, to discredit our own fiscal management reform work. At an intellectual level, the officials couldn't get the connection between the rights issue and financial management. They were right! There wasn't any, beyond the design of the ADB programme loan – it would be stabilisation funds for decentralisation in exchange for a small opening in women's rights – a kind of PC programme condition to encourage the right kind of behaviour.

I had written to an Indian colleague at my firm who was a specialist in government IT systems. In the email I asked him for advice on problems of the SAP R3 system being installed in Pakistan and its likely effects on future local government operations. He responded quickly that he didn't know anything about SAP R3, but wanted to know what was happening in Pakistan which, according to the hysterics of the media, was about to do a first nuclear strike on India. This reply came at the wrong time. I had no one to exchange views with or share my feelings on what was happening. The email served as a release – a kind of catharsis.

> Sanjay – a lot of sabre rattling going on here. Don't know if it will erupt into anything. We are headed for Quetta tomorrow. Gets us away from this nasty border problem and into some good home-grown Al-Queda terrorism. I am more of a traditionalist and prefer the former. But some on the mission are post-modern and prefer the latter, i.e. gender and poverty reduction is part of the new programme. The good news is we have our risks column filled out for the DSP "logframe" – try and beat nuclear war and daily terrorism as an impact on devolution! The ADB should be impressed. (5/25/02)
>
> George

An hour later (at ten in the morning) I called Paul about going to the club that evening. He sounded awfully formal and bureaucratic and wasn't his usual self at all. This was a guy who always seemed to be around – ubiquitous. He was at our meetings at NRB, in the Luna Caprese restaurant with us, with our Team Leader, and someone who somehow knew many friends of mine overseas. Here I was getting treated like someone in line applying for a license.

He went on perfunctorily about his project and some personnel issues he had to attend to as an important man. Then in mid-sentence, "Hey, I hear you prefer war with India over Al-Queda."

Quite a jolt here, but responded, "And how would you know about that, Paul?"

"Ha! ha! ha! See you around," and he hung up.

Fuck! I was really nervous now, starting to imagine all kinds of intrigues and spooks in the hotel. Definitely lost interest in the trip to the club. I found my two colleagues working upstairs.

"Andrew, would you care to go for a short breath of fresh air?"

In front of the hotel there was a roaring water fountain that permitted us to talk undetected – except for the obvious question of why two foreigners would be trying to talk here! I explained what had happened and this jolted him as well. This meant that all of our emails were being monitored, at least for certain words. In my case, probably "border war" and "al-Queda". He checked into the matter and came back a few nights later with the confirmation that Paul was indeed a well-known spook. What made us both curious is why Paul would be so stupid as to let me know he was monitoring my emails. The answer came back through Andrew's sources that Paul was also a well-known drunk and had been juicing it up as usual around ten in the morning – probably didn't know what he had said until later. Now I find Ken Follett novels much less exciting…

Islamabad, Pakistan, 2002

Dear Bill—

You've been in this business longer than me. Ever wonder what kind of impression you've made with the locals after working in a place for a few weeks or months? Often the mission is a complete fiasco. You know the kind – you push paper around, have a few meetings, write something for the "client" bureaucrats and get on the plane. You already know what kind of impression you've made, and as our founder Don Mickelwait might say, "It's time to look at yourself in the mirror when you get home!"

Once, out of situational desperation (to avoid being shut out of a large contract bid because we hadn't put a team of sub-contractors together that would be competitive), I recommended that we work with another firm that he termed "the evil empire". I found a long email referring to topics like why we get into development work, what we hope to accomplish overseas, how we might best achieve our objectives and so on. All this led up to the punch line that if we have to work with a firm like this, we might as well try another profession and even go out of business ourselves – because they are unethical, immoral, corrupt and incompetent. I got the message.

We didn't bid on the contract and remained poor but honest from the sidelines. His observation holds for a lot of the work we do – maybe it's burnout or hangovers that make us mean in the field, or maybe it's that we are just slowing down. It may be time to hang it up. Other times, what starts out a bit wobbly with the locals turns into an unforgettable development experience. On this mission at least, you've bonded with the locals and their institutions. I can't be precisely sure how it happens. I can't really measure the result or empirically prove that it happened. There is definitely greater cooperation by the locals and more respect. It's all there and it creates a foundation for continuing development assistance work. In my case, it happened through basketball.

In Jalal-Abad, Kyrgyzstan, around October–December, 1997, I was working with three colleagues: Bob Collins (who later became our Team Leader in both Bulgaria and Bosnia); Marty McCutchen (Director of International Health Practices at another leading international firm); and John Landquart (now with World Bank) on an ADB project to strengthen the institutional and budgeting systems related to capital projects in the education and health sectors.

Jalal-Abad is a smallish place of forty-five thousand in the dry lowlands of the fertile Fergana Valley near the Uzbekistan border. In fact we had to cross that border daily to work in our other oblast, Osh. The Russians had constructed a health spa on the hill behind the town, so at least you knew the place was good for your health.

Bob was a former Vietnam marine who had lied about his age to go into battle. He had a library of a hundred or so war films in Jalal-Abad. We would watch at least one each evening after we worked together to prepare the dinner. He liked to tell war stories – saving his buddies, being saved from certain death and so on. You might think, what the hell? This kind of guy running a development project – the very antithesis of the sensitive developmentalist. In fact, he was perfect. He gained immediate respect from the locals and our little project team. He ran the office well. I describe him as "good military" (in the sense of getting the job done fast) rather than "bad military" (in the bureaucratic hurry-up and wait sense). He organised us in teams and reported to our firms and clients on time. He could handle visiting snoops from ADB Manila. He ran excellent meetings known as "stand-ups" that (largely for that reason) would last no more than thirty minutes. Imagine that in this day of unendurable posturing sessions to reconfirm one's intellectual and cultural superiority before the colleagues and the boss! He could keep a clean house. He had one serious weakness – which was to criticise my ability to clean dishes and pans. I tried to cook and ruined his kitchen – fried chicken fat flew all over and stuck to his walls and floor that took days to remove. So I was banished from cooking to the clean-up detail. No process or step toward eventual action on this detail – I produced a real accomplishment in the form of a cleaned-up pan. We became the best of friends, worked together later in Bulgaria and still stay in contact though he now works in Bosnia with his wife.

On weekends we played basketball at the Kyrgyz secondary school (#2). In Kyrgyz, there are separate Russian, Kyrgyz and Uzbek schools. For some reason, the Russians had built basketball courts around town in the 1960s, but knowing that they were short of actual basketballs, we brought a few with us. Word spread quickly in the neighbourhood that there were four Americans playing basketball, and we became instant celebrities – packs of kids joined us in the twelve to sixteen year range, and their parents often showed up to watch. Since John and Marty are excellent players, the locals were well rewarded.

An albino kid named Nurmat joined Marty and I one weekend in a half-court game. The typical game included several local kids (boys or girls) playing alongside two of us. Despite the rural outpost quality of Jalal-Abad, there were some very good players among them (certainly better than me). Some even spoke a little English. Nurmat's sister had been in New Jersey on a Soros fellowship so his English was pretty good from being around her. As part of my work evaluating the capital needs of schools, I was asked to give a short talk by the principal, Anarby Toltosonov, on the work of our project, life in the US, and so on. I'm quite sure he didn't care about the content, he just wanted the class to hear some American English. To my surprise, Nurmat was sitting in the class, and gave me the high sign. His peers were obviously impressed that he knew the foreigner and that we could also talk about the basketball games.

As it happened, the following Sunday, Marty, Nurmat and I were close to winning the game. I was running hard, dripping sweat into my contacts which burned like hell. As luck would have it, as I was concentrating on seeing clearly, I got a hard pass from Marty that jammed my finger back and dislocated it. The game stopped and everyone looked at my finger with astonished curiosity. I did too – never seen one of these before. Each player took turns to try and pop it out – but to no avail.

The problem was turned into an immediate opportunity for us to test the quality of oblast health services. We visited the local polyclinic where the doctor diagnosed the problem (for Nurmat who translated) as acute nail-biting! The doctor made motions to indicate that I bit my nails, and this is the kind of thing that happens if you have such habits! Nurmat knew this was wrong and showed him through a series of dribbling and shooting gestures that the finger got screwed up in a basketball game. With a sudden gleam in his eye (you could almost see the light bulb flash over his head), the doctor suddenly grabbed the finger and, with a skilled twisting motion, nearly pulled it off – but it worked. It popped back into the socket.

The story of the great healing got all over town. Our

oblast counterpart officials knew all about it and made the usual jokes – which I won't repeat here. In most government offices that we worked in for the project, they knew about the famous finger dislocation incident of the American during the basketball game with the local kids. I'm convinced that the games and our trip to the polyclinic moved us from formal expatriates to a kind of informal semi-local status. The officials took us more seriously, gave us more time and better information than before. We had bonded with the locals in an unintentional way and this helped us produce better results.

It was more than a month later in early December that I prepared to leave Jalal-Abad. I passed by school (#2) to give the principal the basketball and to try and say goodbye to Nurmat. After the usual exchange of formalities and pleasantries with the principal, I asked to see Nurmat. The principal sent his assistant to retrieve him from class, and, about fifteen minutes later, a shy and frightened version of Nurmat slinked into the principal's office. Apparently he thought he was being called in for another detention or worse!

When Nurmat saw me, he looked a bit confused – then a big smile broke out on his face and he sat down. He was in the clear! But just as quickly, his expression changed and he gave me that look of sad regret that I won't forget.

"Why didn't you come back and play ball with us?" he asked.

I made excuses – the work, the finger healing, the cold weather – all of which bounced right off him. He wasn't buying them – and he shouldn't have. We had created a new obligation to continue playing with them and this should have been written into a revised SOW! In any case, I showed him the basketball we were leaving for the school and told him I would like to come back some day and work there again… but not to visit the polyclinic.

I hope Nurmat believed that – because unlike the excuses, that one was true.

Jalal-Abad, Kyrgyzstan, 1997

Aid to Furniture Micro-Enterprise in Costa Rica

Bob – it's me again!

How do I get into these things? Sometimes I unconsciously flow along with events to see where they lead. Some folks have a problem with the unplanned, unscripted approach to life, and that's why they become seasoned bureaucrats and insurance executives. I have always flowed along to see what turns up, Macawber-style. Sometimes I regret not mustering the courage to act out a new role, or to take a risk and see where it leads. This fear of becoming stale drives me ahead to new problems and opportunities.

Here I was in the summer of 1988 in a seedy industrial slum on the outskirts of San Jose, Costa Rica. I had just had a disastrous appointment with an official at the nearby Ministry of Transport and was headed home for the day. The official never showed up for his appointment, I fell asleep in the chair waiting and, seeing no one around, simply left two hours later when I woke up. Not a good day, but not real unusual either for someone on a Fulbright Research grant from his teaching post at Georgia State University who was doing comparative forestry policy in Costa Rica, Honduras and Belize. The forests and forestry officials had a lot in common. It was apparent that public sector productivity rates roughly mirrored the growth rates of the trees – real slow! Deforestation for beef-cattle production by farmers and ranchers and corresponding elimination of trees for fast-growing, quick-return crops was the trend all over Costa Rica. It had been happening for almost twenty years now. This naturally riled the eco-left who feared global warming and loss of local resources. At the same time, the trends bothered traditional development types (i.e. production foresters) who simply wanted the poor to get jobs and income opportunities from forestry but couldn't really come up with anything workable.

The good news at that time was that eco-types succeeded in installing environmental bond markets and swaps to raise capital and to preserve local forestry resources. On the other side, those who saw real value in production got fiscal incentives put in the law, which applied mostly to small forestry farmers. So research and field work in the trenches of development aid *did* pay off, even if it took a long time.

I plodded along the streets, avoiding the larger potholes, in a major downpour – the kind that hits Costa Rica in the afternoons during the summer monsoon season. Skies are powder blue until around noon, then they turn almost black. The drops sound like large rocks pounding roofs, streets and windows. It is nature's daily attack on mankind and continues until around two or three in the morning. I tried to get things done in the morning, then stay inside in the afternoons if possible. But here I was outside, getting pounded, and there were no cabs or buses. It was not going to be a good day. I was already drenched, but at least my surveys were dry inside my leather briefcase. To gather up thoughts and plot out my next move, I went under a metal awning that was fortunately hanging out over the sidewalk. I heard an electric sound behind me and discovered that inside was a small furniture factory, with a few guys dutifully sawing wood to make chairs and tables. I entered and explained my presence to the head man, a very young and short fellow who ran the place. He was the kind of Costa Rican I had learned to expect – attentive, humble, thoughtful and almost sad. I asked him about his business, and sensing my enthusiasm (at the accidental discovery of a firm that would increase my sample size), he agreed to be interviewed. This was a big break; I could still turn failure into triumph! I sat down and went through my series of questions. At this point, a major clump of wet mud from the leaking ceiling fell onto my questionnaire and made a mess of things. I moved the chair away from the hole and got a new survey for him.

It transpired that the guy (Jesus was his name) employed six people and ran a small business making chairs and other pieces of simple furniture. Many were custom-made for personal customers, and most of his business was picked up by word of mouth. In scoping out his factory, I noticed that the poor guy used a sawblade that looked like my used toothbrush. It was jagged and rusty. The saw itself was a nice old electric model, but it was clear that he couldn't use it for any precision cuts. Jesus never said any of this; I figured he was too embarrassed. His little factory or workshop was about the size of two medium-sized bedrooms. For his trouble I did invite him to lunch at the corner pulperia, frequented by working people in this tiny barrio of San Jose. With the traditional *arroz con pollo* in front of us, Jesus bowed his head, clasped his hand tightly together, and prayed deeply and severely, blessing the food and me for joining him. I paid the large bill – maybe two dollars for both of us, including bread and some juices. I asked him about his family – he had two kids and a wife. I asked him if he had ever been contacted by anyone from the aid community that works regularly with micro-enterprises, e.g. USAID, INCAE training classes, World Bank, UNDP and so on? Nope – never! I am not an expert in enterprises or micro-credit, but hearing this gave me the willies – it actually gave me a chill to think about it. Where was all the money going? What kind of person would be more deserving of credit or training than he?

At the halfway point in my research that summer, I returned to Atlanta and found a sawmill supply company in the yellow pages. I visited the place in some industrial section of town. It was huge, full of sales people and customers who obviously knew this business. The place had been there, apparently, for ninety years. I described the saw and blade to the manager from written measurements I had taken in San Jose using my thumb. I did this when Jesus was not looking and was over talking to his employees. The Atlanta manager was amazed and asked where this saw was. When I told him, he knew immediately what we were talking about. He said that fifty-year-old US saws were still in use in Central and South America (something like the hoards of '52 Chevies that are still functioning in Chile and Cuba). So I was in business.

On return to San Jose a few weeks later, I finally found his workshop. It wasn't easy to find without a storm going on and by someone who was actually intent on finding the place! The firm may have had a sign but I doubt it. But find him I did. At first Jesus was startled to see me. Then, with he and his staff, I did a few brazos. I got that glowing sensation that I often got when I knew I was in the right business as development aide.

"I have a little surprise for you," I said. Jesus was beaming and looked like a kid on Christmas morning!

I laid my gift-wrapped saw blade on top of his table saw and stepped back. He didn't quite get it. I said open it. He opened it and looked at it for a minute or so – top, side, bottom. He then put it next to the old one and it was clear that it would fit. My Atlanta colleague deserved a tip – one more reason to always keep old-time, experienced staff on board!

He looked at me and it was clear he didn't know what to say. He had tears in his eyes. I didn't know what to say either.

"Now you can make more and better furniture, right?" I said.

He agreed and gave me another brazos. Fortunately, I had brought my camera along for the occasion – which is perhaps the most valuable tool in the development business – always take shots after interviews or events like this, however corny that sounds. Others love it, especially when you send them the photos – it cements a lifetime bond.

So out we went to the front of his workshop. His neighbours (an auto upholstery place and an electrical shop) joined us for a few shots. It had been a fortuitous experience and it had all started at the Ministry of Transport. Sometimes Ministry officials serve the world best by not showing up for work.

Chao!

San Jose, Costa Rica, 1988

VIII. Absurdities
Enter, Project Overseers

As one might guess, a foreign or development aide is not totally independent. He or she does not work alone. You work in teams, usually under the watchful eye of the host government Ministry staff and their paymaster, the international donor. You want to work in teams in most places or you go nuts. In rural Albania, they airlifted out a Finn who, after surveying the rusted-out nothingness of his village for a few months, began to hit the bottle seriously. When his EU supervisor came through to search him out a few months later, he found him under the office desk, emaciated and reeking of vodka. So it has to be a team effort. Less likely that the whole team would end up under the table!

In principle, the local team works out project arrangements (bank accounts, phones, offices, cars, mail service and so on) and they are aided by the donor staff in country if possible. USAID backed our cause in Albania, which was to avoid doing maintenance on city hall buildings between training sessions. They also helped us avoid provision of gold watches and shopping trips to Brussels to the Ministry of Interior staff. Some donors, such as World Bank, are almost invisible, and if one ends up in trouble with the host government, that is your problem. In *Tropical Gangsters*, Klitgaard nicely details how a World Bank project team leader in Equatorial Guinea was jailed and the Bank effectively disowned the guy. USAID and British DFID, at least, can help because they maintain relations in most countries at the highest levels of government.

At other times, the donor itself can become a pain in the ass. One should never bite the hand that feeds, but a tactical nip sometimes can ground truth relations with them. This story was recounted by my Pakistan mission leader (a New Zealander) whose friend worked for a UNDP irrigation engineering project in West Africa for three years. The in-country work team were all Italians. The German auditors showed up after the first year. As one might expect, the Germans exhibited all the traits of the "nightmare European" (i.e. German sense of humour, Italian fighting spirit, French moral courage, English work ethic, Swiss flexibility, Indian sense of logic). You could imagine the scene: "Vee half used one thousand pipes und three are missing! Vee half a list of pipes here unt those you installed, no? Three are missing!" (Yell for emphasis.) "Vere are die pipes? Who is responsible?"

The head Italian indicated that according to his records, all were ordered and consumed by the project according to the work plan. The German gave that brilliant smile of complicity and recognition. He first talked quietly and patiently as professor to a dim student. His clever, alert expression told him that, "Of course you recorded it, of course the entries were false, and we both know the pipes were sold illegally on the black market."

"Are you hard uf hearing?" he suddenly yelled at the Italian.

"No, sir."

"Then you must provide evidence of these three pipes or the project must close and everyone must go home."

"Of course, sir. But we only have our records."

The German spun around without a sound and retreated to his colleagues, who all spoke heatedly as if in a rugby huddle. The Italian, meanwhile, returned to his little group and they discussed what to do to avoid being sent home to the local unemployment lines.

The German, viewing them suspiciously out of the corner of his eye, saw one of the Italians hand his chief a clipboard. The foreman (*vorarbeiter*, in his lingo) then approached the German auditor with the good news that the pipes had been found.

"Ver are they?"

"They are in the ground, sir."

"That is obvious, you fool! But ver?"

The Italian shows him a plat map with the number three below a small line. He then moved off in that direction followed by the auditor. Showing him the map, he explained that the three pipes, length twenty yards, were along this line. He paced the line followed by the auditor.

The German then motioned to his colleagues to come quickly. "*Schnell!*"

The three Germans could now be seen goose-stepping in unison with the clipboard in their hands as they reconciled the inventory with the existence of the three hidden pipes below the surface.

In that part of Italy, it is said that villagers still imitate the goose-stepping German auditors as they accounted for the hidden and entirely non-existent pipes. This event still provides roars of laughter and rounds of drinks at any local oesteria.

Unlike the Germans with the Italians, our overseers in Albania became less interested in our work. Many would say this is good. But all foreign aides want confirmation that their works are the most important ever done in the area and are leading to total transformation of whatever system they are working on – procurement, agricultural credit, municipal tax, national customs, national budgeting and so on. So the accepted routine is a report to the donor after finishing a chunk of work. The report typically details the achievement of particular milestones on the management plan for the project.

The head man for our project, Gene Haynes, the CTO or Chief Technical Officer, was a small-town guy who had been a farmer before entering AID. One should be happy to find earthy types like this in the field and, indeed, it was always a joy to hear his responses. That's because there were so few of them.

In late 1996, I gave him a report of our activities for the past five-week period in our five cities – changing budget reporting forms, doing training on treasury management, developing technical notes on municipal services such as urban transit – he didn't give a shit. He read the newspaper while I explained these things in detail. This in no way bothered me as I was out of there as soon as I finished – another box ticked on the form: "report given to CTO"!

At one point, I admitted that our meeting with the mayor in Vlore didn't happen because of his sudden departure to Tirana to meet with central government officials. This was common practise under the old system as the rural party folk would be suddenly reminded of the power of central official supervisors. Under Enver Hoxja, they summoned and you came instantly on threat of prison or an exile village.

It should be noted that Vlore was a hotspot historically and presently. Historically, the Greeks had claimed part of this coastal area and over the years, Albanian and Greek forces had gone at it occasionally. Corfu was just down the road ("road" is used loosely – though only forty miles away from Vlore it could take five hours to get there!). Currently, Vlore was the centre of stolen car, drug and prostitution trafficking for the southern coastal region. Many of the stolen Ferraris and Fiats in the parking lot of our hotel downstairs came through the local port. The hotel was unique, featuring large cows eating the garbage outside. It was quaint, had a little porch overlooking the sea, and overall was not bad. Nearly everyone – waiters, townsfolk, drivers, people walking their dogs –carried large guns, but no one ever fired one – possibly confirming the NRA thesis of deterrence via threat of mutually assured destruction. But gangs of heavies there were! They all looked like John Belushi clones. You know, the kind who try to look friendly or sensitive but end up scaring you. Think of the recent Hollywood tough-guys emulated by as many insecure men as possible. Isn't the disconnect obvious? Their faces are all too scrubbed and pretty; clothes too new and well-cut; blood too red; mutilations too contrived; and bullet holes just too neat. Their muscles are toned from the gym and just too perfect; not from a poorly-paid job of throwing bricks or demolishing buildings all day long. Albanians are cool. Hollywood should send scouts to Vlore immediately to put some of the real local machos on the payroll.

I told Gene that the little delay caused by the mayor was OK with us. (Gene had progressed to the comic page.) Our project team had lunch at a seafood restaurant owned by Artan Ikonomi, who was the son of the budget director. His mother was a fierce, energetic woman who would run to the window of her office carrying her large stick to fight off those with invoices demanding payment from the city. One bright morning as we discussed city finances, I was hit in the forehead by a rock while in her office. She had a treacherous job, but the restaurant was OK. She explained that her son had a day job besides the restaurant, transporting Albanians to Italy in his fast boat for hire, so he might not be back for lunch. But Artan had left word that we were to be given the best in the house as usual – local trout and a carafe of their excellent Chardonnay.

Following several hours of eating and drinking it was time to head out of town for Tirana. Who could blame us for trying to make the best of a bad situation? Just outside of Vlore, it was time to relieve ourselves of the considerable amounts of wine we had consumed. We found a nice olive grove (Albanian olives, the black, pitless kind, are also excellent, by the way) and each worked their own tree.

Suddenly we heard the roar of several black Mercedes coming closer, driving fast towards us across the grove where we were busy pissing.

I explained this to the AID guy who now looked up from his sports page.

"Shit, I thought, it's either the police or a gang of toughs coming to get us. Either way – bribes or robbery – we were screwed."

"What happened then?" Gene asked, now very attentive.

I told him, "They jumped out and ran toward us. We froze until it became clear in all the dust and din that it was in fact the mayor and his team."

"What did you do?" said Gene, suddenly intrigued by my final report.

"We did brazos all around! We held a short meeting there in the grove and explained what we were going to do in the way of training and technical assistance at our next visit. The mayor loved this and gave a short speech on the importance of our work to his little town. He wished us well and said we would dine on him next time we came.

"So all in all, the deviation from our planned schedule built good will and paved the way for an excellent return visit."

Gene frowned. "If you don't follow the work plan, you get me in trouble with the director and we have to ask for a modification. And you know how much shit that causes! Try not to let this happen again!"

"Right chief." I gave him a little salute, clicking the heels and spinning to head for the door. The guy actually appreciated this kind of thing. "See you next trip."

But he was back reading his paper and didn't hear or see me leave. I did like his permanently idiotic grin, though.

Vlore, Albania, 1996

Roof-top Wood Auction in Brazil

John – you won't believe this!

This should remind you of your Peace Corps days. Like you, in more than one instance, I consulted on overseas development assignments without a real clear understanding of what exactly the donor did – or any of them, for that matter! Their office and buildings were impressive. The people were all extremely confident, knew a lot of acronyms (e.g. CASs, PMPs, AOTAs) and had very high self-approval ratings. Their local mission offices were impressive with computers and people arranging meetings feverishly. But what the hell did they actually *do*?

This was a question put to me by an Australian colleague who was a treasury systems expert when we both started work at IMF.

"Do you know what this place actually does? What are we supposed to do here?" he asked quietly.

"Some kind of public expenditure analyses, I think. But let me find out for certain."

I got back to him the very next day with the news that we were in luck. The IMF published a number of brochures that were in fact quite technical and probably aimed at us as well as the public. They had good titles like "What Does the IMF Do?" which was perfect for its own technical staff. It wasn't clear why the public would care about their efforts to fix up the government's books in poor countries. The wider public, fed on websites, sound bites and slipshod journalism, had their simple and often immutable opinions. For example, one website portrayed the IMF as part of the larger world Jewish conspiracy against everything.

Before IMF days, I worked as a consultant for the Inter-

American Development Bank (IADB). My terms of reference (TOR) said that I was to accompany the team and do institutional assessment to implement a new forestry programme which could be financed by IADB on soft terms with local matching contributions of counterpart funds. I could follow that. The larger question which we couldn't answer was whether the IADB forestry programme would fly – whether member and host governments would want something that tied up their lands for the long growth periods required. There were higher return uses, such as coffee, cocaine and resorts. So off we went, five countries in six weeks: Peru, Chile, Brazil, Mexico and Honduras.

Things got a bit strange in Brazil. I like Brazil, nice, can-do people. Women are really OK too – strapping wenches, perfectly proportioned curves, hot, caramel-coloured flesh; positively delicious, all of them. In Brazil, our team moved down the Amazon River and visited three cities, Belem, Santarem and Manaus. We stayed first at Belem, a large coastal port on the Atlantic and the Amazon River. The rule is that if it's in Brazil and you've never heard of the city – e.g. Matto Grosso – it must have at least a million people!

Brazil is a major league country. It has a hundred and seventy million people and is larger in area than Australia. It has cities of seemingly endless size (Sao Paolo, Rio) and at least ten places of over a million that few have even heard of (e.g. Recife). It has unsurpassed beaches (Copacabana), rivers (Amazon), tropical rainforests (with thousands of species), technical innovations (e.g. methanol from wood for cars and trucks), industry (fourth largest steel industry in the world), races (billed as the world's only real multiracial society), and democratic institutions (it is the world's most decentralised system). It has always had potential and many joke that it always will. "Brazil grows at night when the politicians sleep" is an infamous quip here. The difference between Brazil and the Latin countries, in my experience, is the attitude and motivation of the people: Brazilians are can-do and like challenges. Government is viewed cynically as not much of a challenge or place where innovation takes place – so it isn't. The rest of the country flies ahead in spite of government administrators and policies. Productive forces are so strong that policies, however irrational, often cannot keep them back. Definitely positive vibes in this place.

I was riding up the elevator of our Belem hotel one evening after work and a guy said hi to me. This was odd since you couldn't immediately spot an American from their dress, skin colour or way of moving. I mean, I could have been Brazilian, German or Canadian too. Nevertheless, the guy got it right. I asked him what he was doing there in Belem, Brazil.

"Real estate," he said. "I'm from Jacksonville, Florida, and we buy and sell real estate."

"Here in the Amazon? What kind of real estate – forests?"

"Mostly – they have to be cleared and turned into ranches and sites for factories. We also get involved in selling the timber sometimes."

"Interesting, I am here on an IADB mission," I said, and watched if it piqued his interest. Luckily, it didn't.

"We're having a little meeting by the pool after dinner. Why don't you join us?" he said.

"Thanks, I'll try and make it," I said, trying to keep cool and not sound too excited.

What luck! Here we were on an IADB forestry programme mission to assess institutional and economic information to see if countries would support the programme. Brazil, especially this region, was famous for destroying its tropical forests – either via controlled squatters or timber and ranching companies that paid off forest service (IBDF) people to grant concessions or otherwise look the other way. The fact is the interviews with IBDF produced very little new information. The forest service said they were taking regulatory actions that they weren't actually doing. We needed an alternative source of information to ground-truth what they had been saying. The poolside meeting might just do that. I explained this to the mission chief, who heartily supported my attendance there.

It was a romantically tropical scene at the top of the hotel, where people gathered around the roof-top pool for drinks. I could have been on vacation. Strings of coloured lights surrounded the pool and a large deck mixed with potted palms overlooking the city and the harbour on the Amazon River below. It was typically a humid and muggy July night, but the soft breeze made it perfect. With a cold beer in my hand, it was even better than perfect. About ten people were there, maybe seven guys and three women, all clinking glasses of rum or whiskey. Bob, the real estate contact, sat next to me and gave me a running commentary of the game that unfolded. When asked, I introduced myself as a professor (which I was at the time) who was also consulting for IADB (which was also true). Smiles all around and a few strong swigs to loosen things up for the big event. Reminded me of an AA meeting: "My name is Bob!" "Hi Bob!" they chanted in unison after your introduction.

Seemed like a relaxed bunch until I realised that I was missing much of the underlying action. They were shifting topics and making signals so quickly that one would have to have a code book to be aware of what they were doing. The informal timber auction was being driven entirely by the nuances of body language.

"Goddamnist thing about your wife, Eduardo," said one of them. He seemed to be the informal leader. Puffed a local stogie and sat there with his drink in a loose t-shirt covered partly at the neck with a large necklace of wood and bone figures.

"Ya mon. She left me and took my clothes too," he grinned. The others grinned too.

"I got 50,000m^3 of caoba [mahogany] on board," said necklace man.

"But my wife ain't comin' back soon and I need gas in my car."

"I've got seventy-five thousand for it," said the guy to my left.

"The hotel isn't all that bad, and I do like the scenery here. I'll give you sixty-five," he said obliquely.

Necklace man suddenly scratched his left ear. "That means he's made a deal for sixty-five thousand dollars," said Bob.

Nobody even wrote it down, but it was clear that this would be confirmed later and become a written deal. How would they sort it out after all the booze? This was getting interesting. Carving up the forests and selling them off. All done right here by the pool in a superficially business-like way but filtered through a rough code. I listened to a few more timber sales and shipping transactions and tried to work myself in without arousing too much suspicion. I did order several rounds of drinks for them to keep in good stead.

"Question for you. How do you know he will ship you caoba? Caoba is rare even up here," I asked.

Necklace man snickered quietly at this. "Good question. You find that kind of thing in some markets, maybe Central America or Peru. But not here."

"Why not?" I persisted.

"Most of us here are wood people. We come from towns surrounded by tropical forests. We know the wood. There are at least five species that look close to caoba and in other markets traders have to deal with frauds. They deal with it harshly in most cases," he added in the professional tone of a securities salesman.

"We don't have that problem here anymore if you get my meaning. Jao there has a problem with wrong species, don't you Jao? Tell him what happens when you get a bad shipment of wood."

"I get a rash under my left arm," he grinned.

"What about you Eduardo? What happens to you?"

"I have trouble breathing around imitations. It's like an allergic reaction," he said proudly.

"At the other end, you can imagine how upset we must be when, after doing all that paperwork here, and waiting for the shipment for several weeks, we receive the wrong wood. Why, we wouldn't be happy at all, would we, boys?"

"That's right mon," several of them said together as they raised their glasses.

"What about IBDF?" I asked. "Aren't they upset that cattle is replacing all their forests? Won't that put them out of a job?"

All of them stopped talking as the conversation was taking a turn for the serious.

"20,000m^3 of cenizero [a local species of ash]," I heard the guy in the brown coat say.

"I think the IBDF is a good bunch. They don't give us much trouble. OK, Don Daniel [coat man]," says Eduardo, "I give you fifteen."

Coat man says, "Twenty."

Eduardo scratches his ear and nods to Daniel. "IBDF is tough sometimes, right Daniel?"

"Right, last week they surprised us in el Norte with helicopters and we had to pay some hefty fines. That's why our prices are a little higher today."

Pleased with my newfound knowledge on apparent IBDF regulatory capability, I lost the drift for a second and missed the question. There was silence and all of them were staring at me.

"Sorry, what did you say?"

"What did you say you did again?" asked necklace man.

"I consult for the Inter-American Development Bank," I volunteered.

"Development? What is development?" asked Daniel, looking at me with a wry grin.

Following the drift of the banter, Eduardo asked, "You work for a bank? Can I get a cheap loan?"

Ignoring the first unanswerable question, I gave the second one a shot. "IADB loans to governments that want projects financed. If the Brazilian government likes what we propose, and can satisfy conditions, we can lend them money for forestry development."

"Hell, we'll develop the forests for free, won't we?"

"That's right," coat man said, "we'll chop down the forests and sell the timber to the government if they pay what you guys offer, am I right?"

Laughter all around. It was a good one. Given the sorry state of development project progress in Brazil and elsewhere, it might have worked better to pay real stakeholders – i.e. the illegal timber industry – to do sustained yield cutting and manage the forests. That could work better than the expectation IBDF would regulate anything properly or that some corrupt PIU would implement the conditions of a loan. Even better, at least these guys could shift gears quickly – react to timber sale fraud or poaching when it was a "firm matter" (probably rival gang massacre).

"You may be onto something, a new model of development by 'pirate stakeholders'!" I said.

Regards from Brazil!

Belem, 1981

Armenian Goodbye

Mircea—

I was getting used to my new posh life as development aide. IMF was definitely a step up from the usual missions – first-class air travel, five-star hotels, secretary along for paperwork, meetings at the presidential palace and always at the top levels of government. The demeanour of the team members was polished class, quiet discussions among reasonable people of difficult issues, toasts at dinner, a few songs by the operatically inclined. IMF was all class – many had been at Oxford and Cambridge, or the best Canadian, French and German universities for undergraduate and doctoral studies. Clearly, these were the best and brightest in the aid field – many would of course question whether IMF had any intention of "development". Most in IMF would say that's the Bank's job.

As one colleague put it: "We are there to maintain fiscal discipline and watch them keep the books so there's no macroeconomic hanky-panky. Governance, decentralisation, water, health, education – that's the Bank's problem. Defence? Well now, that's our problem since it is such a major source of instability – no defence and the country (or regime at least) gets wiped out in the next war, meaning potentially one less IMF member. Too much defence spending and the economy gets distorted and corrupted."

So the Fund would put us up at five-star hotels or, if possible, guest quarters of the government. Governments often wanted to show maximum class and hospitality to the mission. Who knows, that might get them something in the next stand-by loan programme negotiations? Or in our case, it might not. There are other tactical options as well. The former Minister of Economy in Armenia (whose name was also Armen) told me how he got a negative decision on a loan turned around by World Bank. He had heard that chances of the project loan were slim. The German guy told him all the economic reasons why the project case was weak and probably wouldn't be approved.

Armen said, "Have you heard the joke from 'Radio Yerevan' about the Russian and the American on the elevator right after the 'transition'?"

The German looked a bit stunned and visibly struggled to shift topics. "No."

"The power went off and both were stuck in the elevator for at least an hour. The Russian then asked the American, 'Excuse me. Do you mind, I have to go to the bathroom?'

"'Not at all, be my guest,' said the American.

"The Russian then pulled his pants down and took a dump in the corner of the elevator.

"The American, who was shaken up by this scene, was thinking what a fucked up place this is. He reached for his cigarettes and lit up to calm his nerves.

"'No,' said the Russian. 'You cannot smoke here, it is prohibited!'"

The German guy roared with laughter for at least a minute. This really touched a nerve and the guy seemed to lose complete control of himself. Armen was even getting concerned. They talked a few more minutes, after which Armen excused himself, said his goodbyes, and headed for the door.

At the door, the German, still trying to control himself, said, "It was good talking with you." Two weeks later he received word that his project request had been approved!

So much for exclusively technical project criteria.

Our IMF mission arrived in Yerevan during a 1992 February snowstorm in a corporate jet leased by the Fund in Geneva. The luxurious fifteen-seater had two stewardesses, a

VCR and tapes, fruit and cigars, and full first-class meal service all the way. This was the second Fund mission to Armenia, so for them it was still something like aliens arriving on their earth from outer space. The first Fund mission to Armenia in 1991, rumour has it, landed also in a snowstorm and nobody was at the airport to meet them. The choice was to stay on smoking cigars and drinking after-dinner brandy or step out into the white, freezing nothingness with very uncertain consequences later on.

The deadlock was broken by the Swiss pilot, who informed the mission that he had a schedule to keep. He didn't care what they did, but they were going to have to do it within ten minutes. The Fund guys didn't move – until the realisation hit them that a long trip back to Washington without actually seeing anyone in Armenia could require some detailed explaining. They weren't prepared to do that, though who can blame them for trying! At least our flight was met by a black Lada from the Ministry of Finance. On the tarmac, even at night there were peasant women right out of a Chekhov country story, dressed in bonnets, whisking the snow around for some reason with large brooms. Armenia to me then and now was an intoxicating, almost magical place where you could not possibly take a bad or unforgettable picture! For example, a phalanx of priests in black medieval Christian robes marching through the snow around an old graveyard to the fourth-century church at Ejiamatzin; fifteen different ways to hold a vodka glass for a toast, and so on.

Our technical team was led by a classy but swash-buckling Canadian named McCue. A former wrestler turned economics doctorate, with impeccable manners and charm, he was the perfect fund staffer. He could be cool in French or English. He could practice controlled violence. After our Armenia report was panned by a Fund "murder squad", he smashed up his office and threw things around inside for about twenty minutes before suggesting that we retire to the dining room for lunch. He was a good manager and people person – a rarity at the Fund where cordial relations, manners and personal whim substituted for transparent rules. Just below the surface of manners were daggers, distrust and tribal intrigue.

We were on the usual business of the Fund – tracking down fiscal and budgetary information, tracing steps for key transactions like payments from the budget to ministries and clients; payments to the government from state enterprises and taxable businesses. All this led to a set of loan conditions and recommendations for technical assistance to improve fiscal transparency and that, hopefully, would allow the MOF to control its finances more tightly and enable the country to grow. The idea of fixing up government fiscal plumbing wasn't elegant and it didn't always work, but it was better for most people who lived there than the alternative of uncontrolled inflation and worthless currency!

On the team was another Canadian, Bryan Thomson. Thomson had been with the Canadian Tax Board for many years and was considered one of the best tax experts around. Naturally, an Indian accompanied the mission, Sanjay Gupta. Gupta was a number-cruncher. On the first mission, he quantified the precise value of bread subsidies coming out of the state budget to cover the long bread lines and others starving during those rough years. In 1994, they had to endure an entire winter without electricity. The local nuclear plant had to be shut down before it blew up! To Gupta, the bread subsidy was a major leakage from the state budget that had to be quickly quantified and stopped before it threatened macroeconomic stability. The government naturally took a dim view of his conclusions and simply said to us, "The subsidy will remain. Armenians like bread." McCue nodded, embarrassed slightly by having to be told this, like a dumb student, and that was that.

Our days in Yerevan started early, and were taken up with long official interviews according to a rolling schedule compiled and efficiently distributed to us by the secretary who flew along with us from Washington. Some interviews were in groups; others were one-on-one. I had an especially peculiar meeting the first week that vitiated the old saw that government is dull.

At one of the state banks, I spoke with the Vice President. He was Russian, as many high party officials in Armenia were. The translator was a short, jovial, slightly pudgy woman of around thirty-five. She did her best to stay up with him, he talked fast and it was my duty to listen. I knew nothing in particular about banks other than my own account at home. I should say that I ended up at this meeting more or less by accident as the expert responsible had a schedule conflict. So here I was trying to listen intelligently and ask the appropriate questions at the right time. This could counter the charge that the team had an idiot on board. The best thing to do in these situations is to say as little as possible and show respect. Keep the conversation light and social. Tell a joke or two. Problem is that I could never do any of that.

Thus, it hit me after a few questions and answers from this guy that something wasn't quite right with the operations of his bank. Was it a "bank" at all if they kept the depositor's cash without their permission? The "bank" sounded more like the state tax authority! The procedures for getting deposits out and getting loans approved seemed too complex for me.

"Why are they so complicated?" I asked simply.

"It is the law and that is consistent with the Constitution," he said.

"No," she said to me, "it's because the government has been stealing our money since 1917!"

Christ, I thought, this could turn nasty!

Apparently the bank VP knew some English and became enraged. He pounded his fist violently next to her and blew cigarette smoke at her. I needed to settle things down and to break the ice here.

"Mr Volonoksy, it only seems that in your accounting system, the deposits have become assets and the loans liabilities, or exactly the opposite of what they should be for a private bank."

"Have an apricot, our fruit is the best in the Soviet Union," he said as he moved over to me in the corner of the table. His demeanour was that of a very angry, harassed person, forcing himself to smile while squeezing the little apricot in his fist. He even poured me another cognac.

"You Americans think you can rule the world," he hissed through his teeth. "I will tell you that the Soviet Union was the greatest system the world has ever known. We will defeat you someday," he said as he downed an entire cognac in one swig. I must say that I was getting scared. Somehow I angered him and should this get back to McCue, I could be out of here on the next plane. I was really nervous and afraid to say anything.

I said to the translator, "I think Mr Volonosky has an excellent point. The Soviet Union was the greatest system on earth – on paper. But to defy the laws of supply and demand for so long, you needed a real currency, a store of real value, to finance it. Unfortunately, now you don't have that." I waited for another wave across the bow. But it didn't come.

Just to cover myself I did add, "Please note also that this is an IMF mission and even though I am from the US, the mission has nothing to do with the US government."

He squinted meanly at me. But I couldn't get worked up as this was all a new experience for me. Imagine getting berated by a caricature – that of a defeated Russian bureaucrat! He was tall and had an almost alien-like high forehead with a crop of long and dishevelled white hair. Head full of brains and wild, romantic ideas like Tolstoy. He looked like one of the Metalunans in *This Island Earth*. Unlike the aliens in that movie, led by a kind, understanding scientist ("Please stand back, or you may be harmed," after which the death ray vapourised the nearby interosetor), I think this guy would have liked to rough me up. Instead, he said formally and abruptly, "We must talk more some time, Mr Guess. Now I have another meeting."

I was off the hook for now but sweating profusely. We left in relative silence, given the loud shouting that had just occurred. It was eerie. I moved quickly to get out of there, shaking his hands but saw that he avoided any direct eye contact. No problem offending someone with eye contact here – this was not Navajo Country – by contrast, lack of eye contact here was the offence!

I returned through the Yerevan streets to my room. The guest quarters provided by the Government of Armenia were ample and had hosted many world leaders during the Soviet period. The building complex stretched out into a campus with adjoining halls to allow indoor foot traffic during the rough winters. Our rooms were enormous and filled with the heavy, dark wooden furniture common to the region. This worked out nicely during the fuel crisis of 1994 though – most Armenians burned their furniture and old copies of Marx to keep warm. Meals at the guest quarters were served in a large, gymnasium-sized hall with one table in the middle for us. Thick couches, deep chairs – just don't try and change the floor design or architecture. Like the hidebound Soviet bureaucracy, this stuff was built to stay put and last forever. At the entrance to the pantry stood our waiters, ever-ready to serve and alert to the slightest nod or signal. The dining hall was a good distance from our rooms on foot (maybe we should have taken a cab) and took about ten minutes to get there. Outside were lots of silver birches and magpies, two telling symbols which would let you know what part of the world you were in if you developed amnesia.

At the end of the second day, it was evident that our colleague Bryan had a little drinking problem. I mean, we all drank – harder than usual because of the former Soviet and Russian culture. We tried to control ourselves and, frankly, would have appreciated lighter stuff such as wine and beer – with a few tastes of famous Armenian cognac for dessert. Nothing more was needed. Instead, Bryan swilled lots of vodka during and at the end of his day. I returned home and found that he had stopped by a package store on the way home, i.e. a corner grocery store that sold booze. Might not have bread – but vodka they had! I knew there was a problem with this guy. He showed me a postcard he had with him. It was from a woman he met in a bar in DC. She talked about his crowd there, a veritable tribe of drunks he knew for about a week who got together while he was there and drank the evenings away. An indication of what was to come. Today, Bryan was a bit tipsy. He must have knocked off early and come back to brace himself for dinner.

"Where is Bryan?" McCue wanted to know at dinner.

"He should be here any minute… ah, there he is."

Bryan, who was a lanky guy of around six foot four, sauntered in smiling broadly. He was in a very loud and boisterous mood. He seemed confident in that fortified way – no need to listen to anyone out here. Quite obviously, he was ripped or "pissed", as is said in Commonwealth countries.

McCue had been discussing the latest budget theories with two of us. All the usual stuff about the stability pact rule (three percent of GDP) versus outright balance. McCue called it the "stupidity pact", which it was. Most of us agreed that outright balance was too rigid and unrealistic given the changing needs of the year and difficulty of getting parliaments or presidents to move quickly. So a primary balance was applied to developing and transitional countries (balance before debt service) which was fair. The EU used the three percent rule, which was also plausible until something went wrong (political leaders would be expected to cut such expenditures as social services and unemployment payments and increase taxes even though it was a recession!). The EU rule even imposed penalties as a percentage of GDP for exceeding deficit limits, meaning more deficits for running deficits!

Bryan's grin became a frown rather quickly. Either the booze was wearing off or kicking in, I couldn't tell.

"Goddamn budget has to balance!" he said. Bryan was actually tilting towards McCue and at one point was actually leaning on him. McCue ignored this except for a quick flick of his hand to shove him upright.

There were quick glances all around. McCue and all of us knew something was brewing.

"I worked in Canadian Revenue for twenty-five years. Had to balance the fucking budget or big cock-ups later." He wheezed out a loud laugh.

"Would you balance the budget daily or weekly? How would that work?" said Alice, our lady team member who had worked for the US Treasury for the past six years.

I was watching her lips move and drifting off a bit from fatigue – she reminded me of someone I used to take to drive-in movies in high school and feel up in the back seat. This reverie was shattered by a splash of heavy liquid onto my hands and a loud thud. Bryan's head had fallen into his soup.

"Could you get him out of there?" McCue said quietly to me over his shoulder while looking ahead without the slightest touch of alarm.

I motioned to Aschot our translator for assistance. The two of us brought him upright in his chair, wiped him off and tried to carry him out. He was passed out now and we tried to carry him as one would a long pole. Given his size, this didn't work.

McCue was determined to finish the critical discourse on rules of budgetary balance with his colleague. He and Alice continued their discussion uninterrupted by Bryan, possibly a relief for them. McCue and she talked straight ahead. Apparently there was nothing else going on around them!

Meanwhile, Aschot and I were not getting anywhere with Bryan. His ass dragged on the carpet as we tried to move him out of the hall and up the stairs. He was like a long string-bean – or beanpole. We made it ahead a few yards. Then he lurched violently and we would shoot backwards a few more yards – two steps forward, one step backward. We spent about ten minutes trying this and getting about nowhere. We did have a nice tour of the hall's main floor as the kitchen crew and waiters watched the spectacle in silent horror. On one leg of my odd waltz with Bryan and Aschot, I noticed that the waiters had gone.

Seeing this farce unfold nearby between the finer points in his discussion, McCue motioned to another team member. "Help them out, will you?"

The three of us had better luck. We spirited him across the room log-style and out we went. It was a long haul up the stairs, down the long, dark hall, up more stairs and into his room. Fearing that he could barf and drown in it, or burst out and fall down the stairs in the dark, I took out his keys and we locked him in his room. His feet hung out about a yard from the end of the bed. Unfortunately, the Soviet-era beds were all one-size!

Later that night the mission members talked quietly and in a forgiving, non-judgmental manner about what had happened. Nearly all of us could point to alcoholics in our own families, so this prepared us for the dealing with Bryan. At breakfast, of course, he recalled nothing and we did not raise the issue. Off we went our separate ways to our rounds of interviews. Nothing more was said. Something would appear in his file later and that would about wrap up his IMF consulting career.

Returning to my room that evening, I was about to head down to dinner to see the others in the great hall. No point in sitting around a room like that – actually gave me the creeps, as if Stalin's ghost or some of his victims might be buried underneath the place.

A solid knock on the door. It was one of the staff. "Good evening, sir. Are you ready?"

"Yes, I was just going to dinner."

"Sir, you are moving."

"Not moving, just going to dinner. We are here for another three weeks."

"No. You are moving."

I could see the guy was quite serious and also had been given orders. He wasn't just fumbling around for words. I knocked on McCue's door.

"McCue, the guy says we are moving."

McCue gave the impatient look of one who will deal with this misunderstanding firmly and quickly. "I'm the Team Leader and IMF made arrangements for three weeks here."

"That is true, but our orders are that you are must move now."

"Excuse me, but where are we going?"

"You go to Hotel Razdan."

"We have not packed. We have no way of getting there. How can we move this fast?"

"Sir, there are your cars." He motioned for us to look out the window to the driveway below where three black Ladas were lined up waiting for us.

"But we are not packed."

"You will be shortly, sir. We will pack your bags and move your suitcases now." And with that, several other staff appeared and began putting our things neatly and rapidly into our suitcases.

We were swept out of there in about an hour. Our little show with Bryan the previous evening had clearly and properly offended their dignity and honour. The guest quarters were for high-level guests and they were expected to behave themselves, IMF or no IMF! Like a child scolded by a parent for something he knows he did wrong, my respect for their sense of propriety, their direct action approach and for their standards all increased. The bad news is that we had to go back to the Hotel Razdan! On our last trip there, they didn't take dollars or credit cards!

Best,

Yerevan, Armenia, 1992

Bosnian Serbs Fight it Out in Bed

Sue—

We had some good times, didn't we? Is there anything we didn't do? Is there anything we forgot to do before breaking up and going our respective ways to marriage? I do think of you sometimes. Like recently, for example, though you may not like the connection... I'm here in Eastern Europe surrounded day and night by carnivorous sex pots.

I find it really odd that twelve years after the "opening" to the West, and with legions of returning Western travellers from this region, otherwise intelligent people could still stereotype women here as ex-tram drivers and weight-lifters. They must be blind, stupid or both!

Remember the great Wendy's commercial featuring a Soviet fashion show that brought out a series of screeching, fat, muscular peasant women on stage to the whistles and cat-calls of the audience? The message was that Wendy's fare wasn't all the same – like their competitors'.

The stereotype of Slavic women amazes me – and it is all taste, I grant you – because I have never seen such a collection of fantastic, stylish, cultured, strapping wenches anywhere. They are shapely, luscious, sharp and very educated. Anyone who has trouble with American women and can't find a wife, can come to this part of the world and be "king shit". I know at least one guy who couldn't even get a date in the US. I mean, who would want to listen to this guy talk about supply curves – with their bad English they might even figure it was a come on.

Price theory? He just wants a cheap fuck, one of the ladies might think.

He was obsessed about his economics and still found a fantastic Bulgarian wife! It wasn't going to happen with US women, I assure you! You remember him – always laughed in his face (to my embarrassment) and called him a bore. Hey, you were right!

Hotels in Eastern Europe are built like fortresses – or at least they used to be. The International in Skopje was the typical state hotel: ten storeys, heavy on the grey cement, 1950s futuristic style, dark inside. It had a pub called "Sky Bar" which had the combined dungeon/whorehouse feel to it – you know the type – star lights twirling around on the walls to give it that "with-it", up-to-date feel.

"This is definitely where my kind of action is – Monte Carlo and the Skopje International Hotel Sky Bar!" the cool dude with his shades on might say during a prime-time TV commercial.

Then there was the main restaurant. One morning, I noticed that the large main doors leading onto the porch from the restaurant were inexplicably open and blasts of snow were swirling around the first row of tables. Not a problem. The guests simply sat further back so that the snow wouldn't cover their eggs and toast. I too selected a rear table and strolled up to the big breakfast bar – past the trays of greasy meats, smiling fish, yellowish potato salad and wonder bread that were put out for the gala breakfast buffet. It was what good party members and their families expected. Fortunately, the cut-down Yugoslavs or South Slavs were into cornflakes and milk. There they were! There was also honey to put on the bread so I was really in business. The hotel also had strong black tea! Go for it!

As for the temperature control, the guests were wearing their winter coats and scarves. There was a rational explanation for all this. It was not simply Honduras Syndrome, where someone forgot to close the doors and no one around had authority to make the big decision of closing the doors. No, it turns out the plumbing was broken, pipes had burst upstairs, and raw sewage was spilling down from the ceiling into parts of the restaurant. This smelled and the smells had to be let out! Best way to handle that was to open the door and let the smell out. It was eminently practical, especially given the absence of competition among hotels in Skopje.

And how about that service? There shouldn't have been any since it was buffet style. But there was service anyway – they suddenly came up from behind and took things from you – things that needed to be washed and inventoried for paperwork requirements. My cereal bowl, for example, disappeared even though I had only finished half with it and was getting more tea. One of the girls took my knife while I was going for it. I grabbed it back. She still had hold of the handle and a brief tug of war ensued. These little incidents made life interesting during my introduction to Macedonia and Eastern Europe.

Macedonia is interesting. It is largely Slavic populated with a corridor of Albanians that has grown immensely since the Kosovo war. The Slav portion means an instinctive sense of hopelessness. Even the jokes end with hopeless punchlines: "And the entire village starved!" (Laughter all around.)

"Looks like it's going to be a nice day today, Borislava."

"Yes, but don't worry, it will get worse later," she adds with conviction.

Macedonia was the poor cousin of the Yugoslav federation. That doesn't mean much except it was more agricultural – and also a major wine-producer, which supplied the rest of the federation with primary products. The Slavs here are very proud of their heritage and especially the Serbs. Both, it must be said, detest the Albanians. As my Macedonian translator put it when I said, "You must have been pleased when Clinton put in the five hundred Marines to prevent a Serb attack in 1992."

"You're a fool. You've been brainwashed by CNN," she said, in that inimitable peremptory tone. There can be no contrary response. It simply was true and that was that.

At a Macedonian colleague's farm over lunch, I must have been running at the mouth because my friend Maxim said, "I know that as an American you believe in racial harmony and all that, but if you want to be my friend and come here again, you must not talk to me about working with your Albanian colleagues in Tetovo. I have a few Albanian friends. But I will tell you honestly, as a friend, that we would like to exterminate them all or drive them back to Albania." Would it have been awkward at this point to make the transition and talk about the weather?

So the little landlocked country of around two million people is quite a place. It nearly went to war with Greece over the eight-pointed Vergin Star on its currency and flag. The Macedonian Greeks claimed this as their symbol and were offended that Slavs also claimed it as theirs, so the two Macedonias squared off and were about to have a good row over this major issue when cooler heads prevailed. Each side backed off a bit and the conflict was averted. The irony is that the two Macedonias have more in common than Greek Macedonia and Athens. Athens is regularly accused of cheating Tessaloniki or Salonika out of their fair shares of fiscal transfers from the central government and other service entitlements. With skilful diplomacy, Greek Macedonia could probably get more funding out of Skopje!

In this enlightened racial and ethnic context, I went to bed one evening in my little room at the Continental. I slid off immediately into dreamland, normally forgetful of all the things I should worry about – unfinished work and so on. Around three, I was awakened by what had to be the sounds of people in my room. That gave me a short jolt until I realised that it was all next door. The place had no soundproofing. I lived in a place once where the woman upstairs would take baths and fart so loud it would shake our bedroom just below her bathroom, so it wasn't a total surprise here.

Except the noise was all sex. These were jungle sounds of apes and tigers fucking carnivorously and to the death. The ground shook and the windows rattled, like hearing Chopin the way it should be played on the piano. The woman giggled amidst the sound of bodies rolling around, springs squeaking. Now and then she emitted loud, erotic groans – sometimes they were both groaning. I tried to imagine what was going on, but it was damn hard without being able to see. It was definitely good, whatever it was. Then they really went at it. This had all been the pre-game show. Now she really sang out; the guy was drilling hard now and the bed sounded as if it was going to catapult springs against the walls. The whole place was shaking as if in a violent storm or earthquake. It was a living wet dream.

In a while, they slowed down and both of them let out final groans and fell into a long, very soft academic discussion of something. Christ, would it never end? Could we have more fucking please? Finally, they got tired of groaning and chatting and fell back to sleep. I did too. About five, there was a repeat performance of almost the same intensity and duration. This was unfortunate for the committed foreign aide in that I hadn't had much sleep and had to do interviews all day. Pisser.

The next night was quite normal. I looked around for who it might be in order to place bodies with types and styles of groans. That would allow for addition of the visual dimension and at least increase vicarious thrills. But no people next door. And no noise that night. Must have fucked themselves to death and been buried someplace together. I had a great sleep, dreaming of my vineyard and horses in rural Macedonia in the late summer. Despite being a committed development worker, I had to fantasise occasionally about becoming a country gentleman someplace like this and chucking the whole rat race. California was obviously too expensive, so Macedonia was a natural. Still farfetched but OK as a dream though.

The next night, it was back to work. At around three, the jungle partners revved up their engines slowly – groaning, giggling, squeaking, singing and, of course, all in a language that I couldn't understand. I could deduce, like Watson, that they were friends and this was not some whore deal. Mind you, there were a lot of nice-looking whores around and some hotels, in which I have stayed, actually rented rooms by the hour. Either way the result was the same as two nights ago – I didn't sleep much at all.

After another wintry breakfast in the dining room, with snow swirling close to the food, I approached the reservation/cashier area downstairs. It was the usual customer-friendly design – no signs, no one on duty, just a heavy marble counter to lean on and wait to be given privileged treatment along with the other customers. Even though it was "transition" time, under this system still, the staff were state officials and they could contrive some phoney offence and have you jailed for complaining. More likely, given their demeanour and style, they would simply pound the shit out of you and toss you out in the snow. Either way, it wasn't looking good for customer service.

I approached the guy at the counter who was reviewing receipts from the dining room. I hovered over him for five to ten minutes during which he took no notice of me.

"Good morning," I said loudly and cheerfully. "I have a question for you, my good man. Could you tell me who is in the next room to mine? That would be room a hundred and fifteen."

The man came over. He understood English so I was in luck. "Next to your room? Why do you want to know?" he said suspiciously.

"Do you know you look like Norman Bates? The guy in *Psycho*? Has anyone ever told you that?" Actually he looked more like Manuel Noriega, "*cara pina*" or "pineapple face" behind the counter.

This got him excited. "Yes, Norman! People say that all the time to me. 'You Norman Bates! This Bates Motel!' I never see the movie. I have to see it!"

I now explained to Norman that "the sound-proofing in my room is not so good and the people in one fifteen talk all night. I find it hard to sleep and was thinking of asking them to talk more quietly," I lied.

Another guy came out from the back office. Why did these guys all look like beefy Mafioso and thug athletes? They really looked murderous. The Packers should fly here and recruit the whole place. They could save a lot on pads.

The two of them began looking through a box of files. The files were yellow and moth-eaten, all beat up; some of them were even shredded. Inside was a large row of receipts, the kind the other guy was tallying up to prepare bills. Suddenly, they both reacted insanely to one of the files with short, very loud bursts of laughter. One punched the other in the shoulder. Two drunken bears roaring loudly over a private joke. It was scary and I didn't know whether to laugh too. Norman poked the other guy again and they both laughed even louder!

"Listen, my friend," Norman's colleague began, "the guy is from Bosnia. You know there's been a nasty war there for two years. His girlfriend is a Slav and lives someplace in Macedonia. They got split up and he hasn't seen her for two years! They are making up for lost time in the room next to yours. They will be gone tomorrow. If you want another room, just let us know."

I thanked them and thought about this. What an amazing place. Intense love like that in the middle of a war in a neutral zone, between two apparent enemies. If only their governments spent more time fucking instead of stirring up ethnic hatreds, hotels like this might serve as de-pressurisation mechanisms, war-free love zones, subsidised by the UN. I didn't change rooms. I never saw them though I used to imagine who they might be in the dining room. Maybe they sat in the first row of tables at breakfast to cool off after the heat of the night with wind-driven snow!

Keep in shape, I may visit you again!

Skopje, Macedonia, 1996

IX. Fantasies
Close Shave in Burma: Mission to Myanmar

Coming here has made me appreciate whoever it was invented logic, because before logic, I think the whole world was like this.

John Burdett, *Bangkok 8*

Bill—

This one's for you! You have to agree that on some missions, life imitates art and no imagination is required. The situational absurdities are right there and all you have to do is pay attention and try to remember the details. How many good ones that could be B movie scripts have I already forgotten? On other missions, events and people are strange but you can easily imagine them getting stranger. Is it a perversity that pushes one in this direction? Why did I bring Orwell's *Burmese Days* along to Myanmar? It was perfect – the suffocating heat he described at the beginning of the monsoon season soon to vanish with the rains; Flory the miner who needed a few gin and tonics just to prepare himself for shaving each day so that he could make it down the club for a few more. This would seem absurd and fantastic, unless you were actually in this place and saw its effects on you in a few days. So I fantasised a bit more during my mission there and here is what came out…

Potter was out of shape and it seemed to him that his feet thumped along at an unreasonably slow pace. As he ran through the dense, piney woods, fighting off palmetto leaves slapping his face, he could feel his heart and feet pounding on the sand between wheezy pants and gulps. Now he would remember how his high school PE teacher used to wince with embarrassment at having to put up with a physical wreck in track class. He had more than a grade at stake now.

The soldiers were gaining on him. He slid down the side of a hill covered with pine needles and jumped into the river. Even though the roaring waters deafened him he could hear the shots being fired, not just as they skimmed the water in front of him but the reports of the rifles behind him. The smell of gunpowder whiffed into his nostrils. (Sulphur wasn't an offensive smell – in fact Potter used to sniff bottles of it in chemistry class. More on this later…)

He was a better swimmer than runner so he dove in and stroked on. It was like swimming in molasses – he just sputtered along like an animal who knows it's done for. There it is! Just a few more feet and he'd be on the opposite bank, maybe to freedom. Potter sloshed out and ran hard through the bushes. The steep cliffs rising up from the banks now gave way to a path down hill covered with thorn bushes which impaled him from every side. Here Potter did his famous suicide slide, and low-crawled on all fours through the thorns (his college baseball coach Bob Pifferini would have been pleased). He was getting better with each obstacle. But his excellent athletic moves finally became useless. He was like a cornered rabbit. It all came down to two split-second images – the unmistakable face of his rival Peter Bond dressed in military garb and wielding a large rifle. Bond stood above him in conquest, a malevolent grin on his pockmarked face. Greeted by the sudden powerful jab of a rifle butt in his face, Potter rolled over, seeing light for the last second before Bond fired three rounds into his guts, kicking up the dust on the ground.

As through shifting rents in a fog, he could just make out the face in front of him that stared with idle curiosity.

Potter knew he'd been shot and imprisoned by the military because he couldn't move his head. Potter also realised that actually he'd been dreaming and his head was wedged between the seat and fuselage. During his feverish slumber, Potter's sweat-drenched and twitchy hands had pitched what remained of his drink over the seat and onto a bald head in the row ahead of him. Emerging from the dream he had had so many times, it was always like this. The dream wasn't so bad. Nice to get some exercise while you sleep. It was the result that worried him – a dreary premonition of events to come. He had to know this was a dream by now – how could Bond show up in the Burmese jungle? What was it that caused the recurring dream? Was it like General Buck's recurring Matador dream in Burdick's *Fail Safe*, which turned out to be a major premonition? Was he doomed this time? Or was it a minor premonition that he was going to be sacked from another job? This had happened many times in his short life of forty years.

"Sorry about the Coke. Can I get you a towel?" said Potter in an attempt to cast a sensible light on his odd behaviour. People often thought Potter was improperly alive, a true nutter, but good for a laugh. He had to correct this impression frequently, show them he was thoughtful, sincere and reasonable. It never worked for long.

The drenched man looked at him steadily, almost wistfully with his cow-like eyes. He obviously didn't understand all the peculiar sounds of American English and turned his head away quietly. Peering out of the little porthole of the ancient British jet, growing darkness was muting the normally verdant green and brown colours of the earth. Evidently it was late afternoon. The plane now winged its way through the clouds toward earth. With a few banks and lurches from the wheels and flaps, they were preparing – for what? The question always at this point was, are we going to crash, begin our approach to land, or both?

As the plane settled onto the shimmering Rangoon runway, international consultant Bill Potter braced himself for the work ahead. He was here to straighten out the peculiar systems that governed fiscal policy and the local civil service. He had been doing this kind of process "plumbing" work for ten years now, mostly in Latin America and was on his first trip to Asia. It wasn't real glamorous work, but it gave one the earthy sense of working with real people in government ministries. He often wondered what hope there was to fix a corrupt and tyrannical system governed by a cunning and ruthless kleptocracy through tinkering with civil service laws and budget forms. He deeply believed that his work would change a few minds in important places and that the arithmetic would eventually add up to positive institutional results.

As an added bonus, many of these "real" people were also vivacious women who liked other important things besides calculating cash limits and tax rates, such as cavorting and partying until late hours. At work, however, he showed them how to do things like put budgets together or forecast revenues better. Mostly he did this by relating stories and anecdotes from home and providing a few examples from budgets provided by his friends in government service. As part of his usual routine, he also gave them Double Mint chewing gum, Hershey bars, technical journals and other inducements to provide him information. Invitations to dinner often worked with the ladies. So the work was fun and not too difficult.

The plane circled Rangoon to give its passengers a different perspective on what to expect on the ground. It occurred to him that the pilot was also looking around for the tiny airport through the obscurity of shifting clouds. He recalled the crude simplicity of the old 1946 TWA ads for Constellations: "We feature tricycle landing gears and flaps for your comfort"..."Four engines with the combined power of a locomotive!" Such statements would scare the hell out of most people now. Maybe Myanmar Air should advertise, "Pilots equipped with maps and radios for safe landings at the right airport!"

Life imitated art and, with a series of lurches, grinds and muffled announcements, the plane lumbered itself onto the runway with all the grace and confidence of an overweight albatross. It was one of those buoyant Third World landings that Potter had grown to expect: first, the hard thump and then the bounce of the semi-botched (frequently downwind) landing; followed by a thud of brakes jamming, that would successfully stop the plane just at the end of the runway. No frequent-flyer miles on this run!

Descending the stairs from the faded thirty-five-year-old British jet airliner used by Myanmar Air, the sudden rush of heat slapped him in the face like a ream of hot towels from first class. It reminded him of his sweaty jaunts in Panama and Managua for USAID and anyone else who would send him down and pay his modest daily rate of three hundred dollars – not including meals and booze. It was the same kind of endless expanse too. The flat, tropical wasteland, sandwiched between pastel blue skies and chalky clouds and the cushy black asphalt, turned to gooey mush by the pounding heat. Here one could have a free sauna bath at only ten in the morning!

As he followed the others across the ramp with his beat-up embroidered leather Tex-Mex briefcase, he pushed on through swarms of mosquitoes and assorted flying bugs. Here he entered the warehouse-like structure built to greet international travellers in the Union of Myanmar, formerly known to the world as Burma.

Our arrival is a big event, thought Potter, they're turning on the air conditioners!

Even for someone who had worked in the military

kleptocracies of Latin America like Panama and Guatemala, he thought security was a bit tight. By instinct he shifted into his Third World arrival mode. Concentrating on a focused, singular activity with his mind, Potter had learned to tune out dissonance and rancour. Or most of it, anyway. With this mental trick, he could delete the clamour and din of hundreds of Burmese outside, shouting and waving brightly-coloured green ZLP banners of the only organised opposition to the military junta (State Law and Order Commission or SLORC) that ran Burma. The "ZLP" banner apparently meant "People's Party".

Sounded like a flying monster from a Japanese sci-fi flick: "The Slorcs are attacking again! Take cover!"

As he watched the heavily armed police pushing and shoving demonstrators back from the wire fence on the ramp, he recalled that someone at AID had told him, "Don't worry, we don't get involved in local political matters. We do technical work."

Among the crowd were normal airport fans, cheering to arriving relatives, selling their wares or just letting off steam. The police, brutally egalitarian to a man, seemed to be pushing them all around at random. He saw scores of strategically-placed soldiers around the inside of the staging area.

They're either going to prevent or cause the next coup, Potter thought.

The troops surrounding the airport seemed all ready for the next big war, meaning a good foray against their own people. Dressed in their drab olive outfits featuring chic camouflage (this would help them hide inside the many official white buildings!), Potter observed that their AK-47s were nearly as large as they were.

With the already comforting thought that he would be on the plane out of here in three weeks after teaching his little course at the Ministry of Finance, he moved ahead in line to be greeted by the local minions who ran customs.

One could always get an instant insight into a country's culture from the customs operations. In Thailand, the soldiers looked mean but were always cordial and ran you through with polite efficiency. In Costa Rica, there was an air of relaxed disorder, permitting flexibility for most travellers while allowing officials to be more selective and probably more effective in confronting potential trouble-makers. Their only fault was an obsession with coloured tax stamps and a chronic fear of making individual decisions. This meant multiple, time-consuming clearances of personal documents.

Right away, in Myanmar we were in a different world. Foreigners had to run the gauntlet of customs to make sure they were not subversives (often returning expatriates who had travelled through enemy territory that included places like Japan!) or troublemakers (usually journalists). The desk was raised up so that a petitioner had to stare humbly upwards, giving over his papers like a child returning stolen cookies to his parents. This almost religious ceremony required the errant sinner to humbly and earnestly beseech the robed khaki officials for forgiveness and permission to enter the blessed Union of Myanmar.

Government authority typically works like this in backward, poor societies – locals have to worship petty officials and suffer the abuses (shouts and derision, even an occasional punch or shove) of an intolerant and rigid social structure. Officials used the caste/class system to make subtle distinctions on the basis of caste, colour, dress, and language, and infer other things like intensity and direction of religion and political views. Still the idealist, Potter knew all this but honestly believed that training would change official minds and help create pluralist tolerance and a functioning rule of law protective of citizen rights.

As expected, the little man (bigger because of his military elevator boots) stared down at Potter from behind a pair of designer shades. The silver shades covered both his eyes and many of the waffle-like pockmarks on his face. Manuel Noriega! How did you get here? It was always amazing how such people caricatured themselves. If such characters didn't exist, Hollywood would have to invent them. The chief was thrusting his jaw outward to cover certain undisciplined hesitancies. He was probably a coward and a bully. Still, he could be a caring family man after work. Sitting there in his little starched shirt creased like a potato chip and covered with medals, Potter could see he was a corrupt loser. But it was very important that he avoid any expression which conveyed this.

Such a ridiculous facial expression gave the chief that extra bit of confidence needed to push the arriving rabble about. This posture, along with a peculiar frozen smile revealing fang-like teeth protruding from Betel juice-stained red gums (without a hint of Buddhist inner bliss), equipped him to face the next supplicant who would take up his precious time.

Potter handed him his US passport and flashed an indifferent glance that was neither menacing nor friendly at the soldier. He was good at that – the droopy, half-opened, lifeless eyes that conveyed to the listener exactly what he wanted to convey – nothing! He didn't like soldiers. Following a year in a military academy after being tossed out of his private school in eighth grade, Potter had developed a real distaste for military organisation and the people in it. He figured most of them should be out picking up beer cans in parks or rebuilding slums. The rest of them should be released from duty and allowed to walk around until they ran out of money.

Now it was his turn at the customs window. Potter stepped up and was prepared to hand over his passport and visa. The doll-like official swung gracefully down quickly from his desk like a monkey, slinking over to a larger, hairy man with even more medals on his uniform. The other official was decked out in jewellery and beads that seemed incongruous to the military medals. His chest looked like a salad bar. If he remembered right from military school, the guy was out of dress – the trinkets weren't military issue. But they contrasted nicely with his aviator shades and the hair rolling out between the medals on his chest.

In these humiliating circumstances, Potter expected the officials to get down on all fours where they could be more comfortable. Their work was illuminated by sixty-watt bulbs and oblique sunlight from the outside, which rounded out the picture and gave the place an aura of an indoor animal cage at the zoo.

Potter couldn't hear them, but his passport seemed to be producing an important exchange of words, a few grunts and perhaps some of the best conversation the two had had since they left their treetop homes after mating season.

The men nodded at one another and were waving their hands almost in unison. A bureaucratic dance! Their shades reflected bluish light beams, giving them the inhuman appearance of intergalactic or even subterranean authorities trying to agree on their next victim (they could be "morlocks" from Wells' *Time Machine*). An accord reached, they quickly climbed back up to their tree-top thrones.

Despite Potter's best efforts at concentration, the din seemed to be getting louder in the building. Nor did the wheezing and rattling air conditioner make any difference to the temperature. You could practically see water in the air! The sweltering pre-monsoon heat was chloroforming any attempt to think clearly and remain alert. The slow-moving paddle fans up in the rafters only swatted the bugs and humidity around the room. Small-is-beautiful technology in action. As he stared around aimlessly in line, Potter's head began to swim.

In front of him, the officer's mouth was moving but he couldn't hear anything other than background noise. Potter figured he must have been speaking since he was looking at him all the time. The customs official pointed to the eagle on the cover of his blue passport and showed his gums, apparently a grin. He was a small man but wiry and likely very tough. His head was tiny and two-sided – like a comic-book military character. The head was exaggerated by a cheap crewcut.

"Step up here to the table," he muttered. "You are American. Why are you here? You must know that your visa is not valid."

Despite the apparent offence, it was clear that the remark was off-hand. It was a throw-away statement and Potter treated it as such. Just like bad rap lyrics on the radio. Change the mental station and all would be OK.

Potter had heard this kind of official opener before. The idea was to put you off balance… get you explaining a lot of your moves defensively, stop you in your tracks by reference to their sacred "laws", then in the final act in the play demand payment of an arbitrary but always excessive fee for entry.

Potter often imagined who wrote the "laws" in places where legislatures had never worked in government and were often on permanent vacation. The laws were simply orders written by the junta's more literate people. To deal with the normal uncertainty of contradictory legal provisions and official threats by the customs bureaucracy in places like this, he recalled that in Guatemala he went directly to the airport bar at six for morning flights to brace himself for officials who usually found something wrong. He once even spit on an old visa to smear the date and get himself out of Honduras.

So, looking up at the airport official pushing his pile of documents around, he would usually hear something like: "Oh no, senor, you are missing a stamp and a signature. You can't possibly leave." Sometimes they wanted a bribe. Sometimes offering a bribe could get you jailed which would require a larger payment to get you out later.

Potter tried the cupped-ear move with a confident toss of the head. This allowed him to stall and think of an answer that would satisfy the bastards.

"How long are you staying here?" doll-man asked, apparently forgetting his invalid visa remark.

"Why, just long enough to teach a course at the Ministry of Finance. Several weeks."

"Are you with USAID?" he asked, looking at the other official for complicity. "Have you come from America to give us more essential technical advice? Should our farmers replace their opium crops and grow basic grains for cash? Ha-ha! Do you know that the Tatmadaw exiled the entire AID office a few months ago for their ridiculous multicoloured reports and subversive activities?"

This nonsense began to generate troglodyte impulses deep within his soul. Keep calm. "I am just a college professor who consults for governments like yours paid for by USAID. I am here at the invitation of your government." Well, not exactly true. He was no longer a professor and USAID was paying for the project. But he could always cross those bridges later…

The two drab olive aliens stared menacingly down at Potter from behind their throne. From nervousness, his hand had remained frozen in the cupped-ear position during the conversation. Even they could tell it was some kind of duplicity. If their mouths weren't moving, why was he still trying to listen?

The stocky one raised his right hand as if to salute. Instead it came down with a loud bang on his passport which shook the table. Just like the good old days in Panama where they would hit the passport with the stamp in their fist right next to your ear.

"You may stay in Myanmar for three weeks provided that you do not leave Yangon."

Yangon? Is that what this place is called now? That's what the "Tatmadaw" military junta must call Rangoon now, Potter figured. Who cares, he thought, I don't plan to leave the hotel except to teach the class.

Sucking in air through his missing teeth to get Potter's attention, the big alien pointed behind him to the part of the building where bags were searched and sensitive items like dollars had to be accounted for. Potter moved ahead and got in line behind some Japanese or Chinese businessmen being searched ahead of him. He was parked under a paddle fan. The successive waves of air had a soothing effect of cooling him as they dried up his sweat. It was like emerging from a pool in a breeze. His head began to clear.

As he awaited their decision on him, he watched the drama unfolding ahead of him at the customs station. No, the giggling he heard was not coming insanely from inside his head. Rather, the two Japanese entrants ahead of him were smiling and laughing nervously as the officials pawed their bags. The officials closely watched their reaction as they suddenly thrust their hands in here or there to gauge whether they were getting close. What fun! It was just like the children's game except the penalty would likely be prison or deportation.

Satisfied that the giggling was simply a nervous reaction, like peeing in one's pants, the officials waved them through. Potter placed his bags on the stand and showed them his entry stamp. Several of them began the repetitive task of lining up the suitcases, opening them and hoping to break up the routine by finding something illegal (meaning subversive, anathema to the military or just plain curious). Anything printed might fall in this category. In the airport souvenir stand, local books written by SLORC were on sale with titles like: *Deeds of The Traitorous Minions Against Myanmar* (second edition). So a discovery could mean a big promotion for one of these officials, possibly a place behind a big throne like the senior customs people in the next room. Official discretion had its rewards.

He became aware that all was not well with his efforts to get through customs. They were looking obliquely at one of his bags from various angles, almost like it was talking to them, maybe even giving them orders! He remembered the joke punchline about smart technology – the thermos was smart because it could tell hot from cold. Strange birds were cocking their heads and viewing his bags.

The chief bag inspector glanced obliquely at the carry-on bag, showing his spiked set of teeth and large red gums. Several others also grinned, either from fear of contradicting the chief or from genuine mirth. Like hounds on the trail of game, they all sniffed loudly. The chief reached swiftly in and pulled out the prize – Potter's bottle of duty-free rum which apparently had leaked all over his clothes and produced a pungently alcoholic aroma for their trained noses.

What a stroke of luck, thought Potter, who had once tried this successfully in Honduras. "Would you like a small taste?" he asked.

This was his first mistake. He should have at least known that none of the officials should be seen taking a nip in the presence of others. So, they affected surprise and began searching his bags vigorously. Holding up Potter's *Economist*, which happened to feature Saddam Hussein's angry sunglassed face and the caption "Don't Lose This Face", the chief no longer grinned. Jaw muscles straining and teeth gritted, which Potter hoped was merely a stance, he barked out a few peremptory remarks.

Tapping the magazine for effect, the chief shouted, "Do you realise that the Tatmadaw finds this to be subversive literature?"

"What is Tatmadaw?" Potter asked, digging his hole deeper.

"The Tatmadaw is the State Law and Order Restoration Council, known to you as SLORC, which ensures our safety and security. Communists and subversives with help from officials like your Jesse Helms and others in the House of Representatives seek to undermine our sacred institutions. This magazine thinks we are all clowns in a circus. American imperialists will not be permitted in to contaminate our society. We cannot permit this."

"What should I do with it?"

"It will be kept here until you leave Myanmar. Sign these forms and you can go."

Potter quickly signed, put the bottle back into his carry-on, gathered up his bags and hustled out of the customs area into a large hoard of people. Here was his first view of the multi-ethnic Asian panorama in which he would move for the next three weeks. It was a classic example of Riggs' "prismatic society" where what you saw was really not what you thought you were seeing.

He knew that Burma had at least seventy different races and about two hundred and fifty languages. They all seemed to be outside of airport customs. It was the rainbow without the coalition. Rows of outstretched hands from the shabbiest beggars he had ever seen went out to him for money. Small urchins pulled at his pockets and pants to plead for food or money. The more resourceful among them wanted to carry his bags and serve as his agent and broker a cab for him. Much of the language was unintelligible to him, something like wailing and groaning in unison. The smell of sweat, garlic and old rags followed him through the throng of well-wishers yelling and waving their arms. He was starting to understand that the Central American lens might not fit this place. Wrong framework! Faulty conceptual model!

Between the time he entered the customs station and made it through (probably an hour), the weather had changed from scorching sun to a classical tropical downpour. This was very much like the monsoon season in Central America. It was now almost completely dark outside with rain loudly hammering the corrugated metal roof of the airport terminal. Taking shelter from this, Potter saw one of the passengers on his flight leaning against the wall trying to stay dry.

Looking him over, he thought this was a perfectly reasonable looking fellow, groomed for dinner at some five-star restaurant. He had perfumed and lacquered hair, well-dressed with cuff-links in his white shirt. But his eyes were rolling around in his head uncontrollably like a sick cow or angry pit bull. Potter was so shaken by this that he moved toward the man to have a closer look.

"Are you headed into Yangon?" he asked, to see what kind of sound the man would make.

"Right. Just need a bit of distance from this place, if you know what I mean."

"Are you OK now?"

"I get these attacks sometimes working around here. Attacks of nerves or something from the oppressive surroundings. Maybe it's the heat. Lassiter's the name. I am working here and in Laos on a study of rural boat transport networks for UN. What are you doing?"

"I'm Potter. Just here to give a course on public finance," he said. "I've worked in the Third World before. Never thought I would say this, but Latin America seems somehow more normal than this place."

Neither of them noticed the little man carrying their bags to the taxi. He watched them with a peaceful intensity, trying to discern their real purpose in coming to his land. He had seen many white men come before. Few had any interest in the kind of changes that he and his people wanted to bring to Burma. The foreigners just stayed in the hotels and visited corrupt, lazy bureaucrats who told them enough lies to write their reports. He wondered if these were the same kind of people. Were these more slick, greasy, pimp-like consultants here to make money from the country's plight? Might they be trusted to work against repression, tyranny and injustice the way it should be dealt with – by force?

The ride from the airport in the beaten-up taxi was over a potholed road with very little traffic. There had been a gas shortage despite evidence of enormous oil reserves in the country. Most of it was sold overseas at market prices to pay the junta's wages and to gas up military tanks. Soldiers sporting AK-47s lined both sides of the road. They stood there in the midday heat like mirages, as if they were asleep standing up. Behind them, the tropical panorama included decayed buildings, lots of wiry dogs and little Buddhist monk trainees strolling everywhere. Some of them couldn't have been more than ten or fifteen years old in their bright red robes with shaven heads. Every mile or so there appeared large signs containing uplifting slogans for moral fortitude like: "Fight Eternally for the Motherland!" …"Those Who Council Disorder Must Be Eliminated" and so on. Classically Orwellian drivel from *1984*, but not quite as dramatic in this heat.

Potter already understood what Flory meant in *Burmese Days* when he said, "God! God! How do I get through the rest of this day?" His answer, of course, was the bottle and a concubine. With the possibility of being immobilised by stifling heat and oppressive officials, Potter hoped to fill up at least part of his days by teaching the course.

It was now late afternoon of the first day. On arrival at the Kandaji Lodge, the bellboy opened the door for Potter to his hotel room. Both of them watched a rather well-fed rat go up the curtain and another scurry for safety under a dresser. He had always known there must be classic rats in Burma from authorities like Sherlock Holmes. He commonly saw rats running around parks, streets and subways in Washington and New York. He even caught field mice in his house. But those field mice were clean, like hamsters.

He wondered how much worse these rats could be than the gargantuan roaches of New York. Couldn't be – just have to get used to them like new neighbours. But the thought of having to live inside with them for a few days gave him the chills.

Still, one had to be reasonable about things. Potter was still jet-lagged. Passing the international date line and spending around twenty hours on a jet means your body and mind have different ideas of what day it is and how much sleep you need. He knew that it would be next to impossible to sleep without the usual fortification of about five beers. He passed quickly along the lake in front of the hotel and into the pub. The dark waters of this peaceful lake provided a stunning scene of tropical beauty and pathos. But he also knew the rats and snakes were coming from the lake into the hotel – maybe even his room!

At the Kandaji bar were two other men seated with a stool in between them. So Potter sat between them.

Could mean two more consulting gigs, was the first thought that came to mind. Doesn't pay to be anti-social in work as an independent consultant. He knew that everyone was a potential employer.

As luck would have it, the guy on his left was from the local US embassy office. He was one of the "political officers". He had talked with these types before. As soon as the word "USAID" was out, his eyes glazed over and he looked at him with mild contempt and not a little arrogance. The political officer continued talking with his mate about the latest local political developments (which had come in over the web). Potter then heard him go on about some internal office feud and all the hassle he faced with growing political refugee claims and local US troublemakers. Potter made a few mild attempts to get in the conversation but realised it was a closed club. Predictably, the important Foreign Service Officer excused himself and pushed off. No interest in Potter's assignment. None at all. All answers and no questions. Potter mused: No wonder the US makes such wise and well-informed foreign policy decisions. The senior policy-makers have no idea or interest in what is happening in the field!

Trying the right stool, Potter struck up a conversation with a man from an environmental consulting firm in Colourado. This amounted to only a slight variation on the previous conversation. Still, the beers and talk were helping his jet-lag and soon he could get some sleep. But not just yet. The man turned out to be a neo-Luddite. He was one of those who protested technical progress ("tree-huggers" they were called sometimes) in the name of utopian societies where people would not be alienated from themselves by machines and could live in harmony with nature. He was here to work with villagers on schemes to gather nuts from the forest and process them locally. He was angry about the growing deforestation in Burma, waving his hands around in anguish in reference to the drug deals between the Thai and Burmese governments to deforest in exchange for gaining access to weapons to kill off local political opposition. Potter tried to agree with him but he couldn't figure out where. As with many of these people, he had stopped listening long ago and simply went on. Potter wondered if he even knew what country he was in.

Back in his room, Potter lay down on his stiff little bed and let the air conditioner do its magic. The oppressive heat, the shock of seeing another consultant insanely rolling his eyes in the airport and the spectacle of the rats produced intense fatigue. The neo-Luddite could fuck himself. He wasn't worth getting upset about. Shutting off the lamp, Potter could feel the blasts of air from the one-speed air conditioner.

As he was dozing off a short while later, he felt something hit the top of the sheet by his feet. Like a flash he kicked up his legs and turned the lamp back on. He could just see the shiny tail of one of the rats waddling into a round hole in the wall on the other side of his room.

Potter used the phone to call the desk, and in his most Third World sensitive manner asked if the rats in his room might be moved. He knew that Buddhists liked rats but couldn't recall why. Something to do with their inherent cleanliness and ability to survive for millions of years.

The desk manager was sympathetic. "How many rats are there, sir?"

"Haven't got a clue."

"Were you sleeping with the light off?"

"Hard to sleep with it on."

"No wonder, sir," the clerk said calmly, "the darkness scared the rats. You must sleep with it on and they won't jump on you again."

"Fine, thank you." Potter eventually passed out and woke up soothed at about three a.m. No rat bites, I made it, he mused.

At various intervals all night he awoke from his jet-lagged slumber to the repeated rattling of the air conditioner. Potter wondered if he were dreaming. The chloroformed consciousness of daylight carried over into night.

How did I end up in this place? was always a thought that occurred about this time on his assignments. Maybe I could get into real estate...

But it wasn't adventure or pleasure that motivated Potter. He knew that he was pushed along by events like a cork on the sea. An intellectual blind spot troubled him from childhood and produced precipitate and bizarre decisions for him. He had never been the take-charge, can-do type who commanded respect and ran big offices. Nearly always conversations stopped on his inability to see the obvious. Chills of embarrassment would hit him when everyone saw the answer except him in school. Sometimes he would get the logic backwards and the others would quietly shake their heads and break into red-faced, tearful laughter at him.

Potter's parents had sent him away to boarding school, partly for status and partly to get rid of him so they could fight in peace without feeling guilty for being bad role models. From this experience of semi-rejection, he got confused about right and wrong and who should be respected. He knew right from wrong but couldn't find totally right or wrong people to fit the categories. There were always contradictions.

So despite the fact the Florida boarding school was non-denominational, it had a chapel where all would sing glorious hymns to the accompaniment of discordant tapping at the piano. The intent was to emulate the solemnity and spirit of a British public school. Obviously they couldn't pull it off. Up close the place felt like a prison. From a distance the place sounded more like a saloon. In daily chapel, the headmaster would announce today's miscreants and proceed vigorously to paddle them with hefty, cadenced strokes in front of their peers. The rest of them fought to hold back the laughter from fear that they would be dragged up there next – which often happened! These kinds of spectacles organised by grown men confused him. Potter felt more at home with his own brand of mischief. He spent a lot of time drawing (albeit inaccurate) pictures of nude women. For example, he didn't get the shape of tits right until he first got his hands on the real things at eighteen years of age. This kind of indecisiveness probably ended him up in Myanmar working as a short-termer for a third-rate beltway bandit called Parallax International.

Potter thought of the stable days when he had taught at the university. He had lived under superficially blissful conditions of guaranteed monthly income. Still, he could not romanticise those times, nor did he wish them back. He was simply too impatient to sit around faculty meetings waiting his turn to talk in order of rank (he would be last) and found himself doodling moons, stars and dogs or ending up in shouting matches with the old farts and their wet, doggy eyes from years of drinking and loose living. Nor could he stand their younger boot-licking clones. "You're a liar!" he found himself bawling at one of his colleagues, who grinning at him in triumph would get back at him in the appropriate way – a negative vote for re-appointment in secret at the end of the year.

Being a member of that kind of team required the sham of maintaining awe and respect for really useless colleagues. In exchange for this façade, they might support you. Potter tried this routine for a while. He couldn't hide his naturally challenging demeanour, his wry look of merry ridicule, and his insistently sceptical questions. He was a cynic and obviously a loose grenade. He was a threat to the petrified order of senior deadwood, one unreliable enough (not a team player) to blow the whistle about this glacial retirement community. It was obvious to him that they had never really accomplished a thing in their lives – other than making it to class on time with their worn-out ideas on yellowed notes. So he left the academy. To put it more precisely, he was not re-hired (fired) after three years. So, Potter became an international expert and ended up providing technical advice in places like Myanmar.

Senior Burmese officials invited Potter to lunch before his first public expenditure training class as a gesture of oriental or Tibeto-Burmese hospitality. The setting was a solemn and cathedral-like restaurant near the ancient gilded Shwedagon Pagoda which boasts more gold than the vaults in the Bank of England. Setting the mood was a *saing* or orchestra featuring gongs (*kye-waing*) cymbals (*lingwin*) and flutes (*palwe*). It wasn't really bad if you liked Chinese music, which to him was like the sounds of smashing egg-crates. To his untrained ear, the music sounded something like the rustling of wind through trees. The officials sat around the table, smiling serenely in obedient silence. They had been doing this for two and a half thousand years; no need to change for a foreigner.

Potter took a swig of his beer and asked the priest-like robed man in front of him, "What do you do in Myanmar?"

This seemed to jolt the elderly man but nevertheless produced a pleasant smile. Potter noticed the others also smiled at this. "I am the governor of Rangoon Province."

"Fantastic," he said, trying to think of something appropriate to say. "Do you always have such large lunches?"

"We do not eat much during the full moon. Buddhists generally fast for the holiday. This is in your honour."

"Thanks. I'm learning more each day about Myanmar people and culture. One thing that interests me is the number of 1955 Chevrolets just in Rangoon... er... Yangon alone. Ever notice that? Just today, I saw a '55 Chevrolet go by the hotel with about ten people in it. A car collector could have a field day here. Only problem is the steering wheel was on the right side. I used to have a friend who drove on the left side of the road in Washington. Since he got out of the hospital he only walks now. Ha-ha!" But they weren't laughing.

Some looked at him with tolerant concern, like he was sick and should be taken to a hospital. From one perspective, the officials were looking right through him. They had never heard such sounds uttered before and wanted to treat him like a special animal, even a child. They smiled serenely and graciously nodded their heads in forgiveness.

Potter realised from their stares of amused curiosity that he had to control himself. It surprised him that despite his Mexican strategy of consuming large amounts of beer to prevent digestive problems the trots actually arrived four days into his stay.

It must be the food, he thought. Either I've not had enough beer to kill the parasites, or possibly I've had too much and can't function properly, he reasoned.

Fortunately, table conversation was kept at a higher plane than cars or the trots by the eloquently bombastic local director of the United Nations office, Curt Reiner. Reiner had been stationed here for six years and knew virtually every official. He could provide good counsel on how to survive palace treachery and intrigues. His predecessor had been kicked out by the Burmese for meddling in local affairs. The UN sought out and found a man with a booming, authoritative voice, an articulate command of English and who acted cautiously if at all.

Potter fumbled about with the chopsticks in an attempt to do things the local way. Raised in an ethnic neighbourhood of West Side Manhattan, he was used to cultural and ethnic smorgasbord. On the one hand, his lack of pretence seemed to work with his Burmese guests. On the other, they were also offended.

Aung Chang, the finance minister, watched in amusement as Potter dumped the rice out of his chopsticks several times. Potter was hungry and determined to eat. He aggressively went at the chicken, meat and rice but couldn't get them into his mouth.

"Try holding the sticks closer to the end and clip them together around the meat," the minister suggested. Trying it this way, Potter and his onlookers were surprised to see it work. The American was feeding himself without using his hands. Wonders never cease!

At his other side, Reiner proffered confidential observations for his benefit. In that peculiar Germanic accent that gives English a more precise meaning than it really deserves, Reiner noted how, "decades of psychological conditioning under tyrannical rule had made the Burmese civil service lethargic".

"Zay are afrait to speak out," said Reiner, flashing a beaming smile of brilliant complicity. "I am told that a legal provision remains requiring every Burmese to report conversations mit foreigners. This encourages silence to avoid zee burden of reporting conversations. As zee agency of the United Nations concerned mit human reichs vee must question zee very legitimacy of a government vich perpetuates this technical apparatus," Reiner continued.

Potter pushed some meat and most of the chopsticks into his mouth in one big gulp. He didn't know much about the Myanmar government. Not really required for his terms of reference – beyond knowledge of the budget laws. But it struck him how stereotypically people of different nationalities often behaved. The Germanic feature of exaggerated respect for authority, mindless fascination with numbers and systems and a rigid hierarchical view of the world, which he read someplace, fit this guy to the letter. Nor did he consider them negative qualities. They were simply programmed to behave like this, just as the French had a way of reinforcing their most brilliant conversational points with those famous knowing smiles that wrinkle up at the corners of their mouths. These were the cultural nuances that foreigners ignored at their peril, like New York smugness – which to Potter was simply a learned defence mechanism rather than an intentional insult, as outsiders see it. Orwell saw this among the British colonials in Burma. They mistakenly saw sneers instead of the personal shame and inferiority at their real inability to speak English. This created problems for the future of their empire.

Following this capacious lunch and the quiet exchange

of cordialities, the group filed into a large adjoining room where the class was to be held. A modern classroom next to the dining room. How sensible! First we eat, then we educate. One could almost see the Kafka-esque logic of having a torture chamber behind the courthouse.

Training in Potter's mind was a device to share experiences and facilitate lesson drawing. He was never good at didactic displays of textbook learning. Something from his inner city basic education produced a life-long scepticism of scholars as pedants. This is all bullshit, he would muse. How can I simplify it and make it stick in their minds? Usually it amounted to lectures spiced with jokes, stories and anecdotes, none of which were considered acceptable methods of scientific analysis. More usually, it involved regular meetings with students in nearby pubs after class.

The architecture of the room was predictably authoritarian chic – laced with dark, heavy wooden panels that surrounded a long wooden table at which the students would sit. To one side, a miniature jury of observers would sit in implied judgment of student comments. The room was modern but sterile. The oppressive context was really more conducive to silence, rote learning and pain than intellectual excitement.

Curt Reiner introduced the course with a short expansive address that probably had been given elsewhere. The only item hopefully different here was that his delivery was punctuated by short belches inaudible to all but the first few rows. "Ladies and gentlemen, zee worlt progresses in linear proportion to the number of courses delivered on cost control and technical budget processes... rrreeak—" (here Reiner let out a big one which drew smiles and even laughter from the back of the room). What a really stupid man, thought Potter.

After this stunning introduction, Reiner wiped his

mouth and moved aside, leaving the floor to Potter. Potter hustled up to the front of the room, between the blackboard and the little lectern. He had faced all kinds of classes in his brief but intense career as university lecturer. He liked to break up the monotony by saying outrageous things which he hoped would stimulate discussion and challenge intellects. Usually nothing happened and Potter would walk out feeling empty and exhausted. He rationalised his plight (he had to – otherwise it was simply that he was a poor lecturer) by reminding himself of just how dull a technical subject like governmental budgeting would be to the average mind. With the wrong kind of approach, the topic could degenerate into a discussion of rules and forms!

Naturally there was some truth to the charge that the whole topic was dull.

How could a bunch of mid-level bureaucrats do anything to change fiscal administration when their strings were pulled by a set of military thugs who ran the country with an iron hand? he thought.

The problem as he saw it was that thinking Burmese were too scared to say anything good or bad in response to his lectures. Their minds had been depoliticised by living in a regime in which expressing the wrong idea could get them executed. What remained was a passive instinct to merely survive. He had to fix that. How else could progress be spread, democracy take root and minds be expanded? He wasn't just a consultant anymore; Potter had a mission. He would be the vehicle through which critical intelligence and understanding would spread, multiplying from small changes into large ones. Society would flower through his determination to change lives through capacity-building! This would lead to new kinds of trust between working people, to whole new societies based on trust, hard work and the pursuit of knowledge. Social capital would increase. This minor budgeting course would serve as a catalyst and model for future efforts by other consultants who came after.

His eyes brightened and his mind raced ahead in different directions. Potter drew boxes and arrows on the board, paused and pondered his creations, erased them and added more boxes and arrows. It was his famous budget process flow chart.

Potter particularly liked the topic of budget implementation. It allowed him to set up the apparent contradiction (or tension) between treasury control of public finances and entrepreneurial independence needed by line ministries for delivery of basic services like health and education. This gave him the chance to defend the lowly practitioner out in the field delivering healthcare services to the poor, against the evil city bureaucrat interested only in boxes checked properly and regular reports. It also allowed him to argue for major new public management changes and against rigid, intrusive, corruption-inducing inspections and controls by central government units. All this, and getting paid too!

So, moving to the topic of budget implementation he asked, "How can we control expenditures and still ensure community benefit at minimal cost? Suppose as a manager you are charged with a portion of overhead expenses that you know aren't your responsibility? You didn't create them but must pay them as part of your budget. You know it can be measured as a direct cost and allocated right to a particular job and cost centre. Suppose also that you want passionately to do your job – deliver healthcare, provide transportation to the poor and elderly? What do you do? Is it ethical to hide behind the cost and say I can't deliver the service? Or should you skimp by over committing budget funds to do the job? Should an ethical manager forget the rules and costs and push ahead with the job? Can we assume that a good fiscal manager can always sort things out later? Aren't the many central Ministry of Finance rules and the forms simply devices that prevent your proper delivery of services? Shouldn't we say, 'screw the green eyeshaders'?"

The class murmured among themselves. Some of them smiled and were starting to get into it. Potter was getting excited. He darted here and there for emphasis. Chalk smoke was puffing off the board as he pounded it with hefty strokes. At one point, Potter jumped up and spun around completely in the air. It was an academic harvest dance that surprised some of the thirty or so students in the class. Others continued to stare at him in bewilderment as if he were an insect during mating season. His intellectual hormones were now in high gear.

"Performance is what counts. Cost controls should include fiscal incentives for performance assessments. Traditional controls only tie the hands of management. You can't motivate performance with threats to go to jail for exercising reasonable discretion," he added.

Potter was almost at his peak of orgiastic intellectual excitement. His instructional energy radiated around the room like powerful laser beams, bouncing off the students and hitting the floor.

"Suppose the internal auditors threatened you with jail for establishing a special bank fund when you knew that if the money went through the front office instead, they would steal the money and the medical equipment you needed to deliver services could not be purchased? Would you risk jail to get these purchased? Would you exercise your budget skills to hide the account and its deficits, knowing that if you could replenish it later with next year's funds, you could pay off the bills and even close the account before anyone knew? What do you think?"

Eyes blazing wildly, Potter scanned the room for an uplifted hand, that universal sign of acknowledgment that they not only understood the issue problem, but wanted to creatively come to grips with it. Yet, there was a telling silence before him. Nobody even moved an eye. He saw that a bearded man in the back was snoring and had probably been asleep during the whole presentation. Undaunted, Potter asked it a different way. "Should fiscal control rules always be obeyed?" More silence, more blank stares.

A hand uplifted! God has given him reason. "Tell us!" he said, gesturing upwards to encourage the words from the student's mouth.

But the student was only pointing toward Potter's crotch. An odd response. A quick glance downward and Potter moved to zip up his open fly.

Recovering quickly, he tried to move ahead to the next topic on the board. He took a glass of water and thought of his best chance to get back on track and regain the momentum: a joke. Looking around one more time, Potter stared briefly into his glass of water half expecting to see bacteria and parasites floating around. This is bad, need to break the ice, he thought.

"Have you heard the one about the elephant?" Still no hands.

He began to tell the one about the guy who won an elephant in a raffle. His eyes rested briefly on the bare shoulders of the slim Burmese brunette in the first row. She was showing some interest! A flush came to her and hit Potter like an electric shock below the belt. A few calculated moves of her deliciously shaped legs and he moved ahead with recharged batteries, a man driven by erotic determination to enlighten his students.

"The owner's friend offered to train the elephant. He said he could teach it to sit down." As the duller students actually took this down in their notebooks, the brunette's face flashed a clever smile. She knew they were being set up and liked to be teased.

"So the friend went over and kicked the elephant in the balls and sure enough it sat down. Education is a wonderful thing." Some students blinked in disbelief; others still wrote without changing expressions; the brunette moved her legs around in erotic joy and giggled a few times.

"Since the owner didn't like this kind of education, he asked his friend if he couldn't teach the elephant something without being so cruel. His friend said yes, he could teach it to shake its head. So he went over to the elephant and whispered in its ear, 'Do you want another kick in the balls?' The elephant shook its head."

A few students muttered nervously. If they got it, they weren't showing it, he thought. Sometimes it's like that teaching public finance. If you don't get student attention first, the rest is a waste of time.

"Now, I'd like to get your attention," he said, looking over at the nubile brunette with more than intellectual interest. It was really getting hot now and he was out of water.

After putting a few more diagrams on the board for the next part of the module, Potter thought he might energise himself again with another survey of the brunette's legs. Wheeling around on the pretext of reference to his diagram, the view was blocked by a wall of khaki. Two beefy uniformed Burmese soldiers stood before him with stern expressions. As the class stared in hushed silence, one pointed his drill stick at Potter.

"The joke appears to be on you, sir. The students have informed us. You have offended Buddhist cosmology, a crime against the Tatmadaw. You must come with us." Potter had worked in enough authoritarian places to know that protest was a waste of time and simply gave them further pretext to apply more rules. He would behave as always until the opportunity to tangle them up in their own logic arose; or until the expected *deus ex machina* arrived from within or without Burmese officialdom. Potter put down his chalk, gathered up his coat and meekly went along with them out the door. He was too surprised and embarrassed to say anything to the class and simply left without facing them.

On the way to the interrogation centre, the commandant turned to him and repeated his slogan that no foreigner would mock the most cherished gem of Dharma (law), the white elephant. It suddenly hit Potter what had happened. He knew something about the idea that Buddha was supposed to have been a white elephant in his one and last incarnation. He also knew that the god Indra rode on one called Erawon (it made him think of Samuel Butler's *Erewhon*, roughly "nowhere" spelled backwards! Ho-ho!). It was well-known in local lore that King Thibaw gave one white elephant a palace guarded by a hundred soldiers, complete with servants, singers and umbrellas of its own. To cover expenses, the elephant was granted earmarked revenues from its own province. When the British took over, they couldn't pay for recurrent expenses from the colonial budget of Burma. So they put the elephant in the Rangoon Zoo in 1886 where many say it died of a broken heart.

So, in the muddled confusion compounded by Burmese monsoon heat, his joke was taken as an offence against white elephants. One of the more alert students must have slipped out and informed on him while the rest snored. Hell of a class! Lucky he hadn't referred to "white elephant" capital projects – that was the next module for tomorrow! So he was in a fix. The brunette got him excited and he forgot what he was doing! And where was Reiner when you needed him?

Potter was taken to the Tatmadaw's interrogation centre, a wooden barracks where nothing much seemed to be going on. The ceiling fans moved around slowly and noiselessly.

The only noise during mid-afternoon were the electrical pings of cicadas outside.

Sitting alone in the whitewashed room at the little wooden table, Potter wondered whether his luck had finally run out. The sound of cadenced boot-steps pounded down the hall. His door flew open and two soldiers entered. Like their colleagues at the training centre, they wore their shades indoors. This could have been a custom. More probably, generalising from his Latin American experience with tin-pot regimes, it was designed to conceal any emotional expressions and to make them more menacing.

The one with the chest full of medals spoke first. "We're not going to waste a lot of our time with you. We never do with spies. You either tell us what we want or we'll deal with you harshly."

Potter knew that accusation of spying for the CIA was standard practice against Americans because there was no retort. If you denied it you sounded like a fool; if you claimed you were they wouldn't trust you because you were accused of being a spy, and so on.

"Any suggestion on how I might be spying while teaching my class? Is there something going on around here that anyone couldn't gather from reading the *New York Times*? If I were on a secret mission disguised as a consultant, why would I sabotage it by apparently slandering elephants?" Such questions were great seminar discussion, and Potter knew they wouldn't get him anywhere.

"We're not as stupid as you think. You mocked the white elephant because you are obviously ignorant of Burmese history and cultural traditions. But we know you are here to gather information on SLORC operations from officials participating as students in your class."

"Actually I said nothing about a white elephant because I knew about King Thibaw's pet. I told a story about an

251

elephant – it could have been any colour. As for your traditions, we love your people and want them to thrive without being under the thumb of bullies like yourself."

"Which brings us to the point," said the commandant. "We don't give a shit about elephants. But we do care about opponents of this government." Here the commandant placed the end of his drill stick against Potter's chest. To increase the pain, the commandant's colleague placed his foot on the chair to prevent Potter from reclining away from the stick. As Potter cried out, the commandant continued.

"You expect that American economic sanctions against us will put your friends, the ZLP and the Karen into power. But you are backing losers. We may trade drugs and forests for arms, but they thrive also from smuggling just like we do. Too bad you have such a simplistic view of the political world over here."

Potter gathered his wits as the commandant retracted his stick. The commandant's mouth continued to flap in front of him, something about sharing information with the Karen tribe (which he knew were one of their opponents – they had about sixty-five other opponent groups too!). He also knew that the Karen had originated about four and a half thousand years ago in the Gobi Desert and were considered by many to be one of the lost tribes of Israel because they had a book of legends and stories similar to Hebrew scriptures in the Bible.

"Look here, I am just a consultant giving a course." He spoke in almost a whisper so the commandant might move in a little closer. Potter waved his hands around in front of him and softly explained, "I don't want any trouble," after which he thrust his fist forward and popped the commandant a good one on the chin, sending him reeling backwards onto the floor. Somewhere in his personnel file it said that Potter had a tendency to "go tropo". Almost predictably, he employed the feral solution of a growl and spring, if he honestly believed that further rational discussion was impossible. This tendency had cost him an earlier university post, where he had decked the department chair. Similarly, this outburst felt real good at the time. It always brought pain later.

Potter continued loudly to explain things from his seat to the amazed commandant and his colleague. It was like an insane continuation of his class. He started to explain how overvalued exchange rates merely helped crony importers of the regime and hurt the average Burmese. In response, the soldier behind Potter soundly thumped him on the side of the head with the back of his fist. Despite the loud crack, he felt no real pain from this in contrast with the knot in his chest from the drill stick. He was even gratified that the guy paid attention.

The commandant faced him again, his fists tightly gripped around the stick and red faced. "You say we are thugs. Why, you little turd, you are nothing more than an international whore, working for whomever gives you money! We don't need your assistance here. You don't help anyone but yourself. Take him below."

The other soldier pulled Potter out of his chair, pushed him out the door and down the hall. As he was getting ready for another good shove, Potter heard the commandant shouting. The other stopped and faced the commandant. "You obviously will want to speak with your embassy. Give him the phone in your office."

Actually, Potter never thought of asking this, any more than calling Parallax International. He had forgotten because he knew it was a waste of time. The "firm" consisted of no more than a telephone, a secretary and a roller-dex file of consultants. The US Embassy was notorious for ignoring Americans in trouble overseas. He first tried his luck by calling Curt Reiner at UNDP, but

Reiner simply told him that what they were doing violated the Geneva accords on human rights.

"I know that, Curt. What can I do about it?"

"Vell, nothing – the government wants nothing to do mit UN or any of dee ander international organisations. Vee are all subversives in their eyes. I vill do vat I can."

In his next attempt, he reached the US Embassy and asked for the political section. As luck would have it, it was the guy he had met in the pub of the Kandaji Lodge, a man called Chip Strong. Curiously, Strong spoke in an imitation British accent. Must be required for foreign service officers… He spoke of the many protocol difficulties and political sensitivities that prevented him, officially, from doing anything on Potter's behalf other than lodging a protest with the Myanmar Government. Functionally, this meant the Tatmadaw, which was holding hundreds of its own political prisoners and had many more under house arrest.

Strong continued. "I will fax this protest immediately. I wish I could be of more assistance, but my hands are tied. I hope you know that I would see this differently if I were leaving his post tomorrow or were acting as a fellow American comrade. I will check up on your case tomorrow."

The next day, Potter was back at his table in front of his accusers. It was obvious that the game was turning sour. The commandant told him, "You are in a fix, my friend. Your government doesn't like you anymore than it likes us. We get the sanctions and all you get is a protest, another one which we just toss on the pile," he said with a cruel grin on his face.

No mark where I poked him. All that effort for nothing, thought Potter.

"So when we make you 'disappear' like the others, we simply get another protest from your government and a few more negative votes on IMF loans. Do you think that kind of shit matters to us? We are in command. We sell our wares and receive lots of weapons and spending money in return. We will show you how we deal with ridiculous people like yourself. Our people have been dealing with subversive foreigners for five hundred years. We don't boast about our strength, but as Sino-Tibetans, we always crush our opponents and their apologists. You will disappear shortly and nobody will know or care until it is too late." Despite his tone, the commandant offered Potter a cigarette, which he took.

Potter could see that he was in deep shit this time and needed something like the proverbial ninety-yard touchdown pass in the last ten seconds to pull this one out.

"I am a spy. You were right about the whoring. I work for the highest bidder. If you want more information on the Karen, pay me as well. Kill me and you lose a source. Release me and you also lose a source. Fifty thousand dollars *per diem* and I'm on retainer."

"Don't waste our time. You are nobody to us. Since you would sell out to anyone, you have no backbone, no integrity and we need nothing from you except information on what you were doing here. We know who you are. If you want to live, you will tell us where the Karen National Liberation Army commander Bo Mya is. You will also tell us what the Karen are planning to do against us."

Potter realised he was down to his last move. If he played martyr, they would kill him. If he gave them phoney information, they would kill him too. And Parallax International would replace him in about fifteen minutes. So he looked into his hands and pondered his fate.

The incredible thing to Potter was that these people took themselves seriously. They killed and imprisoned to keep control of a little patch of overheated jungle and its starving inhabitants. They were all going to die anyway. Why didn't they just go to the beach and forget about it?

The commandant stared at him silently through his

shades. He slapped his drill stick against his boots a few times to help Potter think up a response.

Maybe this is where you call for a priest, thought Potter. No, they would send some joker like the frocked idiot in Kubrick's *Paths of Glory* who muttered a lot of religious platitudes about things being OK in the next world. He recalled that one of the prisoners even tried to deck the priest and had to be restrained. That was risky – he could have been executed twice!

Nevertheless, Potter needed higher spiritual reassurance. He wasn't a believer or a church-goer, but he knew that there was a higher force governing his life. After all, there was someone in the Bible who had been unjustly condemned, knew the world was filled with sleazy, rotten, power-grabbing people, who, if given absolute control over others without legal constraints, would become torturers. Their behaviour would not be changed by showing the other cheek.

Quickly, he reconciled his accounts and began to close the books of his life. He knew he had been a bad person but one who had done some good along the way. Where would his soul go – hell, heaven or purgatory? No matter. His spiritual liabilities outweighed the assets and his time was up.

"Give me some paper and a pen. I will tell you. I don't know who Bo Mya is or where he hides out, but I can describe the Karen army plans for you."

"You have until tomorrow morning to think it over. Take him back to his cell and bring him back to me tomorrow. If he refuses to tell us where Bo Mya is, you may execute him on the spot," the commandant said casually to the other soldiers.

Potter of course had no idea where Bo Mya might be. He had never met a Karen and had only read about them. But he had a sense of the absurd. It had come down to this.

His career and probably his life was finished. He had no family, and only a few superficial friends who liked to work out at the gym and eat expensive food. He had nothing to go back to really. His consulting job was really quite irrelevant in the scheme of things. There was nothing more to do.

Potter spent another night in his cell. The cell actually had fewer rats than his hotel room. It was a four-star cell. He saw the moon slice across the sky through the window just before dozing off. In his dream he was running from the soldiers again, and he knew that Bond would shoot him while he was down, just like last time. His recurring dream was a premonition after all.

He slid down the side of a hill covered with pine needles and jumped into the river. Even though the roaring waters deafened him he could hear the shots being fired, both as they skimmed the water in front of him and as reports of the rifles behind him. The smell of gunpowder wafted into his nostrils. He was a better swimmer than runner, so he dove in and stroked on. It was like swimming in molasses – he just lumbered along like a groundhog fleeing a fox, a groundhog who knows its done for. There it is! Just a few more feet and he'd be on the opposite bank, maybe to freedom. But this time the dream was different. Now he was running through the jungle, he felt the shimmering spray of the waterfall, noticed a small riverside encampment consisting of a few shacks and a pier, with a sign nearby that read "Wang Kha".

In the morning, the soldiers came for him. He heard their cadenced boot-steps around dawn. No point in taunting them. They were just doing their jobs like he probably would too. Potter saw them trapped like their superiors in a web of cronyism in which they made their own rules. It wasn't their fault.

Back in the interrogation room again, he got out his pen

and wrote down "Wang Kha" from the dream – which might have come from staring at a map of Burma on the plane into Rangoon. He recalled that it was on the Thai border and if Bo Mya wasn't there, hey, one of his close relatives might be.

Seeing this name, the soldiers began chattering in Burmese with animation. The commandant began shouting orders until all of them were shouting and yelling together. It sounded like a kennel at feeding time. The big hungry dogs were ordering the little ones around and the latter obeyed out of fear and the need to be given a share of the evening's booty.

Christ, what a bunch of losers, he thought.

"Take him away!" shouted the commandant to his underling. Despondently, Potter was led away without a word down some stairs, through a long corridor where he imagined that he would be thrown into a room and shot. There he stayed for the next two days.

Expecting the worst, Potter concentrated on his public finance material to prevent terror from overtaking him. This worked for a day. But the next day, he sweated like a pig in anticipation that they would end his fine career prematurely. The next morning the usual entourage of khaki came for him.

Potter was shoved into a waiting truck from the Ministry of Defence.

Racing through the streets of Rangoon past dusty slums and wiry dogs, Potter was surprised that the commandant spoke to him. "At Wang Kha, we were ambushed by the Karen. After several hours of shooting, we captured their headquarters. The headquarters contained drugs, arms, money and best of all for you, Bo Mya, who was taking a shit when we caught him. We also got one of his conspirators."

Potter noticed that they had brought back the bodies in a

truck nearby – just like deer on the front of the car so everyone knows what a great hunter you are. The commandant took him over to the truck. There on the front, Potter saw the body of Lassiter, the guy he had spoken with at the airport. He must have been working with the Karen. Potter also noticed that the body next to him was that of the airport baggage handler. The carrier must have recruited Lassiter. Who knows? He felt sickened by his good fortune.

"I am not going to ask how you knew them or where they were. Consider yourself lucky this time. But go back and tell your kind that we are not open for your democratic reform business. We make the rules and nobody tells us about elections. Here is your passport. Those are your belongings. Don't come back."

Potter felt a combination of giddy nausea and ecstatic relief. His head swam and he seemed to lose consciousness. After a dream in which he was on top of his classroom brunette this time, he woke up in a sweat on the Myanmar Air plane to Bangkok. It was a good sign that his great escape dream had moved on to better topics.

"Hell of a play to win last week's Tech game! Says right here in the *Herald Tribune* they used the Statue of Liberty play against Maryland! Imagine! One of the oldest plays in the book and it still works," said the bovine-looking fellow next to him slobbering out his sandwich onto the tray between chugs of scotch. "BJ Riley from Lubbock, Texas, at your service. God, this food is disgusting, but I love it!

"These Burmese, or whatever the hell they call themselves now, they aren't such bad people. They understand good capitalist principles just like Adam Smith and George W Bush. You don't think so? I just sold them a few luxury hotels in Rangoon. But they made me pay a premium price for the teak I bought. They're real smart. Someday Myanmar will be a tourist mecca. No muggers or crime – hell, everyone's already in jail. Ha-ha!"

Potter listened to the man next to him in gaunt disbelief. What an imbecilic description of dealings with one of the world's most thuggish governments – right there in league with Saddam Hussein! He couldn't martial enough strength to tell the man what a fool he was. Besides, he probably meant no harm. It was just that collectively, people like him were keeping regimes like this in power. Potter no longer really cared. He was already thinking about his next job in Latin America…

Hang in there and avoid places like Yangon.

Myanmar, 1991

So Ken—

After reading these tales, you must be saying, "I told you so. You should have gotten a real job. Development aid is fine, it just doesn't produce any development! Prop up tin-pot dictators like Mobutu in Zaire with project aid? What did you expect him to do, invest it benevolently on behalf of his people? Computerise the accounting system to stop theft of public funds? Look at transparent and accountable Washington DC with its state-of-the-art procurement and fiscal control systems! Give even more aid to the best performing countries? Give me a break – they could all do even better if there were no development aid at all!"

You stated these points bolstered by your merry grin *ad nauseum* in rebuttal to my feeble arguments. You said they merely justified what I was doing. They gave me purpose.

I still think you are wrong, but if I often suffer from tiny worms of doubt about all this, the worms gnaw away at my insides and grow larger. Of all people, I shouldn't ask you, but what is it with the aid business, especially the American variety? We try to involve the rest of the world in our own virtue. We have the definitively correct visions of what the world should be like – all vegetarian, environmentally-sensitive, feminist, non-smoking democracies. Wasn't Hitler also a vegetarian? Of course, foreign aid is one means of achieving visions like these. But has development assistance ever created such a system with such values? Should it? Or has the aid business merely let loose a lot of consultants and foreign aides to hen-peck the world with their virtuous platitudes? As you and I have argued, military force in pursuit of our democratic vision is another means. We both think force is a necessary part of the equation to get any serious change at all, especially with thug regimes. The fact is that the rest of the world (at least "old Europe") is reluctant to trumpet our cause and fight for democratic governance. They are cynical and try to say US aid really means oil or markets for US companies. Maybe there's some truth to what they say, but look at the disaster in Darfur while the EU sits on its bureaucratic ass. The US is too bogged down in Iraq now to intervene there. What's the point of humanitarian aid if thugs prevent it from being delivered? You've heard all this before from me...

We still want to impose our virtuous ideas on our fellow men and women, don't we? Unlike other world history great powers, America is a colossal power but at heart still not an imperial one. We want women to be free to choose their paths and partners just like US women do. We want the US Constitution exported – freedom of association, press, speech and safeguards against police searches and arbitrary arrests. Brutal regimes do not like to hear these things and scoff at us through their supporters and willing dupes. This explains a lot of the resistance to foreign aid workers and why aid often doesn't achieve anything. You know that the design of aid projects to reduce food shortages and increase farm yields have been relatively straight-forward for the past forty years. They recommend such items as: secure land tenure for farms; provision of extension services; and cheap credit. Ethiopia has received a lot of grants and loans for these purposes. Nevertheless, the government is now resettling two million peasants from dried-out plots in the highlands to the fertile soil of the west. The Prime Minister indicates that it is not working and wants two hundred million dollars from international donors to finance the scheme.[15]

---

[15] "Ethiopia: People Aren't Cattle", *The Economist*, July 17, 2004, p.50

What can donors do to demand that proper actions be taken by host country governments? Not much. How can wrong-headed government policies be changed by outside donors and institutions? Not easily. Aid workers caught in the middle of such conflicts (and they are common) can become frustrated and depressed. Working with such governments can cause cynicism and encourage aid workers to quit the business altogether. I have been there several times. As it is said, just when you think you've hit the bottom of your aid career, you can still go lower.

At the same time, with our colossal powers, the US at least may have become children of the Grand Inquisitor. The more we talk of spreading democracy, governance and welfare around the world, the crueller we have become. Many of us become hardened in our positions, so cocksure that we are right. How can we be guilty when we have in mind the welfare of so many others? In Trilling's *Middle of the Journey*, Maxim broke with the communist party because he was cynical of its hypocrisy and cruelty. We need to take pains that our "great experiments" imposed by force, such as in Iraq today, do not turn us into cruel bullies and monsters, leading to cynicism of our real tasks that need to be performed to help the poor and underdeveloped people of the world with aid.

For those contemplating becoming foreign aides and taking their own safaris, there is still a lot of good work that can be done. One should enter the aid business contrite, to learn and not to teach – despite one's impressive academic credentials. One should learn how to deal with aid bureaucrats, stroking their egos, making them feel important, being patient and not striking out in rage or frustration. These are the people – in the projects, in the aid bureaucracies, in the aid firms and NGOs – who will make your life easier or more difficult. The dispatches and tales above indicate how professional life can be made difficult by failure to perform the feat of regularly "sucking up" to authority. Do it with dignity! Prospective foreign aides will have little difficulty working with overseas local officials and citizens. Ironically, this may be the easiest part of the business! Most people with whom I have worked overseas have been personally warm and professionally receptive to technical advice. I am still doing aid safari work.

Ken, I would gladly do it all again.

Budapest, Hungary, 2005

Acknowledgments

The idea for a book of foreign aid anecdotes was suggested to me by my friend, Malcolm Holmes, a few years ago. Late one night after dinner in Washington, as we exchanged tales from our respective technical assistance and training experiences on overseas projects, he said: "You should write these stories up. Everyone in this business says they will but no one does. They either have no time, forget the details of their experiences, or are afraid of getting kicked off the consultant's roster."

"But I only write technical reports and articles, not human interest stuff," I told him.

"Give it a shot, mate," he replied and we had yet another glass of excellent Australian Shiraz.

The preceding pages represent my efforts to make sense of experiences that often lacked narrative structure or apparent purpose at the time. Writing this book was a chance to reflect on my aid fieldwork experience. It enabled me to review how I got into this; to think about the future; to engage in some cathartic venting about things in aid work that bother me and about which I could do little; to fantasise about what might have been. I would like to acknowledge Malcolm's support for this "project". The dispatches are derived partly from memory and my notes taken during missions. As an opportunist, I adapted parts of what actually happened for narrative purposes. The experiences and opinions herein are entirely my own. I take full responsibility for errors and any offence caused by my barbs and fantasies.

I also want to acknowledge those who got me into this work and encouraged me to stay. Jim Rowles got me into this through his work in Costa Rica years ago. I was impressed with how interesting his life was working in San Jose on the Stanford Law Reform Project compared to my own. That was a turning point for me and I decided I wanted to work in development assistance. Others added fuel to the fire. My favourite MPA professor at the School of Public Administration, University of Southern California, Alberto Guerriero-Ramos, encouraged me to continue studying and working in comparative policy and administration. My doctoral thesis advisor in political science, Ron Chilcote, at the University of California, Riverside, encouraged me to work with the rural poor in Latin America and elsewhere. They said it was my "destiny" and knew what they meant from experience.

It should be said, that field of development assistance is full of hard-working specialists who risk their lives every day in tough places to reform systems, and deliver the goods to the less fortunate of the world. This book is dedicated to my friends who are still at it and to the many solid aid workers who need recognition for the valuable work that they do.